COST, PRICES, AND PROFITS:
THEIR CYCLICAL RELATIONS

NATIONAL BUREAU OF ECONOMIC RESEARCH

Studies in Business Cycles

COST, PRICES, AND PROFITS: THEIR CYCLICAL RELATIONS

THOR HULTGREN
University of Wisconsin—Milwaukee

ASSISTED BY MAUDE R. PECH

Published by
National Bureau of Economic Research, New York

Distributed by
Columbia University Press, New York and London
1965

Relation of the Directors to the Work and Publications
of the National Bureau of Economic Research

1. The object of the National Bureau of Economic Research is to ascertain and to present to the public important economic facts and their interpretation in a scientific and impartial manner. The Board of Directors is charged with the responsibility of ensuring that the work of the National Bureau is carried on in strict conformity with this object.
2. To this end the Board of Directors shall appoint one or more Directors of Research.
3. The Director or Directors of Research shall submit to the members of the Board, or to its Executive Committee, for their formal adoption, all specific proposals concerning researches to be instituted.
4. No report shall be published until the Director or Directors of Research shall have submitted to the Board a summary drawing attention to the character of the data and their utilization in the report, the nature and treatment of the problems involved, the main conclusions, and such other information as in their opinion would serve to determine the suitability of the report for publication in accordance with the principles of the National Bureau.
5. A copy of any manuscript proposed for publication shall also be submitted to each member of the Board. For each manuscript to be so submitted a special committee shall be appointed by the President, or at his designation by the Executive Director, consisting of three Directors selected as nearly as may be one from each general division of the Board. The names of the special manuscript committee shall be stated to each Director when the summary and report described in paragraph (4) are sent to him. It shall be the duty of each member of the committee to read the manuscript. If each member of the special committee signifies his approval within thirty days, the manuscript may be published. If each member of the special committee has not signified his approval within thirty days of the transmittal of the report and manuscript, the Director of Research shall then notify each member of the Board, requesting approval or disapproval of publication, and thirty additional days shall be granted for this purpose. The manuscript shall then not be published unless at least a majority of the entire Board and a two-thirds majority of those members of the Board who shall have voted on the proposal within the time fixed for the receipt of votes on the publication proposed shall have approved.
6. No manuscript may be published, though approved by each member of the special committee, until forty-five days have elapsed from the transmittal of the summary and report. The interval is allowed for the receipt of any memorandum of dissent or reservation, together with a brief statement of his reasons, that any member may wish to express; and such memorandum of dissent or reservation shall be published with the manuscript if he so desires. Publication does not, however, imply that each member of the Board has read the manuscript, or that either members of the Board in general, or of the special committee, have passed upon its validity in every detail.
7. A copy of this resolution shall, unless otherwise determined by the Board, be printed in each copy of every National Bureau book.

(Resolution adopted October 25, 1926,
as revised February 6, 1933, and February 24, 1941)

CONTENTS

TABLES

xx

CHARTS

ACKNOWLEDGMENTS

William I. Greenwald and Elma Oliver were very helpful in the preliminary exploration from which the present study evolved. Dorothy Dorfman Green assembled the material on manufacturing costs, profits, and prices.

Sophie Sakowitz and Charlotte Boschan advised on questions involving seasonal adjustment and identification of turning points. International Business Machines Corporation contributed electronic computer time.

Harold M. Groves and Maurice W. Lee of the National Bureau's Board of Directors and Ilse Mintz, Geoffrey H. Moore, Robert P. Shay, and Richard T. Selden of the research staff made helpful comments on earlier drafts of the manuscript.

H. Irving Forman drew the charts and Joan Tron prepared the manuscript for press.

FOREWORD

The relations among costs, prices, and profits, which Hultgren treats in this volume, are among the most intricate of any with which students of business cycles are concerned. They are also among the most controversial. The reader, therefore, is likely to welcome both the careful compilation of data that Hultgren has made and his painstaking efforts to extract dependable generalizations from them. Many will be tempted to push the data farther and to find in them support for this or that theory of inflation or recession. Such attempts may well be justified, but those who are so inclined will do well first to ponder the difficulties that Hultgren's explorations reveal. They will, I believe, have cause to be grateful for the warnings as well as for the solid ground from which they can then set forth.

This is a field in which the analyst must generally use what statistics he can get, rather than those he would like to have. Nevertheless, Hultgren constructs a number of new measures adapted to his problem. Because available indexes of manufacturing output are based in part on data on labor input, and hence prejudice comparisons with labor input, he develops new quarterly indexes of the physical volume of sales and output in a number of manufacturing industries, independent of measures of input. These new estimates, together with those for a few industries for which adequate physical output indexes are already available, cover roughly three-fourths of manufacturing output, and the industries included constitute a fairly representative group.

The measurement of the physical volume of activity in manufacturing is only one of a number of problems of data comparability and coverage that the author encounters. The data on total costs, profits, and sales pertain to corporate enterprises, often widely diversified; indexes of output and of labor cost are compiled from

reports by individual plants or establishments, including firms that
are not corporations; price quotations refer to specific products.
Most of the monthly industry statistics on labor costs cover only
the wages and hours of production workers, omitting the increasingly numerous clerical, sales, and other white-collar employees,
as well as the growing costs of fringe benefits. Price quotations
often cover a very limited range of the products of an industry,
may not take adequate account of quality changes or of concessions
in terms, and generally refer to goods being currently ordered
rather than (as costs do) to goods being produced or delivered.
Each of these matters is considered by the author and, to the extent
possible, evaluated in terms of its potential effect on his conclusions.

In the face of these obstacles to precise measurement and comparison, Hultgren uses industry data chiefly in anonymous fashion.
Each industry (and each cycle in sales or output) provides an observation on cost-price relations. From this collection of observations
he draws generalizations with respect to cost-price behavior at
large, rather than with respect to any particular industry. With
this procedure, inadequacies in the data for a given industry (or
cycle) are less crucial, although biases that affect the data generally
can still, of course, be present. Those who are concerned with a
single industry, on the other hand, may find the defects in the data
too great to warrant conclusions specific to that industry. The fact
that Hultgren judges them useful for his analysis is no guarantee
that they will be sufficiently reliable for other uses.

Despite the limitations of the data and the restrictions they impose on empirical analysis, Hultgren extracts important findings
from them. For example, in tracing the source of the well-known
tendency for profits of manufacturing concerns to rise and fall
with their volume of sales, he finds, first, that margins (profits per
dollar of sales) also rise and fall with sales; next, that prices, at
least in the postwar period, do not regularly rise and fall with sales;
and finally, that unit costs tend to move inversely with sales.
Hence the inverse movements in costs turn out to be more important, as a rule, than the movements in prices in accounting for the
characteristic cyclical conformity of profits. Before World War II,
and especially in the more severe contractions in business that the

economy experienced, movements in prices apparently contributed more to the swings in profits than in recent years.

In another respect, too, unit costs play a significant role. Their
pattern, while broadly inverse to sales, is not merely an inverted
replica of sales, as it would be if total costs remained fixed throughout the cycle. Instead, an expansion in sales is typically accompanied by a decline in unit costs initially, but as the expansion
proceeds, unit costs tend to rise. The rise usually continues, indeed
may even accelerate, after sales begin to contract, but this advance
in costs frequently is reversed before the contraction in sales comes
to an end. These reversals in unit costs, which may be thought of as
either lagging behind similar turns in sales or leading opposite
turns in sales, tend to produce opposite reversals in profit margins.
That is, the cyclical upturn in costs often generates a downturn in
margins before sales reach their peak, while the cyclical downturn
in costs helps to bring about an upturn in margins before sales
reach their trough. Prices usually do not contribute to this tendency. More often than not, they tend to offset it by continuing to
rise at least as long as sales do and by declining, if at all, toward the
end of the contraction in sales. But these movements in prices
are typically not as sharp as those in costs. The upshot is that early
reversals in margins are fairly common, particularly during expansions in sales, and they are chiefly attributable to the behavior
of costs. This process has important implications for the generation
of business cycles because of the importance of profits in motiva-
ting economic activity.

As already noted, Hultgren's analysis is largely carried out in
terms of the upswings and downswings in the sales or output of the
industry whose costs, prices, and profits are being considered. This
is warranted by the important influence that an industry's volume
of activity has on these variables, particularly on its unit costs. On
the other hand, prices of materials, selling prices, and wage rates
are often less influenced by an industry's own activity than by
the general state of business. Indeed, an industry's activity itself is
typically governed, in part, by the general state of business. Hence
the analysis reveals a complicated set of interrelationships among
the sales or output cycles of the several industries, their costs,
selling prices and profits, and the general business cycle. By weav-

ing such relationships together, one can see what happens to these
factors during business cycles, and why they behave the way they
do.

Take, for example, the course of unit labor costs during a business cycle expansion. In the early months of such an expansion
unit labor costs, as a rule, decline. This is a period when many industries, though not all, are experiencing a rise in output and sales.
For those whose activity is increasing, unit costs go down because
of rapid increases in output per man-hour in this early stage of
expansion in their own activity and because the general labor
market situation is not such as to produce equally marked increases
in hourly earnings. For those whose activity is still declining, unit
costs may also decline, or at least fail to rise as rapidly as before,
both because output per man-hour frequently rises in the late
stages of an industry's contraction, and because the labor market
situation is even easier for such industries than for those that are
extending their workweek or hiring more labor. As the general
expansion proceeds, however, the unit labor costs of those industries that began their expansion early tend to rise, because increases in output per man-hour have become more difficult to
achieve, payment of overtime rates is more common, and labor
market tightness for particular trades or skills begins to exert
upward pressure on wage rates. This may be balanced for a time
by the declining costs of industries that are just beginning to enjoy
an increase in sales. But sooner or later, increases in unit costs
become more prevalent, partly because in some industries sales
begin to decline. The result is that few industries fail to find themselves with rising unit costs at the end of a business cycle expansion.

What will surely be remembered as Hultgren's chief contribu-
tion in this study is his exploration of unit costs. The behavior of
costs has been one of the great unknowns in business cycle analysis.
Current statistical data on unit costs are rarely seen; it was only in
1961 that a federal government agency began publishing, for the
first time in history, I believe, a monthly index of unit costs—labor
costs per unit of output. Hultgren's work should lead to new efforts
to improve the statistical base for measures of labor and other costs
of production, comparable with prices. A broad program of statistical improvement in this area is needed.

GEOFFREY H. MOORE

COST, PRICES, AND PROFITS: THEIR CYCLICAL RELATIONS

1

FACTORS THAT
INFLUENCE PROFITS

Upswings and downswings in business activity mean, for most industries, upswings and downswings in the quantity of goods or services they sell. These fluctuations are accompanied by changes in the prices they receive and in their cost of doing business, changes which, in turn, affect their profits. The main purpose of the present study is to explore these effects.

By cost we mean not aggregate expense but cost per physical unit of product sold. Prices received and cost affect profit per unit sold and profit per dollar of sales. For example, if the price received for a product and its cost both increase, but the price rises by a greater amount than the cost, profit per unit of product increases. If the price rises by a greater percentage than the cost, profit per dollar of sales increases.

Aggregate profits are also affected by quantity sold. If profit per unit falls a little, but the quantity sold increases substantially, aggregate profit will rise. If profit per dollar of sales falls a little, but the aggregate dollar value of sales rises substantially, aggregate profit will rise.

It is therefore instructive to analyze profit changes in two steps. First, what happens to profits per unit, and second, what happens to quantity sold? Alternatively, what happens to profits per dollar of sales, and what happens to aggregate sales (in dollars)?

Either alternative has its merits. Profit per dollar of sales appears to figure more commonly than profit per unit of product in the thinking of businessmen and investors. The profit-per-dollar figure is often found in reports of management to stockholders, while profit per unit of product is hardly ever found, doubtless because most companies sell a variety of products and feel no need for a single composite measure of quantity sold. Often no information as to cost or profit per physical unit is available to the out-

side analyst, although the managers of enterprises have frequent
occasion to compute such figures for individual products.

ARITHMETIC OF PROFIT MARGINS

In this volume we shall therefore inquire what has happened to
profit margins during the course of upswings and downswings in
quantity sold or sales. (Information is available only for some parts
of the national economy.) By the margin we mean the ratio of
profit to sales. Sometimes it will be more convenient to talk of its
complement, the ratio of expenses to sales. By profit or profits we
mean the aggregate as distinguished from the margin; by sales we
mean the revenue, not the quantity sold.

The sales of any commodity, thus measured in dollars, equal the
quantity of the commodity sold multiplied by the average price the
vendor receives. Difficulties in the definition or measurement of
quantity often make it impossible to separate the two factors.
Where these difficulties can be overcome, however, it becomes possible to compute cost per unit of product. Since aggregate cost
equals cost per unit times quantity, and sales equal price times
quantity, the ratio of cost per unit to price is the same as the ratio
of aggregate cost to sales.

Changes in cost ratios and margins can reflect various combinations of changes in prices and unit cost. A rise in prices received
tends to widen margins, but they will not actually widen if cost per
unit rises by the same or a greater percentage. A fall in cost also
tends to widen margins but, again, margins will not actually widen
if prices fall as fast or faster. The logically possible combinations
of changes in prices and cost and their effects on cost ratios and
margins are worked out in Table 1. Combinations involving no
change in the price or cost factor, or equal percentage changes
in cost and price, are rare and statistically suspect. The important
combinations boil down to six. Wherever possible we shall analyze
changes in margins in terms of these combinations.

Demand and Margins

Even when the analysis just described has been performed, margin
changes have been explained only in a proximate and rather super-

TABLE 1

Possible Combinations of Change in Price and Unit Cost and Their Effect on Cost Ratios and Profit Margin

Change in Price	Changes in Cost Per Unit	Change in Cost Ratio	Change in Profit Margin
Rise	Greater percentage rise	Rise	Fall
Rise	Same percentage rise	No change	No change
Rise	Smaller percentage rise	Fall	Rise
Rise	No change	Fall	Rise
Rise	Fall	Fall	Rise
No change	Rise	Rise	Fall
No change	No change	No change	No change
No change	Fall	Fall	Rise
Fall	Rise	Rise	Fall
Fall	No change	Rise	Fall
Fall	Smaller percentage fall	Rise	Fall
Fall	Same percentage fall	No change	No change
Fall	Greater percentage fall	Fall	Rise

ficial sense. One still does not know under what circumstances prices and costs change at different rates or in opposite directions. To carry the analysis farther raises questions that may be summarized under the heading of supply and demand. In particular, we shall often find that prices rise faster than cost, so that the margin widens in spite of rising cost. This can occur, as we shall show, only if something happens that economists call an upward shift of demand. It should be useful at this point to review some of the ideas economists have developed on that subject and to note their relevance to fluctuations in margins.

Careful thinking about supply and demand almost inevitably leads to the notion of a demand schedule. "Other things being equal," people in a specified market will buy a small quantity of a commodity in any specified period of time if the price is high, a larger quantity if the price is lower, an even larger quantity if the price is lower still. For a graphically minded reader, the relation may be represented by a line like *DD* in Chart 1.

Actually we can observe only one point on the curve at any one time. If a certain quantity was in fact sold at a certain average price in one period, we infer that this price and quantity represented a point on the schedule for that period. The curve as a whole is an inference from other information, or perhaps it is just a useful hypothesis. If "other things" change from one period to another,

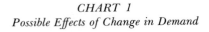

CHART 1
Possible Effects of Change in Demand

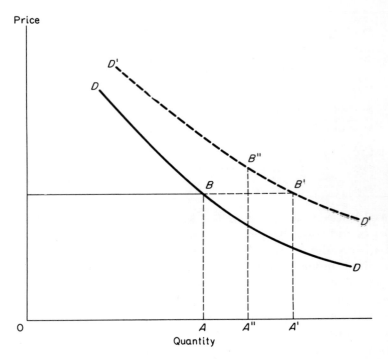

the curve shifts to a new level. When the economically sophisticated speak of a change in demand, they mean that such a shift has occurred. (In Chart 1, if we observed *OA* and *AB* in one period, we would infer that the curve then passed through *B*. A rise in demand would mean that the curve shifted, for example, from *DD* in the first period to *D'D'* in a later period.)

If price and quantity sold change in opposite directions from one period to another, it is usually hard to tell whether the new observation is on the old curve or on a new, shifted curve. If they change in the same direction, however, one may infer that the curve has shifted, i.e., that demand has risen or fallen. In a business upswing both prices and quantities sold usually rise; that is why we say that the demand for most commodities rises.

DEMAND, QUANTITY SOLD, AND PRICE

A rise in demand (i.e., an upward shift in the demand curve), although it raises the price at which the initially marketed quantity could be sold, does not necessarily result in an actual rise in price. One must also take into consideration the response of suppliers. If they increase the quantity supplied fast enough as demand rises, the price will not rise; it may even fall. In Chart 1, if demand rises from DD to $D'D'$, while quantity sold increases from OA to OA', the price will not change. Only if the quantity sold increases to some intermediate amount, such as OA'', will price rise, as from AB to $A''B''$. In later chapters, however, we shall find many actual instances in which the rise in quantity is sufficiently limited to permit a rise in price.

Conversely, if demand falls price will not necessarily fall; it may even rise, if quantity is cut back sufficiently. In Chart 1, if demand is initially at $D'D'$ and falls to DD, and quantity falls from OA' to OA'', price will fall. But if quantity is cut back to OA, price will not change.

DEMAND, QUANTITY, COST, AND MARGIN

Even if an upward shift in demand and the change in quantity sold lead to a rise in price, the combination does not guarantee a rise in margin, for cost may rise simultaneously with demand. If cost rises by a greater percentage than price, the margin will fall; only if it rises by a lesser percentage will the margin rise. Conversely, if a fall in demand and the change in quantity sold lead to a fall in price, the margin will not necessarily decline; that depends also on what happens to cost.

SHIFT IN DEMAND ESSENTIAL
TO SOME CHANGES IN MARGIN

Certain combinations of changes in quantity, cost, and margin cannot occur without certain shifts in demand. If quantity and cost both rise, there must be a rise in demand if the margin is to rise. For if demand did not rise, the increase in quantity would not be accompanied by a rise, but by a fall in price, and the margin would be squeezed between falling price and rising cost. Conversely, if quantity and cost both fall, there must be a downward shift in demand if the margin is to fall. Otherwise, the fall in quantity would be accompanied by a rise in price; with cost falling and price rising, the margin would widen.

Statistical Procedures

CLASSIFICATION OF EXPENSES

The expenses a business enterprise incurs can be divided conveniently into three groups. One is labor expense, including salaries of officers and general office employees as well as salaries and wages of those workers more directly engaged in productive processes. The second is expense for commodities and services purchased from other business enterprises, including not only materials that enter into the products, such as cotton yarn used in a shirt, but other commodities and services needed to carry on operations, such as fuel, power, light, and business stationery. It is hard to find a single word to describe the third group of expenses, but for lack of a better term one may call them general or overhead expenses. They include such items as insurance, interest, depreciation, and taxes. For reasons presently to be described, we exclude taxes on profits. Payroll taxes might well be included in labor expense although the statistics often do not permit this to be done.

INCOME ACCOUNTS VERSUS INCREMENTAL COST

Cost to a vendor, as estimated by him, influences price insofar as it sets a minimum beneath which he considers it would not be worth his while to sell. The expense data we use to compute cost per unit of product sold are obtained, in effect, from business income statements. They include some items, such as depreciation, interest on fixed debt, and others that are not affected immediately by the volume of sales. At times businessmen may figure that these costs cannot be fully covered in any case, and it may be better to take a price which will cover some portion of them than to ask a fully inclusive price at which customers will not buy very much. On the other hand, income statement expense does not include any return on the capital of owners. A businessman who could not expand sales without buying new plant or equipment would count some return on any equity capital that might be involved as part of the minimum price at which he would accept additional orders.

FOCUS ON PROFITS BEFORE TAXES

Only profits after income taxes (and excess profits taxes, when levied) indicate what proprietors or stockholders actually earned from the operation of their properties; but profits before taxes reflect more accurately the impact of changes in demand and in the cost of labor and materials. Profits after taxes have been affected by changes in the rate of income tax and also by the imposition and later expiration of the excess profits tax. Sometimes the exact taxes due on the profits of a quarter cannot be determined when the accounts for that quarter are made up and published. Under such circumstances corporations include a more or less arbitrary round sum in their quarterly income statements to represent their tax accrual. Tax liability for past periods may be readjusted, resulting in extra taxes or in refunds which are often included in the current income statement, although they do not result from current operations. We therefore center our attention on before-tax figures; by the margin, we mean the ratio of profits before taxes to sales unless we indicate otherwise.

FIGURES ARE SEASONALLY ADJUSTED

Wherever possible in the following chapters, we use quarterly or monthly data, since annual figures tend to minimize and blur the cyclical fluctuations in which we are interested. On the other hand, quarterly and monthly figures often show evidence of seasonal influence. Whenever we find such evidence, the figures have been adjusted for seasonal variation.[1] In an industry selling products like garden tools or swimsuits, the seasonal analysis might

---

[1]The usual technique of seasonal adjustment cannot be applied to a series of figures that contains both positive and negative items. Profit margins are sometimes negative. Where this was the case, we circumvented the difficulty by seasonally adjusting the ratio of cost to sales and deducting the seasonally adjusted cost ratios from unity (or, in percentage form, from 100) to get seasonally adjusted margins. Seasonally adjusted profits could then be obtained by applying the adjusted margins to adjusted sales.

indicate the quantity sold should rise 20 per cent from the first quarter of the year to the second for purely seasonal reasons. If, in a particular year, the unadjusted quantity rose 30 per cent between those quarters, the seasonally adjusted figures we use would show a rise. If unadjusted quantity rose only 10 per cent, the seasonally adjusted figures would show a fall. In an industry that sells products like electric heaters or ski togs, a seasonal decline of, say, 20 per cent might be expected between the same two quarters. If the unadjusted figures declined only 10 per cent, the adjusted figures would show a rise; if the unadjusted figures declined 30 per cent, the adjusted figures would show a fall.

DIVIDING A CYCLE INTO STAGES

Cost, price, the margin, or profit may not change in the same direction throughout an upswing or downswing in quantity sold. For example, the margin may rise during the earlier portion of an upswing but fall during the later portion. To explore such possibilities, every expansion or contraction of quantity can be divided into a standard number of segments; and we can then ask what, if anything, usually happens in first segments, in second segments, and so forth.

Specifically, we cut up each expansion into the following periods: the trough quarter, the first third of the quarters between trough and peak, the second third, the last third, and the peak quarter. We divide each contraction in the same way, the trough quarter now of course being the last period. We call each period a stage. In a full trough-to-trough cycle the last stage of the expansion is identical with the first of the contraction, so there are nine stages in all, which we number consecutively from I to IX. Stage IX of one cycle is identical with stage I of the next. Usually II, III, IV and VI, VII, VIII contain more than one quarter, in which case we strike an average of the figures for the several quarters. If the number of quarters between I and V or V and IX is not evenly divisible by three, we make III or VII one quarter longer, or shorter, than its neighbors. The procedure is illustrated for the machinery group of industries in Table 2.

With five-stage averages, the change in a variable during a phase — i.e., an expansion or contraction — of quantity can be examined

TABLE 2
Illustrative Division into Stages of a Cycle in Quantity Sold, Machinery Industry, 4Q 1949 – 4Q 1954

Stage	Quarters Included			Profit Margin (per cent)
	First	Last	Number	
I	4Q 1949	4Q 1949	1	9.1
II	1Q 1950	4Q 1950	4	12.4
III	1Q 1951	1Q 1952	5	13.1
IV	2Q 1952	1Q 1953	4	10.9
V	2Q 1953	2Q 1953	1	10.7
VI	3Q 1953	4Q 1953	2	8.2
VII	1Q 1954	1Q 1954	1	9.0
VIII	2Q 1954	3Q 1954	2	8.9
IX	4Q 1954	4Q 1954	1	7.8

in four successive segments. In an expansion, the first is the change from I to II, the second the change from II to III, and so on. In the machinery industry we observe that the margin rose in the first segment of the expansion from 9.1 to 12.4. By examining the first segment of other expansions in this industry and others, we can determine whether a rise commonly occurs in first segments.

Although the foregoing procedure indicates the characteristic direction of change in margins in any class of segments, it does not indicate what pattern of change margins follow in any single quantity expansion or contraction in any single industry. In one expansion in one industrial group, a variable may rise in every segment; the changes in the order of time may be $+ + + +$. In another expansion in the same or another industrial group the variable may fall in the first two and rise in the last two segments; the pattern of change may be $- - + +$.

There are sixteen logically possible patterns of change in four successive segments. To simplify the discussion, some of these patterns can be grouped into eight categories; for example $+ + + -$, $+ + - -$, and $+ - - -$ can all be described as cases of rise, fall (Table 3).

The five-stage procedure cannot be applied to quantity expansions and contractions less than five quarters long. We can, how-

TABLE 3

Possible Patterns of Change in Four Successive Segments of an Expansion or Contraction

Direction of Change in				Description of Pattern	Category Number
First Segment	Second Segment	Third Segment	Fourth Segment		
+	+	+	+	Continuous rise	1
+	+	+	−	Rise, fall	2
+	+	−	−	Rise, fall	
+	−	−	−	Rise, fall	
+	+	−	+	Rise, fall, rise	3
+	−	+	+	Rise, fall, rise	
+	−	−	+	Rise, fall, rise	
+	−	+	−	Rise, fall, rise, fall	4
−	−	−	−	Continuous fall	5
−	−	−	+	Fall, rise	6
−	−	+	+	Fall, rise	
−	+	+	+	Fall, rise	
−	−	+	−	Fall, rise, fall	7
−	+	−	−	Fall, rise, fall	
−	+	+	−	Fall, rise, fall	
−	+	−	+	Fall, rise, fall, rise	8

ever, note the quarter-to-quarter direction of change in shorter phases, and can apply some of the categories in Table 3. If the phase is two quarters long, the sequence of change can be $++, +-,$ $-+,$ or $--$; it can be classified in category one, two, five, or six. If it is three quarters long, it may be assignable to one of these categories or to category three or seven. In this manner we can exploit our information for short as well as long phases.

2

MANUFACTURING: PRICES
AND COST DURING CYCLES IN
QUANTITY SOLD OR PRODUCED

COMMODITIES CAN BE STUDIED ONLY IN GROUPS

In the preceding chapter the factors that influence profits were outlined in terms of the market for a single commodity. In practice, however, it is not possible to study profits derived from individual commodities on an extensive scale. Most business enterprises produce many products. Some of the costs such an enterprise incurs are exclusively connected with the sales of one product or another. They are direct or out-of-pocket costs. Other expenses are common to several products and cannot be apportioned among them except by some more or less arbitrary formula. Statistics that show the profits derived from individual items, after deducting either out-of-pocket or fully-allocated cost, are not ordinarily available.

We can, however, study the profits derived by industrial groups of firms from all the products they sell. Especially detailed data are available for manufacturing corporations. Beginning with the first quarter of 1947, the Federal Trade Commission and the Securities and Exchange Commission have jointly published estimates of the sales, expenses, and profits of all manufacturing corporations. They have also published the same information for each of twenty-two subdivisions of manufacturing, and have computed profit margins for all. We shall refer to each subdivision simply as an "industry," although in most cases each includes a wide range of manufacturing activity.

In dealing with the complex of commodities produced by such an industry, it is necessary to think in terms of index numbers combining the quantities of the various products and index numbers combining their prices. If the index numbers are accurate and consistently designed, however, the relations among cost, prices, and margins which were outlined at the beginning of the last chapter hold good. [1]

Although the FTC-SEC figures were designed to provide totals for all corporations in each major industry, in the earlier years they fall short of the true totals because of difficulties in sampling and estimation. It is possible to raise the figures in such a way as to make allowance for the shortfall; the technique used to make that allowance is described in the appendix.

These data, when adjusted for coverage and seasonal variation, show what happened to the margin and aggregate profits of an industry between any specified dates. They do not indicate the extent to which the changes in margin were the result of changes in prices received or of changes in cost. They do not tell whether the changes in demand and quantity supplied were such as, for example, to permit both costs and profits to rise. To explore the influences affecting profits, data on prices received and quantity sold are also needed.

Often the available price data do not closely match the sales and profit data. One reason is that a corporation assigned by FTC-SEC to one industry makes not only products characteristic of that industry but items usually regarded as products of another industry. Suppose, for example, that a corporation makes both glass and paint, but derives more revenue from the sale of the

---

[1]For example, composite quantity sold in either of two periods can be defined as the sum of the quantities sold, each quantity being weighted by its average price in the first period. The composite quantity in the second period can then be symbolized by $\Sigma p_1 q_2$, and that in the first by $\Sigma p_1 q_1$. Using this definition of composite quantity,

$$\frac{\text{Unit cost II}}{\text{Unit cost I}} = \frac{\text{Cost ratio II}}{\text{Cost ratio I}} \times \frac{\text{Price index II}}{\text{Price index I}}$$

where the price index is weighted by quantities sold in the second period. For, if c = unit cost, E = aggregate expense, and S = aggregate sales revenue, then

$$c_2 = E_2/\Sigma p_1 q_2 = (E_2/S_2)(S_2/\Sigma p_1 q_2) = (E_2/S_2)(\Sigma p_2 q_2/\Sigma p_1 q_2)$$

$$c_1 = E_1/\Sigma p_1 q_1 = E_1/S_1$$

$$\frac{c_2}{c_1} = \left(\frac{E_2/S_2}{E_1/S_1}\right)\left(\frac{\Sigma p_2 q_2}{\Sigma p_1 q_2}\right)$$

From this formula, all the relations in Table 1 can be deduced.

former than of the latter. FTC-SEC count sales of paint as well as of glass in the sales of the stone, clay, and glass products industry. Paint prices are included in the wholesale price index for chemicals, not in that for stone, clay, and glass.

How serious are such discrepancies? A special study by the Census Bureau makes it possible to tell, for corporations assigned to each industry in 1954, how many of the employees of these corporations worked in factories making products of the industry, and how many worked in establishments making other products or performing some kind of nonmanufacturing service.

In most cases it appears that over 85 per cent of the workers employed by corporations assigned to an FTC-SEC industry made

TABLE 4

Employees of Manufacturing Corporations: Number in Industry to Which Corporation Is Assigned and in All Other Industries, Fifteen Industries, 1954

	Number (thousands) in Establishments in				Percentage in Industry to Which Corporation is Assigned (3) ÷ (4) (5)
Industry to Which Corporation is Assigned	Subindustry to Which Corporation is Assigned (1)	Other Sub-industries in Same Industry[a] (2)	Industry to Which Corporation is Assigned (1) + (2) (3)	All Industries Including Nonmanu-facturing (4)	
Food and beverages[b]	1,507.0	44.5	1,551.5	1,676.9	92.5
Tobacco	94.4	0	94.4	97.8	96.5
Textiles	952.6	37.0	989.6	1,052.6	94.0
Apparel	1,135.6	4.9	1,140.5	1,162.1	98.1
Lumber and products	598.7	15.1	613.8	638.2	96.2
Paper and products	403.3	73.6	476.9	514.7	92.7
Chemicals	582.9	29.6	612.5	794.2	77.1
Petroleum refining	235.3	1.9	237.2	359.6	66.0
Rubber	226.1	0	226.1	305.9	73.9
Leather and products	337.6	7.7	345.3	364.2	94.8
Stone, clay, glass	428.5	3.0	431.5	483.8	89.2
Primary metals	923.2	35.5	958.7	1,298.2	73.8
Fabricated metals	819.7	3.8	823.5	929.0	88.6
Machinery	1,232.1	29.3	1,261.4	1,456.5	86.6
Electric equipment	746.5	12.3	758.8	1,079.8	70.3

Source: *Company Statistics,* 1954 Censuses of Business, Manufactures, and Mining Industries. Does not include employees in central administrative offices, auxiliaries, sales branches, and sales offices of these companies.

[a]Incomplete; some subindustries not reported by Census.

[b]Does not include single-industry companies in sugar subindustry. Employment in miscellaneous food products estimated from payroll data.

products of that industry (Table 4). For petroleum refining, however, the figure is only 66.0, and for primary metals only 73.8
per cent. But the Census data show that many of the remaining
workers were engaged in mining, transportation, or distribution.
Most of them produced, carried, or sold raw materials or products
for the companies. Their pay, and other expenses of the "establishments" in which they worked, are included in the expenses of
the FTC-SEC industry, and the revenue from which the companies
obtain compensation for such expenses is included in the FTC-SEC
sales. The ratios for chemicals, rubber, and electric equipment
(see col. 5, Table 4) are also rather low. Census antidisclosure
rules prevent full reporting of the information called for in
column 2. If it were available, the ratios in column 5 would be
higher.

Quantity Sold

ESTIMATING QUANTITY SOLD

Price indexes are available for all of the twenty-two FTC-SEC
industries except printing and publishing, motor vehicles, other
transportation equipment, instruments, and miscellaneous. The
indexes refer to products characteristic of an industry, not to all
products made by corporations in the industry. But the ratio of
the value of characteristic products to the value of all products
must be somewhat similar to the ratios in the last column of Table
4, or rather to the higher, true ratios suggested in the discussion of
that table. Accordingly we assume that the price index for an
industry approximately represents the course of prices received by
corporations in the industry.

We use the price index not only to measure that course but to
estimate the quantity of goods the industry sells. An index of corporate sales in each industry is divided by its index of prices to get
an index of quantity sold.

In the labor statistics to be considered later, the primary iron
and steel and primary nonferrous metals industries are combined.
We therefore combine the FTC-SEC data for these industries.
Comparison of the FTC-SEC data for the furniture industry with
labor data suggests that the former lose coverage rapidly with the

passage of time. Accordingly, we omit furniture. Of the twenty–
two FTC-SEC industries, therefore, one is lost by statistical merger,
one is dropped because of coverage, and five have no adequate
price indexes. We are left with fifteen for which we can estimate
quantity sold and compute indexes of cost per unit. They accounted for 81 per cent of the sales of all twenty-two industries in
1947 and 80 per cent in 1961.

CYCLES IN QUANTITY SOLD

The quarterly indexes of quantity sold were charted for each
industry, and peaks and troughs in each were determined by in-
spection of the charts.

Most of the upswings and downswings in the several industries
corresponded roughly in time to those in business at large, as
indicated by the National Bureau business chronology (Table 5),
and can be divided into three groups of expansions (1949–53,
1954–57, and 1958–60) and four groups of contractions (1948–
49, 1953–54, 1957–58, and 1960–61). Only four industries
– food, tobacco, rubber, and machinery – had upswings approximately as long as the 1949–53 business expansion. For others,
this expansion was interrupted by a contraction of quantity sold
after the surge of demand resulting from the outbreak of the
Korean War subsided. We are therefore obliged to recognize
two extra groups of industry expansions which we shall call early
Korean and late Korean, and an extra group of contractions in
the vicinity of 1951 which we shall call Korean.

The quantity sold by the food, leather, and stone-clay-glass
industries was already contracting when the data began in 1947;
hence these industries are not included in the 1948–49 group of
contractions. The apparel industry was expanding at the beginning
and continued to expand until 4Q 1952. After 3Q 1954, the food
industry continuously increased the quantities it sold; it is therefore not represented in most groups of "phases" (expansions or
contractions). The tobacco industry likewise increased its quantity
from 4Q 1954 onward. For such reasons, the number of industries
represented in the several temporal groups varies; and only one
group includes all fifteen.

The index of quantity sold by each industry was weighted by the

TABLE 5
Peaks and Troughs in General Business and in Quantity Sold, Fifteen Manufacturing Industries, 1947–61

	Peak	Trough	Peak	Trough	Peak	Trough	Peak	Trough	Peak	Trough
General Business	4Q 1948	4Q 1949	—	—	2Q 1953	3Q 1954	3Q 1957	2Q 1958	2Q 1960	1Q 1961
Manufacturing Industries										
Food and beverages	—	3Q 1948	—	—	2Q 1953	3Q 1954	—	—	—	—
Tobacco	2Q 1948	1Q 1950	—	—	4Q 1952	4Q 1954	—	—	—	—
Textiles	2Q 1948	1Q 1949	3Q 1950	3Q 1951	4Q 1952	2Q 1954	3Q 1957	1Q 1958	3Q 1959	1Q 1961
Apparel	—	—	—	—	4Q 1952	4Q 1953	3Q 1956	4Q 1957	2Q 1959	1Q 1960
Lumber and products	1Q 1948	1Q 1949	1Q 1951	3Q 1951	4Q 1952	1Q 1954	3Q 1956	3Q 1957	1Q 1959	2Q 1961
Paper and products	3Q 1948	2Q 1949	2Q 1951	2Q 1952	3Q 1953	1Q 1954	3Q 1955	4Q 1957	3Q 1959	4Q 1960
Chemicals	3Q 1948	2Q 1949	3Q 1950	4Q 1951	1Q 1953	4Q 1953	1Q 1957	1Q 1958	2Q 1959	4Q 1960
Petroleum refining	—	—	—	—	2Q 1953	4Q 1953	4Q 1956	4Q 1957	2Q 1960	1Q 1961
Rubber	4Q 1947	4Q 1949	3Q 1950	2Q 1951	1Q 1953	1Q 1954	3Q 1957	1Q 1958	3Q 1959	1Q 1961
Leather and products	—	1Q 1950	3Q 1950	—	4Q 1952	1Q 1954	1Q 1957	2Q 1958	2Q 1960	4Q 1960
Stone, clay, glass	—	2Q 1949	2Q 1951	2Q 1952	1Q 1953	1Q 1954	2Q 1956	2Q 1958	2Q 1959	4Q 1959
Primary metals	2Q 1948	4Q 1949	2Q 1951	2Q 1952	2Q 1953	2Q 1954	1Q 1956	2Q 1958	2Q 1959	1Q 1961
Fabricated metals	1Q 1948	2Q 1949	1Q 1951	3Q 1951	2Q 1953	1Q 1954	2Q 1957	2Q 1958	3Q 1959	2Q 1960
Machinery	2Q 1948	4Q 1949	—	—	2Q 1953	4Q 1954	2Q 1956	2Q 1958	2Q 1959	1Q 1961
Electric equipment	3Q 1948	1Q 1949	1Q 1951	3Q 1951	1Q 1953	3Q 1954	1Q 1957	1Q 1958	3Q 1960	1Q 1961
15-Industry composite	4Q 1947	4Q 1949	—	—	2Q 1953	1Q 1954	1Q 1957	1Q 1958	2Q 1960	1Q 1961

ratio of its 1947–49 sales to the 1947–49 sales of all, and the weighted indexes were combined to get a composite index of quantity (Chart 2). This index had upswings and downswings corresponding to those in business at large. There was no decided contraction after the Korean outbreak, but the curve is irregular with only a small upward tilt in the middle of the 1949–53 period.

Having located the upswings and downswings of quantity, we can now consider how changes in prices received, cost, and margins were related to fluctuations in that variable.

Prices Received

DEFECTS OF THE PRICE INDEXES

To indicate the course of prices received by the several industries, we used the Bureau of Labor Statistics wholesale price data. These represent prices "in the first important commercial transaction" and are therefore more appropriate to use in conjunction with data for revenues of manufacturing corporations than they would be if they pertained to later stages of distribution. BLS combines its price relatives into various groupings, some of which represent as nearly as practicable the group of products made by one or another of our fifteen industries; in other cases, it was necessary to make our own groupings. Details are shown in the appendix.

The percentage changes in the price index for an industry are probably only rough approximations of the true course of prices received by companies in the industry. Each industry sells a great variety of products, and each product is often sold in a variety of grades, models, sizes, and other specifications. Only a sample of the many separately priced items are included in the index, in the hope that their movement represents that of the whole complex of prices. Correspondingly, the weights of the index are crude; they do not represent the full diversity of production. Moreover, the weights of the index are changed only at intervals of years, while the composition of quantity sold varies more or less continuously. Products of other industries sold by corporations assigned to any one industry are not included in that industry's index. Even if price indexes for such products were available, we would not know what weight to assign to them.

CHART 2
*Quantity Sold and Quantity Produced, Composite of Fifteen
Manufacturing Industries, 1947 – 61*

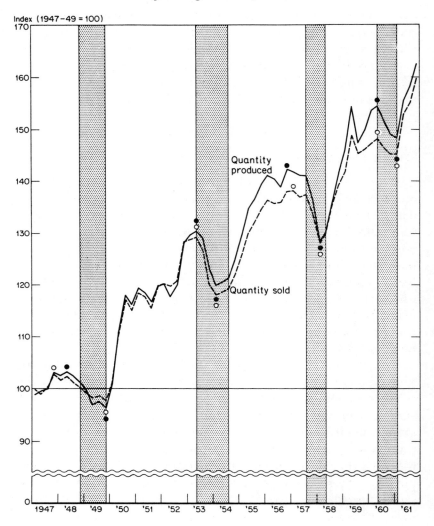

SOURCE: Appendix Tables B-1, B-2.
   NOTE: Shaded areas are contractions in business. Dots are at peaks
and troughs of quantity produced; circles are at peaks and troughs of
quantity sold.

There is reason to suspect that the prices of the items included in the indexes fluctuate more than the BLS relatives for those items do.[2] Some critics think that true prices have a greater tendency to rise during periods of expanding output or business and a greater tendency to fall during periods of contraction than the indexes indicate. On the other hand, if the indexes included more items and products, there might be more offsetting changes and the indexes might fluctuate less than they do.

Our sales data for any quarter reflect the prices involved in contracts on which delivery is made during the quarter. Some of those goods may have been ordered in a previous quarter, and the price may have been determined at that time. According to BLS, "The prices reported for the wholesale price indexes are those in effect as of the mid-month pricing date. They are generally the prices at which new business will be booked."[3] There is some danger, therefore, that the sales reported for any quarter may best be represented by the BLS index for the previous quarter, or perhaps by some kind of weighted average of indexes for the current and earlier quarters. The accuracy of our work could be affected in either of two ways. Deflation by a price index that took account of prices preceding the quarter of delivery might change the comparative level of the quantity-sold index in successive quarters; in particular, it might locate the turning points in quarters different from those indicated by the procedure we regularly employ. Even if the turning points are correctly noted, perhaps we should use earlier indexes to indicate the change in prices reflected in deliveries. For example, if a trough in quantity sold occurred in 3Q 1954 and a peak in 2Q 1957, the prices applicable to these sales may have been the prices in 2Q 1954 and 1Q 1957, respectively.

We have 900 quarterly figures for sales in one industry or another, each of which has been deflated by the BLS index for the same quarter. To see how much difference allowance for the lag between contract and recorded sale might make, we could divide

[2] See the staff papers by Harry E. McAllister and John Flueck in Price Statistics Review Committee, *The Price Statistics of the Federal Government,* New York, NBER, 1961.

[3] Letter of October 31, 1962, from Arnold E. Chase, Chief, Division of Prices and Cost of Living, BLS.

each sales figure by the price index for the preceding quarter, or the second preceding quarter, or an arbitrarily weighted combination of quarters; but the operation would be tedious. We did, however, make a limited experiment for one industry in which the lag may be substantial, machinery; we deflated the sales in each quarter by the price index for the preceding quarter. Of eight turning points in quantity sold, two are changed (Table 6). The direction of stage-to-stage change in cost is the same in twenty-five of twenty-eight instances; in price, the same in twenty-three of twenty-eight. Percentage changes are not much affected.

TABLE 6

Effect of Alternative Deflation Procedures on Turning Points in
Quantity Sold and on Amplitudes of Change in
Cost and Price Indexes, Machinery Industry, 1947 – 61

Kind of Turn	Date of Turn		Cost Per Unit		Price Index	
	A	B	A	B	A	B
			(percentage change from preceding peak or trough)			
Peak	2Q 1948	3Q 1948	--	--	--	--
Trough	4Q 1949	4Q 1949	9.3	9.8	6.9	7.2
Peak	2Q 1953	2Q 1953	11.4	12.8	16.5	14.9
Trough	4Q 1954	4Q 1954	5.6	6.5	2.2	3.1
Peak	2Q 1956	4Q 1956	5.6	6.8	9.0	11.3
Trough	2Q 1958	2Q 1958	13.2	12.5	9.3	7.5
Peak	2Q 1959	2Q 1959	-1.9	-2.4	2.1	1.5
Trough	1Q 1961	1Q 1961	6.6	6.7	2.2	2.2

Note: Sales in each quarter are divided by price index for same quarter to compute A columns, for preceding quarter to compute B columns. Example of computation of price index, column B: price index for 3Q 1949 ÷ by price index for 2Q 1948 = 1.072.

On the assumption that turning points were correct, we made a simpler but more comprehensive test of the effect of various assumptions on the direction of changes in price. The first line of Table 7 gives the results of our standard procedure: the price change between trough and peak quarters in quantity is calculated from the price indexes for the same two quarters. The price change on the second line is computed from the price indexes for the respectively preceding quarters. Rises predominate both in expansions and in contractions, with or without the lag (Table 7). Allowance for a two-quarter lag, or a three-quarter lag, does not upset the predominance.

TABLE 7

Price Indexes: Number of Rises and Falls During Phases of Quantity Sold, Based on Various Assumptions About Quarter in Which Price Is Determined, Fifteen Manufacturing Industries, 1947–61

Time at Which Price of Quantity Sold is Assumed to be Determined	Expansions		Contractions	
	Rises	Falls	Rises	Falls
Quantity peak and trough	35	13	42	18
One quarter before quantity turn	31	17	47	13
Two quarters before quantity turn	33	15	48	12
Three quarters before quantity turn	35	13	41	19

It is clear that the price indexes should be used with caution. It is also clear that major changes in the indexes reflect real movements in prices, although perhaps with some delay and some degree of overstatement or understatement. If we ignore the evidence of the indexes entirely, our understanding of changes in profits will be poorer than if we employ that evidence with circumspection.

PRICES ROSE APPRECIABLY IN SOME EXPANSIONS

The price indexes themselves have a net rise in most expansions and most contractions. The percentage of rises is larger, however, in the former than in the latter. There are also considerable differences among successive groups of cycles. In the late Korean group, six of nine indexes declined, and the median change is a small decline (Table 8). In the 1958–60 group, most indexes rise, but the median rise is small. A majority of the indexes rise in every group of contractions, except 1948–49, but again the median changes are small. Price rises were universal in the early Korean period and in 1954–57.

An over-all price index for the fifteen industries may complete

TABLE 8
Price Indexes: Changes in Successive Groups of Expansions and
Contractions in Quantity Sold,
Fifteen Manufacturing Industries, 1947−61

Group of Phases	Number of Observations	Number of Net Rises	Median Percentage Change
Expansions			
Early Korean	9	9	9.2
Late Korean	9	3	−1.2
1949−53	4	3	11.1
1954−57	13	13	7.1
1958−60	13	7	0.8
Total	48	35	2.4
Contractions			
1948−49	10	6	2.6
Korean	9	5	0.1
1953−54	15	12	2.2
1957−58	13	11	1.2
1960−61	13	8	0.5
Total	60	42	1.1

the picture. To construct it, we weight the price index for each
industry by the ratio of its 1947−49 sales to 1947−49 sales of the
fifteen, and sum the products. This index rises substantially in the
1949−53 and 1954−57 expansions; the other changes are small
(Table 9). Using prices for the quarter preceding each turn in
quantity alters the direction of change in one phase.

TABLE 9
Composite Price Index: Net Change During Phases of Quantity Sold,
Fifteen Manufacturing Industries Combined, 1947−61

		Percentage Change				Percentage Change	
Date of Turn in Quantity Sold	Price Index (1947−49 =100)	To Peak from Trough	To Trough from Peak	Quarter Preceding Turn in Quantity Sold	Price Index (1947−49 =100)	To Peak from Trough	To Trough from Peak
4Q 1947	99.7	--	--	3Q 1947	96.0	--	--
4Q 1949	98.2	--	−1.5	3Q 1949	98.5	--	2.6
2Q 1953	112.2	14.3	--	1Q 1953	111.5	13.2	--
1Q 1954	113.5	--	1.2	4Q 1953	113.8	--	2.1
1Q 1957	122.7	8.1	--	4Q 1956	121.4	6.7	--
1Q 1958	124.1	--	1.1	4Q 1957	123.9	--	2.1
2Q 1960	125.1	0.8	--	1Q 1960	125.0	0.9	--
1Q 1961	125.7	--	0.5	4Q 1960	125.6	--	0.5

PRICES ROSE MORE OFTEN AND FASTER NEAR PEAKS
THAN NEAR TROUGHS IN QUANTITY

Even when there is little net change in price over an expansion or contraction as a whole, there may be a difference in this respect between early and late expansion, or early and late contraction. When sales are low and unused capacity is abundant, manufacturers may be eager enough for new business to cut prices; when production is running near capacity and demand is high, buyers may be eager to bid prices up. The price indexes rise much more often in the neighborhood of peaks in quantity than in the neighborhood of troughs. The frequency of rises increases steadily from the first to the last segment of expansions, and decreases steadily from the first to the last segment of contractions (Table 10).

TABLE 10

Prices Indexes: Direction of Change from Stage to Stage of Cycles in Quantity Sold, Fifteen Manufacturing Industries, 1947–61

From Stage	To Stage	Number of Observations			Percentage		Median Percentage Change
		With Rise	With Fall	Total	Rising	Falling	
I	II	19	27	46	41	59	−0.3
II	III	29	17	46	63	37	0.6
III	IV	34	12	46	74	26	0.8
IV	V	37	9	46	80	20	0.4
V	VI	34	6	40	85	15	1.5
VI	VII	31	9	40	78	22	0.8
VII	VIII	18	22	40	45	55	−0.1
VIII	IX	14	26	40	35	65	−0.2
I	V	35	13	48[a]	73	27	2.4
V	IX	42	18	60[a]	70	30	1.1

[a] Includes phases too short for division into five stages.

The differences between first and last segments are quite consistent from one group of phases to the next. In every group of expansions, except the 1949–53 group, price increases are more frequent in the last than in the first segment (Table 11). The exception reflects the sharp rise in prices following the Korean outbreak early in the long phase. Again with the same exception, the median change in price is algebraically larger in the last segment than in the first. In every group of contractions, rising prices are more numerous during the first segment than during the last; in every one, the median change in price is algebraically greater in the first segment than in the last.

It is hard to believe that these progressive and systematic differences can result from errors in the price indexes.

TABLE 11

Price Indexes: Changes in Early and Late Expansion or Contraction During Successive Groups of Phases in Quantity Sold, Fifteen Manufacturing Industries, 1947–61

Group of Phases	Number of Observations	Number of Net Rises		Median Percentage Change	
		I–II	IV–V	I–II	IV–V
Expansions					
Early Korean	8	1	8	−2.5	4.5
Late Korean	8	1	7	−1.2	0.4
1949–53	4	3	2	3.0	−1.2
1954–57	13	10	11	0.4	1.6
1958–60	13	4	9	−0.3	0.2
Total	46	19	37	−0.3	0.4
		V–VI	VIII–IX	V–VI	VIII–IX
Contractions					
1948–49	6	6	1	6.0	−0.8
Korean	5	4	1	0.4	−0.6
1953–54	11	10	5	1.6	0.0
1957–58	11	9	5	1.1	−0.1
1960–61	7	5	2	0.2	−0.2
Total	40	34	14	1.5	−0.2

In twenty-one, or 44 per cent, of the forty-eight quantity expansions, prices followed a fall-rise pattern (Table 12). In each such instance, the prices received by an industry apparently declined, at least from the first to some intermediate stage, and rose from that stage to the fifth. Continuous rises, however, occurred in a substantial block: fifteen, or 31 per cent.

In twenty-eight, or 47 per cent, of the sixty contractions, the pattern was rise-fall. In each of these cases, price rose at least from stage V to some intermediate stage, and fell from that stage to IX. The most common pattern of price change in contraction was therefore the exact opposite of the most common pattern in

TABLE 12
Price Indexes: Patterns of Change During Expansions and Contractions in Quantity Sold, Fifteen Manufacturing Industries, 1947–61
(number of phases)

Pattern	Expansions			Contractions		
	Long Phases	Short Phases[a]	Total	Long Phases	Short Phases[a]	Total
Continuous rise	13	2	15	7	5	12
Rise, fall	4	0	4	20	8	28
Rise, fall, rise	2	0	2	6	0	6
Rise, fall, rise, fall	0	--	0	1	--	1
Continuous fall	2	0	2	2	6	8
Fall, rise	21	0	21	0	0	0
Fall, rise, fall	3	0	3	3	1	4
Fall, rise, fall, rise	1	--	1	1	--	1
Total	46	2	48	40	20	60

a
Too short for division into five stages.

expansion. The second most common pattern, however, was the same in both — a continuous rise.

The percentage of net rises was larger in expansions than in contractions. Prices usually declined during the last half of contractions and the first segment of expansions. Price changes, therefore, showed some tendency to fluctuate with quantity, but with a lag.

RELATION OF PRICES TO QUANTITIES ORDERED

Table 10 shows that prices rose in some instances during the first segment of an expansion in quantity sold, and in most cases during the second, third, and fourth segments. The data suggest that advances in price were not sufficient to discourage customers from increasing their purchases; in other words, demand rose fast enough to more than offset those advances. But, as noted earlier, goods delivered late in expansion may have been ordered at an earlier time when prices were lower. To analyze the relations among price, demand, and purchasing, it might be more illuminating to study changes in prices during cycles in orders. The Department of Commerce estimates the value of new orders received by the fabricated metals, machinery, and electric equip-

TABLE 13
Price Indexes: Direction of Change from Stage to Stage of Cycles in
Quantity Ordered and Sold,
Three Manufacturing Industries, 1948–61

		STAGES OF QUANTITY ORDERED			STAGES OF QUANTITY SOLD		
		Number of Observations		Per-centage	Number of Observations		Per-centage
From Stage	To Stage	With Rise in Price[a]	Total	Rising	With Rise in Price[a]	Total	Rising
I	II	2	11	18	4	11	36
II	III	8	11	73	8	11	73
III	IV	10	11	91	11	11	100
IV	V	10	11	91	9	11	82
V	VI	9	9	100	8	8	100
VI	VII	8	9	89	7	8	88
VII	VIII	8	9	89	4	8	50
VIII	IX	4	9	44	3	8	38
I	V	10	12[b]	83	8	11[b]	73
V	IX	11	14[b]	79	13	14[b]	93

a
  Price fell in all other observations.
b
  Includes phases too short for division into five stages.

ment industries—three of our fifteen groups. We deflated the
orders estimates by the price indexes to get estimates of quantity
ordered, noted the turning points and hence the cycles and
stages in these figures, and computed a price index for each stage
of each orders cycle in each of the three industries.

The orders data do not change the picture much (Table 13).
In most instances, prices rose in the last three segments of expansions in quantity ordered. Prices often rose during segments of
contractions in quantity ordered, presumably contributing to the
decline in the latter. On the other hand, five price declines in
fourth segments did not keep quantity ordered from declining.

Total Cost

COST ROSE IN MANY EXPANSIONS BUT IN EVEN MORE CONTRACTIONS OF QUANTITY SOLD

In each industry and quarter, we computed aggregate expense
by deducting profits from sales. An index of aggregate expense was
then divided by the index of quantity sold to get an index of cost.

TABLE 14

*Cost Per Unit: Direction of Change from Stage to Stage of Cycles
in Quantity Sold, Fifteen Manufacturing Industries, 1947−61*

From Stage	To Stage	Number of Observations			Percentage		Median Percentage Change
		With Rise	With Fall	Total	Rising	Falling	
I	II	10	36	46	22	78	−1.2
II	III	18	28	46	39	61	−0.2
III	IV	31	15	46	67	33	0.8
IV	V	34	12	46	74	26	0.7
V	VI	34	6	40	85	15	2.0
VI	VII	36	4	40	90	10	2.0
VII	VIII	26	14	40	65	35	0.4
VIII	IX	18	22	40	45	55	−0.2
I	V	27	21	48[a]	56	44	0.9
V	IX	54	6	60[a]	90	10	3.9

a
Includes phases too short for division into five stages.

TABLE 15

*Cost Per Unit: Changes in Successive Groups of Expansions and
Contractions in Quantity Sold,
Fifteen Manufacturing Industries, 1947−61*

Group of Phases	Number of Observations	Number of Net Rises	Median Percentage Change
Expansions			
Early Korean	9	7	4.9
Late Korean	9	4	−0.9
1949−53	4	3	10.4
1954−57	13	10	5.0
1958−60	13	3	−1.6
Total	48	27	0.9
Contractions			
1948−49	10	9	6.0
Korean	9	9	7.1
1953−54	15	13	5.2
1957−58	13	12	3.8
1960−61	13	11	1.9
Total	60	54	3.9

Since our price index for an industry does not include products of other industries produced by corporations in that industry, our estimates of quantity sold are in error insofar as a more inclusive index would have moved differently from the available index. If the more inclusive index would rise more than the available one when sales expand, our growth in quantity sold is too large. If it would fall more when sales were contracting, our decline in quantity sold is too large. If our quantity index rises too much, cost per unit may appear to fall in cases in which it actually rose. If our quantity index declines too much, cost per unit may appear to rise in cases in which it actually fell. Such cautions are especially relevant to figures for the chemicals, rubber, and electric equipment industries (cf. Table 4 and discussion).

Cost indexes prepared in this way indicate a net rise in a narrow majority of upswings in quantity, 56 per cent (Table 14). In downswings, net rises were much more numerous, occurring in 90 per cent of the observations.

INFLATION AND COST

Whether cost rises with increases in quantity sold appears to depend on the degree of inflation prevailing. In the early Korean, the 1949–53, and the 1954–57 expansions, cost rose in a majority of the industries, and the median net change was a rise (Table 15). In the late Korean and the 1958–60 groups, on the other hand, cost fell in most industries, and the median change was a decline.

COST, LIKE PRICES, ROSE MORE OFTEN AND FASTER NEAR PEAKS IN QUANTITY

Cost rose in only a minority of first segments of expansions in quantity (Table 14). It rose in a larger minority of the second segments, and in more than half of third and fourth segments. During contractions, it rose more often than not in all segments except the last. But the percentage of rises declines continuously from the first to the fourth segment.

The differences between early and late expansion is fairly consistent from one temporal group of expansions to another (Table 16). From stage I to stage II, cost fell in a majority of the expansions in each group except 1949–53, and the median change was

a fall. From stage IV to stage V, however, the median either rose
or declined less than from I to II, again with an exception in the

TABLE 16

Cost Per Unit: Changes in Early and Late Expansion or Contraction During Successive Groups of Phases in Quantity Sold,
Fifteen Manufacturing Industries, 1947 – 61

Group of Phases	Number of Observations	Number of Net Rises		Median Percentage Change	
		I–II	IV–V	I–II	IV–V
Expansions					
Early Korean	8	0	8	−3.4	5.2
Late Korean	8	3	6	−0.8	0.0
1949–53	4	2	2	0.4	−1.5
1954–57	13	3	12	−1.1	1.7
1958–60	13	2	6	−1.1	−0.1
Total	46	10	34	−1.2	0.7
		V–VI	VIII–IX	V–VI	VIII–IX
Contractions					
1948–49	6	6	2	5.5	−0.9
Korean	5	5	3	2.1	1.0
1953–54	11	9	6	1.6	0.0
1957–58	11	8	5	1.4	−0.1
1960–61	7	6	2	0.9	−1.0
Total	40	34	18	2.0	−0.2

1949–53 group. In every group of contractions, the median rise
in the first segments was larger than the median rise, if any, in the
last segments. In every group most industries had rising cost as the
quantity they sold began to decline, but rising cost was less common
toward the end.

The most frequent sequence of change was a fall in the earlier
and a rise in the later part of a quantity expansion (Table 17). In
contractions the most common sequence was a continuous rise.

The frequently expressed belief that prices generally rise only
when "full" employment or some other rigid barrier to expansion
is encountered needs to be modified. Price increases predominated
in the third, not only in the fourth, segment of expansion. Increases in earlier segments were by no means rare. Early rises
were found in supposedly competitive as well as in supposedly
"price-administered" industries. Considerable possibilities of physical expansion still exist when prices begin to rise. Furthermore,

TABLE 17

Cost Per Unit: Patterns of Change During Expansions and Contractions in Quantity Sold,
Fifteen Manufacturing Industries, 1947–61

(number of phases)

Pattern	Expansions			Contractions		
	Long Phases	Short Phases[a]	Total	Long Phases	Short Phases[a]	Total
Continuous rise	4	1	5	11	12	23
Rise, fall	3	1	4	15	5	20
Rise, fall, rise	3	0	3	6	1	7
Rise, fall, rise, fall	0	--	0	2	--	2
Continuous fall	3	0	3	0	1	1
Fall, rise	26	0	26	1	1	2
Fall, rise, fall	6	0	6	5	0	5
Fall, rise, fall, rise	1	--	1	0	--	0
Total	46	2	48	40	20	60

[a]
Too short for division into five stages.

prices often continue to rise after sales begin to recede — i.e., as an industry moves away from, not toward, a capacity level of operations.

Labor Cost

In the introductory chapter, we noted three major categories into which the expenses of an industry can be divided. If we had separate data on each, we could compute each kind of cost on a per-unit-of-product basis. There are no data on expenditures for purchased products or on property taxes, etc., for our fifteen manufacturing groups; but we can make rough estimates of labor cost per unit. The latter is the product of man-hours per unit and average hourly earnings; both factors can be studied.

ESTIMATING MAN-HOURS PER UNIT OF PRODUCT

For each manufacturing group, the Bureau of Labor Statistics publishes figures on hours per week for production workers and on the number of such workers in the middle week of each month. Multiplying these figures together for any month gives aggregate man-hours for the middle week. Averaging the products for three months gives quarterly figures. Dividing each quarterly figure by average quarterly man-hours in 1947–49 gives a quarterly index of man-hours. Dividing this index by the index of quantity yields an index of production-worker hours per unit of quantity.

BLS also reports the number of other than production workers, although not their hours per week. Assuming that they worked the same hours as production workers, we estimate aggregate midweek man-hours of all workers in each industry and, proceeding as before, get an index of all-worker hours per unit.

ESTIMATING QUANTITY PRODUCED

The BLS data are for "establishments" making the products of an industry, regardless of whether those establishments are owned by corporations assigned to that industry. The figures for any quarter do not include any labor performed in an earlier quarter on goods sold in the quarter for which the figures are reported. They do include labor performed during a quarter even if the goods were not sold until later. The estimates of quantity sold include goods drawn from initial finished inventory and do not include quantities produced during the quarter but left in inventory at the end. The labor data are, therefore, not ideally comparable with data on quantity sold. In computing indexes of man-hours or payrolls per unit of product it would be preferable to use indexes of production, rather than of quantity sold, in assigned establishments, rather than in assigned corporations.

A large number of production indexes are constructed monthly for the Board of Governors of the Federal Reserve System. They are combined into groups which are more nearly on an establishment than a corporate basis, and they aim to measure production, not quantity sold. On first thought they appear to be comparable with the labor data, and in fact we have used quarterly averages of the Federal Reserve indexes for four industries — tobacco, paper and products, petroleum products, and primary metals — to compute indexes of man-hours per unit of production and labor cost per unit of production.

But there is a basic objection to using other FR indexes for this purpose, however useful they may be for other purposes. Because no direct monthly (or quarterly) figures are available for many kinds of production, the FR statisticians construct annual indexes of "productivity," dividing an annual index of man-hours of production workers into an annual index of production based on independent annual data for output (or, in some cases, deflated value). A monthly index of productivity is interpolated between the annual data by a standard formula. The course of the monthly index during any calendar year is governed entirely by the annual figures for that year, the preceding year, and the following year (Table 18). Almost always, productivity is assumed to move

TABLE 18

Effect of Direction of Change in Annual Productivity Ratios on Direction of Monthly Change in Ratios Interpolated by Federal Reserve Method

Annual Ratio		Monthly Ratio in Second Year	
First Year to Second	Second Year to Third	Jan. to June or July	June or July to Dec.
+	+	+[a]	+[a]
+	0	+	−
+	−	+	−
0	+	−	+
0	0	0	0
0	−	+	−
−	+	−	+
−	0	−[a]	+[a]
−	−	−[a]	−[a]

Note: Call three successive annual productivity indexes r_1, r_2, r_3. Each index is multiplied by a factor which varies from month to month. Call them f_1, f_2, f_3. Call the productivity index desired for any month in the second year m. Then $m = f_1 r_1 + f_2 r_2 + f_3 r_3$. For example, in January 1953, $m = .421 r_{52} + .616 r_{53} + (-.037) r_{54}$.

Let a = the numerical value of the difference between r_1 and r_2, and c = the numerical value of the difference between r_2 and r_3. Then $m = f_1 (r_2 \pm a) + f_2 r_2 + f_3 (r_2 \pm c)$. Although the individual factors vary from month to month, their total is always unity. Consequently, $m = r_2 \pm f_1 a \pm f_3 c$. The directions of change in the table above were worked out from this formula.

[a]Except when changes in annual ratios are numerically very unequal, i.e., the larger is at least 2.73 times the smaller.

in one direction continuously for half a year or throughout the year. A monthly index of man-hours is multiplied by the inter-polated index to get monthly production.

A group index may consist entirely of components based on independent monthly production data, or it may be composed largely of components based on productivity interpolation. The monthly Federal Reserve indexes for the four industries previously mentioned are based entirely on independent production data. All the other groups rely, at least in part, on productivity interpolation (Table 19).

The effect of the interpolator on the index of output itself may be small, and not objectionable if all one desires is a rough

TABLE 19

Federal Reserve Production Indexes: Importance of Components Based on Deflated Value and Man-Hours

Industry Group	Weight of Entire Group, 1957 (1)	Annual Series Based on Deflated Value[a]		Monthly Series Based on Man-Hours	
		Weight (2)	Per Cent of (1) (3)	Weight (4)	Per Cent of (1) (5)
Food and beverages	9.87	3.62	37	4.19	42
Tobacco	.77	.00	0	.00	0
Textiles	2.78	1.45	52	.50	18
Apparel	3.44	.45	13	1.33	39
Lumber and products	1.65	.00	0	.74	45
Paper and products	3.27	.00	0	.00	0
Chemicals	7.10	4.90	69	4.67	66
Petroleum refining	1.93	.00	0	.00	0
Rubber	1.91	1.25	65	.47	25
Leather and products	1.10	.26	24	.26	24
Stone, clay, glass	2.92	1.80	62	2.06	71
Primary metals	7.73	.00	0	.00	0
Fabricated metals	5.42	4.89	90	4.89	90
Machinery	8.92	8.44	95	8.78	98
Electric equipment	6.39	4.95	77	4.60	72
Total of 15 groups	65.20	32.01	49	32.49	50
Furniture and fixtures	1.48	1.48	100	1.48	100
Printing and publishing	4.66	3.13	67	3.13	67
Motor vehicles	5.04	.66	13	1.97	39
Other transportation equipment	5.72	3.00	52	5.72	100
Instruments	1.66	1.54	93	1.66	100
Miscellaneous and ordnance	2.73	2.26	83	2.73	100
Total of 21 groups	86.49	44.08	51	49.18	57

Source: *Industrial Production, 1959 Revision,* Board of Governors of the Federal Reserve System, Washington, 1960, pp. S-4 through S-19.

[a]Includes a few series, not separately indicated by the Federal Reserve, based on man-hour data.

measure of the approximate course of output. But precise comparison of output with related variables is another matter. Changes in man-hours per unit of product influence cost, and information about them is therefore highly pertinent to the present inquiry. But suppose "production" in an industry is estimated from labor data. Then if we divide man-hours by production, all we get is the reciprocal of the interpolated productivity ratio. If half of the production is so estimated, it is difficult to describe just what we do get, but it can hardly be a true index of hours per unit.

If the interpolated productivity factors are in error, the changes in production from quarter to quarter may be overstated, understated, or wrong in direction. If aggregate expenses are divided by such an index, the true change in cost may be understated, overstated, or reversed.

An alternative would be to divide man-hours and payroll indexes by the indexes of quantity sold used in earlier sections of this chapter. True, in addition to their more general imperfections, these indexes reflect corporate quantity sold rather than establishment quantity produced. On the other hand, they make no explicit or systematic assumption about hours per unit of product. Comparisons of their year-by-year, industry-by-industry changes with those in the annual FR indexes (which do not depend on "productivity" assumptions) indicate much similarity of movement, but some divergence. Over the fifteen years from 1947 to 1961, the trend of the annual FR index for some industries differs considerably from that of the annual deflated sales, and it probably reflects the trend of production more accurately. We therefore use the annual FR indexes to indicate the general level of quantity produced within each calendar year, and the deflated value indexes to indicate the distribution of quantity produced among the four quarters. In every industry where the FR quarterly indexes depend in part on productivity assumptions, and a price index for the industry is available, we have adopted this solution. Specifically, for each industry we calculate for each calendar year the ratio of the FR index to the deflated sales index. The ratio for any year is assumed to be correct for the middle of the year. One-fourth of the change in the ratio from one mid-year to the next is assumed to occur in each quarter. The resulting ratios for

TABLE 20

Peaks and Troughs in General Business and in Quantity Produced, Fifteen Manufacturing Industries, 1947–61

	Peak	Trough	Peak	Trough	Peak	Trough	Peak	Trough	Peak	Trough
General Business	4Q 1948	4Q 1949	--	--	2Q 1953	3Q 1954	3Q 1957	2Q 1958	2Q 1960	1Q 1961
Manufacturing Industries										
Food and beverages	--	3Q 1948	--	--	--	4Q 1954	--	--	--	--
Tobacco	2Q 1948	4Q 1949	--	--	3Q 1952	2Q 1954	--	--	--	--
Textiles	2Q 1948	1Q 1949	3Q 1950	3Q 1951	2Q 1953	4Q 1953	4Q 1955	1Q 1958	3Q 1959	1Q 1961
Apparel	--	--	3Q 1950	3Q 1951	4Q 1952	1Q 1954	3Q 1956	4Q 1957	2Q 1959	1Q 1960
Lumber and products	1Q 1948	1Q 1949	1Q 1951	2Q 1952	1Q 1953	1Q 1954	1Q 1955	2Q 1958	2Q 1959	2Q 1961
Paper and products	2Q 1948	2Q 1949	2Q 1951	4Q 1951	3Q 1953	1Q 1954	3Q 1956	1Q 1958	3Q 1959	4Q 1960
Chemicals	3Q 1948	2Q 1949	--	--	1Q 1953	4Q 1953	1Q 1957	1Q 1958	--	--
Petroleum refining	2Q 1948	2Q 1949	3Q 1950	3Q 1951	3Q 1953	1Q 1954	3Q 1957	1Q 1958	3Q 1960	1Q 1961
Rubber	4Q 1947	1Q 1949	3Q 1950	3Q 1951	1Q 1953	1Q 1954	3Q 1957	1Q 1958	3Q 1959	1Q 1961
Leather and products	--	1Q 1950	3Q 1950	3Q 1951	4Q 1952	4Q 1953	1Q 1957	2Q 1958	1Q 1959	4Q 1960
Stone, clay, glass	4Q 1948	2Q 1949	2Q 1951	2Q 1952	1Q 1953	1Q 1954	2Q 1956	2Q 1958	2Q 1959	4Q 1959
Primary metals	3Q 1948	4Q 1949	2Q 1951	2Q 1952	2Q 1953	2Q 1954	4Q 1955	1Q 1958	2Q 1959	1Q 1961
Fabricated metals	1Q 1948	2Q 1949	1Q 1951	3Q 1951	2Q 1953	1Q 1954	2Q 1957	2Q 1958	3Q 1959	3Q 1961
Machinery	1Q 1948	4Q 1949	--	--	2Q 1953	4Q 1954	2Q 1956	2Q 1958	2Q 1960	1Q 1961
Electric equipment	2Q 1948	1Q 1949	3Q 1950	3Q 1951	2Q 1953	2Q 1954	1Q 1957	2Q 1958	2Q 1960	1Q 1961
15-Industry composite	2Q 1948	4Q 1949	--	--	2Q 1953	1Q 1954	4Q 1956	1Q 1958	2Q 1960	1Q 1961

the beginning and end of each quarter are averaged. The deflated sales figure for the quarter is multiplied by the average ratio to get an index of quantity produced. It was possible to apply this method to eleven industries; lack of adequate price data prevented its application to five; lack of comparability in sales and output coverage prevented its application in one (furniture). The eleven industries for which the method was used, plus the four for which the FR quarterly indexes were used, are the same as the fifteen industries discussed earlier in this chapter.

Turning points in quantity produced, like those in quantity sold, corresponded in a general way to turns in business, with numerous "extra" turns in 1950–51 (Table 20).

TABLE 21

Man-Hours Per Unit: Direction of Change from
Stage to Stage of Cycles in Quantity Produced,
Fifteen Manufacturing Industries, 1947–61

From Stage	To Stage	Number of Observations			Percentage		Median Percentage Change
		With Rise	With Fall	Total	Rising	Falling	
		PRODUCTION WORKERS					
I	II	2	42	44	5	95	−5.6
II	III	7	37	44	16	84	−2.8
III	IV	12	32	44	27	73	−1.8
IV	V	7	37	44	16	84	−2.0
V	VI	31	13	44	70	30	2.0
VI	VII	13	31	44	30	70	−1.4
VII	VIII	17	27	44	39	61	−1.0
VIII	IX	22	22	44	50	50	−0.1
I	V	0	48	48[a]	0	100	−11.0
V	IX	34	27	61[a]	56	44	0.7
		ALL WORKERS					
I	II	1	43	44	2	98	−5.5
II	III	5	39	44	11	89	−3.0
III	IV	11	33	44	25	75	−1.6
IV	V	8	36	44	18	82	−2.0
V	VI	34	10	44	77	23	2.4
VI	VII	15	29	44	34	66	−0.6
VII	VIII	21	23	44	48	52	−0.2
VIII	IX	24	20	44	55	45	0.2
I	V	0	48	48[a]	0	100	−11.4
V	IX	45	16	61[a]	74	26	1.9

[a]Includes phases too short for division into five stages.

INVERSE RELATION OF MAN-HOURS
PER UNIT TO QUANTITY

In each industry, we have computed production-worker man-hours per unit at each stage in each cycle of quantity. Hours per unit were lower at the peak than at the preceding trough in all of the forty-eight upswings of quantity (Table 21). They were higher at the trough than at the preceding peak in 56 per cent of sixty-one downswings of quantity.

Production-worker hours per unit were also studied in my report on *Changes in Labor Cost during Cycles in Production and Business*.[4] Quantity was measured without the aid of price deflation; only industries with output measured in physical units or weighted indexes of physical measures were included. Because of this restriction, the portion of manufacturing covered was much smaller than in the present study. On the other hand, the "industries" were more narrowly and precisely defined; there was less danger of mingling industries with unlike characteristics in one set of figures; each of our present fifteen "industries" is usually a combination of more specifically definable industries. The span of time varied from industry to industry, beginning in 1932 or later and ending in 1958 or earlier. A few nonmanufacturing industries were included in the tabulations. Nevertheless, the conclusions of the two studies are similar. The earlier study revealed a net fall in hours per unit during 92 per cent of the expansions, and a net rise in 71 per cent of the contractions.[5] Both investigations suggest that hours per unit are inversely related to quantity.

For the present study, we have also all-worker hours per unit. Once more we find a net fall in every expansion. There was a net rise in 74 per cent of the contractions, much higher than the 56 per cent for production workers only. When all workers are considered, the inverse relation between hours per unit and quantity is even more strongly marked. Rises outnumbered declines in each temporal group of contractions, except 1948–49, and the median change was a rise in every group (Table 22).

Although it was, in effect, assumed that hours per week of other workers fluctuate by the same percentages as hours of production workers, it is likely that they fluctuate somewhat less. Consequently,

[4]New York, NBER Occasional Paper 74, 1960.
[5]*Changes in Labor Cost*, Table 10, p. 26.

TABLE 22

Man-Hours Per Unit: Changes in Successive Groups of Expansions
and Contractions in Quantity Produced,
Fifteen Manufacturing Industries, 1947–61

Group of Phases	Number of Observations	Number of Net Rises	Median Percentage Change
PRODUCTION WORKERS			
Expansions			
Early Korean	9	0	−14.8
Late Korean	10	0	−7.4
1949–53	4	0	−18.2
1954–57	13	0	−12.7
1958–60	12	0	−9.1
Total	48	0	−11.0
Contractions			
1948–49	12	4	−1.1
Korean	10	8	6.6
1953–54	14	10	1.4
1957–58	13	6	−0.3
1960–61	12	6	0.2
Total	61	34	0.7
ALL WORKERS			
Expansions			
Early Korean	9	0	−15.0
Late Korean	10	0	−6.4
1949–53	4	0	−15.5
1954–57	13	0	−12.4
1958–60	12	0	−10.1
Total	48	0	−11.4
Contractions			
1948–49	12	6	0.4
Korean	10	9	8.2
1953–54	14	11	2.9
1957–58	13	10	1.9
1960–61	12	9	1.3
Total	61	45	1.9

aggregate hours of all workers may have increased less during expansions of quantity and fallen less during contractions than assumed. In that case, the declines in hours per unit during expansions and the rises during contractions were even more pronounced than our figures would indicate. With respect to our conclusion, the assumption about hours per week is on the conservative side.[6]

[6]In estimating annual productivity, the BLS has assumed that nonproduction workers always work a 40 hour week. Using that figure, the inverse fluctuations of all-worker hours per unit would be even greater.

HOURS PER UNIT FELL EVEN IN LATE EXPANSION

In every segment of quantity expansions, instances of falling man-hours per unit outnumbered instances of rising man-hours per unit (Table 21). Declines were most common in first segments, where they occurred in 95 per cent of the observations for production workers and 98 per cent of those for all workers. But even the lowest percentage is 73 (production workers, third segments). In my earlier work on labor costs during cycles, declines in production-worker hours per unit were also found to outnumber rises in every segment. There was a somewhat more systematic progression. The percentage of observations with rising man-hours

TABLE 23

Man-Hours Per Unit: Patterns of Change During Expansions and Contractions in Quantity Produced, Fifteen Manufacturing Industries, 1946–61
(number of phases)

Pattern	Expansions			Contractions		
	Long Phases	Short Phases[a]	Total	Long Phases	Short Phases[a]	Total
PRODUCTION WORKERS						
Continuous rise	0	0	0	0	6	6
Rise, fall	2	0	2	11	6	17
Rise, fall, rise	0	0	0	15	1	16
Rise, fall, rise, fall	0	--	0	5	--	5
Continuous fall	20	2	22	1	2	3
Fall, rise	6	2	8	6	2	8
Fall, rise, fall	15	0	15	5	0	5
Fall, rise, fall, rise	1	--	1	1	--	1
Total	44	4	48	44	17	61
ALL WORKERS						
Continuous rise	0	0	0	0	7	7
Rise, fall	1	0	1	12	6	18
Rise, fall, rise	0	0	0	18	1	19
Rise, fall, rise, fall	0	--	0	4	--	4
Continuous fall	23	2	25	0	0	0
Fall, rise	7	2	9	5	3	8
Fall, rise, fall	12	0	12	4	0	4
Fall, rise, fall, rise	1	--	1	1	--	1
Total	44	4	48	44	17	61

[a]Too short for division into five stages.

per unit of product increased steadily from 8 in first segments of production expansions to 29 in fourth segments.

A continuous fall from stage to stage was the most common pattern of change during individual expansions (Table 23).

HOURS PER UNIT ROSE MOST OFTEN AT BEGINNING OF CONTRACTION

During contractions of quantity, there is less similarity between the early and late portions. The net rises over the phase as a whole seem to be concentrated in the earliest segment. Hours per unit rise in a large majority of first segments, fall in a large majority of second segments; thereafter, the observations are more evenly divided. In my earlier study, a more regular progression was found. The percentages of rises, for production workers, in successive segments, were 74, 60, 57, 56. The absence of an equally smooth rise and fall in the present data may be a consequence of the smaller number of observations (forty-four instead of eighty-nine expansions, forty-four instead of ninety-seven contractions), the poorer comparability of the labor and production data, or the broader and less homogeneous industrial categories. Although the progression in the earlier study was downward, the figures indicate a predominance of rises in every segment. In any case, there seems to be little doubt that hours per unit rise sharply immediately after a downturn in quantity, or that the early rise usually exceeds any later decline.

During the contractions in the present study, the most common pattern of change was an initial rise and a subsequent fall or a rise-fall-rise pattern.

HOURLY EARNINGS ROSE IN ALL SEGMENTS OF EXPANSION AND CONTRACTION

Labor cost per unit of product depends not only on hours per unit but on the amount of wages paid per hour. Average hourly earnings (available only for production workers) were higher at the peak than at the trough in every quantity expansion (Table 24). They were higher at the trough than at the peak in all but two of the contractions. In every segment of expansion and of contraction, rises greatly outnumbered declines. Hourly earnings followed a continuously rising pattern in forty, or 83 per cent, of the

TABLE 24

*Hourly Earnings of Production Workers: Direction of Change from
Stage to Stage of Cycles in Quantity Produced,
Fifteen Manufacturing Industries, 1947 – 61*

| From Stage | To Stage | Number of Observations | | | Percentage | | Median Percentage Change |
		With Rise	With Fall	Total	Rising	Falling	
I	II	42	2	44	95	5	1.4
II	III	38	6	44	86	14	2.4
III	IV	44	0	44	100	0	3.0
IV	V	43	1	44	98	2	2.2
V	VI	40	4	44	91	9	1.3
VI	VII	42	2	44	95	5	1.3
VII	VIII	37	7	44	84	16	1.0
VIII	IX	37	7	44	84	16	0.4
I	V	48	0	48[a]	100	0	9.2
V	IX	59	2	61[a]	97	3	3.7

[a]Includes phases too short for division into five stages.

TABLE 25

*Hourly Earnings of Production Workers: Patterns of Change During
Expansions and Contractions in Quantity Produced,
Fifteen Manufacturing Industries, 1947 – 61*
(number of phases)

| Pattern | Expansions | | | Contractions | | |
	Long Phases	Short Phases[a]	Total	Long Phases	Short Phases[a]	Total
Continuous rise	36	4	40	29	13	42
Rise, fall	1	0	1	6	3	9
Rise, fall, rise	5	0	5	5	1	6
Rise, fall, rise, fall	0	--	0	0	--	0
Continuous fall	0	0	0	0	0	0
Fall, rise	2	0	2	2	0	2
Fall, rise, fall	0	0	0	1	0	1
Fall, rise, fall, rise	0	--	0	1	--	1
Total	44	4	48	44	17	61

[a]Too short for division into five stages.

quantity upswings, and in forty-two, or 69 per cent, of the down-swings (Table 25).

In many cases, however, earnings rose faster when quantity was expanding than when it was contracting. We have compared the change per quarter in each phase of quantity with the change per quarter in the following phase of opposite character. In seventy-one of ninety-five comparisons, hourly earnings increased more rapidly in the expansion than in the contraction. The figures are affected by changes not only in wage rates but in the proportion of overtime, which tends to rise in expansion and fall in contraction. Overtime accounts for at least part of the differences in the rate of increase.[7]

Average hourly earnings in manufacturing as a whole had a similar history from 1932 to 1961. They increased in the six expansions of manufacturing production (measured between turning points in the Federal Reserve index of production) and also in five of the six contractions, falling slightly in 1937–38. The rate of increase in each of the five contractions was smaller than in the neighboring expansions.

ESTIMATING LABOR COST

Since rising hourly earnings were so common in all segments of expansions and contractions, one would expect rises in labor cost to be more numerous than rises in hours per unit. Unfortunately, the payroll data relate to production workers only; there is no quarterly information on the compensation of other workers in separate industries. Even the production-worker data do not include social security taxes or the cost of other "fringe benefits." But at least we can construct indexes of payrolls for production workers in each industry, and can divide them by our indexes of quantity to get indexes of production labor cost per unit.

PRODUCTION LABOR COST FELL IN MOST EXPANSIONS

The indexes do show that labor cost per unit increased more often than man-hours per unit. The "percentage rising" figure on

[7]Separate indexes of wage rates are scarce. For a discussion of some that are available, see Daniel Creamer, *Behavior of Wage Rates during Business Cycles*, New York, NBER, OP 34, 1950.

TABLE 26

Labor Cost Per Unit (Production Workers): Direction of Change
from Stage to Stage of Cycles in Quantity Produced,
Fifteen Manufacturing Industries, 1947–61

From Stage	To Stage	Number of Observations			Percentage		Median Percentage Change
		With Rise	With Fall	Total	Rising	Falling	
I	II	6	38	44	14	86	−4.2
II	III	18	26	44	41	59	−1.0
III	IV	36	8	44	82	18	1.6
IV	V	21	23	44	48	52	−0.2
V	VI	37	7	44	84	16	3.8
VI	VII	27	17	44	61	39	0.6
VII	VIII	26	18	44	59	41	0.3
VIII	IX	25	19	44	57	43	0.4
I	V	15	33	48[a]	31	69	−2.8
V	IX	52	9	61[a]	85	15	4.3

[a]Includes phases too short for division into five stages.

TABLE 27

Labor Cost Per Unit (Production Workers): Changes in Successive
Groups of Expansions and Contractions in Quantity Produced,
Fifteen Manufacturing Industries, 1947–61

Group of Phases	Number of Observations	Number of Net Rises	Median Percentage Change
Expansions			
Early Korean	9	2	−3.4
Late Korean	10	5	−0.4
1949–53	4	2	−1.4
1954–57	13	4	−2.7
1958–60	12	2	−3.7
Total	48	15	−2.8
Contractions			
1948–49	12	10	3.2
Korean	10	10	11.0
1953–54	14	11	3.6
1957–58	13	11	4.1
1960–61	12	10	3.5
Total	61	52	4.3

every line of Table 26 is higher than the corresponding figure in Table 21. Nevertheless, labor cost, like hours per unit, fell in a majority of the expansions and rose in a majority of the contractions. The inverse relation predominated in every group of phases except the late Korean and 1949–53 expansions, in which the number of falls equaled the number of rises (Table 27).

The changes during expansions ranged from a decline of 19.7 per cent to an increase of 15.9 per cent; the median change was −2.8 per cent. The changes during contractions ranged from −7.6 to +33.8 per cent; the median was +4.3 per cent.

In the earlier and more precise labor cost study, it was likewise found that production labor cost fell in a majority of the quantity expansions (62 per cent) and rose in a majority of the contractions (91 per cent).[8]

Man-hours per unit, including all workers, fell in every expansion. The more inclusive figure rose even more often in contractions than the less inclusive one (Table 21). If the hourly compensation of other workers fluctuated by about the same percentage as that of production workers, labor cost per unit, including all workers, must have had a net fall in most expansions and a net rise in most contractions.

RISING PRODUCTION LABOR COST
MOST COMMON IN FIRST HALF OF CONTRACTION

Declines in labor cost outnumbered rises in all except third segments of expansions (Table 26). Rises in cost were most numerous immediately after the peak, in first segments of contractions, when they occurred in 84 per cent of the observations. The percentage declines progressively thereafter; but rises outnumber falls in all segments.

In eighteen, or 38 per cent, of the expansions, labor cost fell at first but rose later (Table 28). The more complicated fall-rise-fall pattern, however, was almost equally common. In seventeen, or 28 per cent, of the contractions, labor cost rose continuously; in an equal number it rose at first, but later fell.

[8]*Changes in Labor Cost,* Table 15, p. 39.

TABLE 28

Labor Cost Per Unit (Production Workers): Patterns of Change
During Expansions and Contractions in Quantity Produced,
Fifteen Manufacturing Industries, 1947–61
(number of phases)

Pattern	Expansions			Contractions		
	Long Phases	Short Phases[a]	Total	Long Phases	Short Phases[a]	Total
Continuous rise	1	0	1	7	10	17
Rise, fall	2	0	2	13	4	17
Rise, fall, rise	2	1	3	14	1	15
Rise, fall, rise, fall	1	—	1	3	—	3
Continuous fall	4	2	6	0	0	0
Fall, rise	17	1	18	3	2	5
Fall, rise, fall	16	0	16	3	0	3
Fall, rise, fall, rise	1	—	1	1	—	1
Total	44	4	48	44	17	61

[a]Too short for division into five stages.

AGGREGATIVE FIGURES CONCEAL CYCLICAL VARIATION

We have constructed indexes of hours per unit and labor cost for the fifteen industries combined, i.e., treating them as one vast industry, by the methods used to construct the individual indexes.[9] Nobody who looked at the composite indexes only, however, would suspect that there is an inverse relation between hours per unit or labor cost and quantity. Composite hours per unit declined in contractions of composite output as well as in expansions (Table 29). Composite cost rose in two of the three expansions and fell in some of the contractions. The differences between the composite "industry" and the individual industries is explained by differences in the size of the quantity fluctuations in conjunction with technological change and the upward trend of hourly earnings.

A composite tends to have smaller cyclical fluctuations than its

[9]Composite man-hours and labor cost are aggregates of the fifteen-industry data. Composite quantity produced is an average of the quantity indexes for the fifteen industries weighted in the same manner as the composite price index, namely, by the percentage distribution of sales in 1947–49.

TABLE 29

Quantity Produced, and Man-Hours and Labor Cost Per Unit:
Percentage Changes in Composite and Individual Cycles, 1947 – 61

		Hours Per Unit		Cost Per Unit		Hourly Earnings, Production Workers
	Quantity Produced	Production Workers	All Workers	Production Workers	All Workers	
		EXPANSIONS				
Composite						
4Q 1949–2Q 1953	35.3	−7.8	−6.8	16.3	19.5	26.2
1Q 1954–4Q 1956	18.6	−11.0	−9.8	1.3	3.5	13.9
1Q 1958–2Q 1960	20.3	−9.9	−9.8	−2.2	−1.0	8.6
Average	24.7	−9.6	−8.8	5.1	7.3	16.2
Individual						
a. Between composite						
dates	25.4	−10.5	−9.4	2.8	--	14.8
b. Between own dates	30.8	−11.9	−12.0	−3.4	--	9.8
		CONTRACTIONS				
Composite						
2Q 1948–4Q 1949	−6.6	−8.3	−6.7	−4.4·	−1.4	4.2
2Q 1953–1Q 1954	−8.0	−3.3	−1.5	−1.4	3.1	1.9
4Q 1956–1Q 1958	−9.8	−3.3	−0.6	0.3	5.7	3.7
2Q 1960–1Q 1961	−3.9	−5.3	−3.4	−4.0	−2.0	1.3
Average	−7.1	−5.0	−3.0	−2.4	1.4	2.8
Individual						
a. Between composite						
dates	−7.1	−3.4	−1.7	−0.1	--	3.4
b. Between own dates	−12.8	1.3	3.2	5.6	--	4.2

components. One reason is that turning points in a component often do not coincide with turning points in the composite. In such cases, the change in the component between turning points in the composite is smaller than the change between the component's own turning points, and may even be in the opposite direction. The situation is illustrated by lines a and b of Table 29. To derive line a, the percentage change in each industry between the composite peaks and troughs is computed, yielding fifteen changes from 4Q 1949 to 2Q 1953, fifteen from 1Q 1954 to 4Q 1956, and so forth. The average of the forty-five changes during composite expansions, and of the sixty for composite contractions, is shown on the line. For example, from the composite peak in 2Q 1948 to the composite trough in 4Q 1949, the quantity of lumber products fell 5.3 per cent; this figure is used in calculating the average of −7.1 per cent.

In computing line b, the percentage change in each industry from each trough in its own quantity to the following peak, or vice versa, is computed, and the average of the changes in the forty-eight specific cycle expansions and the sixty-one contractions is shown on the line. From its own peak in 1Q 1948 to its own trough in 1Q 1949, the quantity of lumber products fell 19.7 per cent; this figure is used in calculating the average of −12.8 per cent.

Falling quantity tends to raise hours per unit. But technological progress tends to reduce hours per unit not only in expansions but in contractions of quantity. If the fall in quantity is small, the rise in hours per unit that it would cause in the absence of technological change is likely to be small, and the influence of technology may preponderate over the influence of volume.

Since the rise in quantity during the composite expansions is smaller than in the individual expansions, the fall in hours per unit during the composite expansions tends to be smaller than during the individual expansions. If the fall in hours per unit is small, the influence of the rising hourly earnings factor in labor cost can preponderate over the influence of the falling hours per unit factor.

Although cost including nonproduction workers is not available for individual industries, it was possible to make estimates for the composite. The Department of Commerce supplies quarterly estimates of total labor expense—salaries, wages, and fringe benefits received by all workers—for all manufacturing; and production-worker wages can be computed for all manufacturing from BLS data. The ratio of total compensation to total production-worker payrolls can therefore be computed. The cyclical variations in the ratio are probably similar to those in the corresponding ratio for the fifteen industries combined. Multiplying our index of production-worker cost per unit by an index of the ratio yields an approximate index of all-worker cost per unit.

The downward trend in composite hours per unit was remarkably persistent. So was the upward trend in hourly earnings (Charts 3 and 4). The effect of one trend on production-worker cost virtually neutralized the effect of the other. But there was also an upward trend in the proportion of nonproduction to production workers, and hours of all workers per unit trended downward more slowly. Rising rates of pay more than offset falling hours per unit; the more inclusive measure of labor cost per unit had an upward trend at least through 1958.

ANNUAL FIGURES SUPPORT CONCLUSIONS ON LABOR COST

Our quarterly indexes of output, and therefore the indexes of hours and cost per unit, are defective to some extent because of

CHART 3
*All-Worker Man-Hours and Labor Cost Per Unit,
Composite of Fifteen Manufacturing Industries, 1947–61*

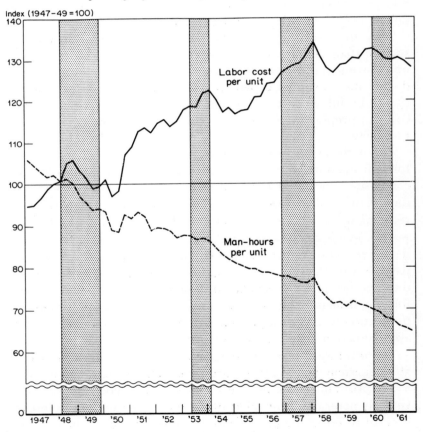

SOURCE: Appendix Table B-2.
NOTE: Shaded areas are contractions in composite quantity produced.

inaccuracies in the price indexes used to derive them. Deflation of sales by prices was used as a means of obtaining quarterly from annual figures. If the deflation by price indexes is distrusted, can anything about cyclical fluctuations in hours per unit and cost be learned from annual figures alone? In the first place, the distrust would presumably extend to the yearly figures for industries where

CHART 4

Production-Worker Man-Hours Per Unit, Hourly Earnings,
and Labor Cost Per Unit,
Composite of Fifteen Manufacturing Industries, 1947–61

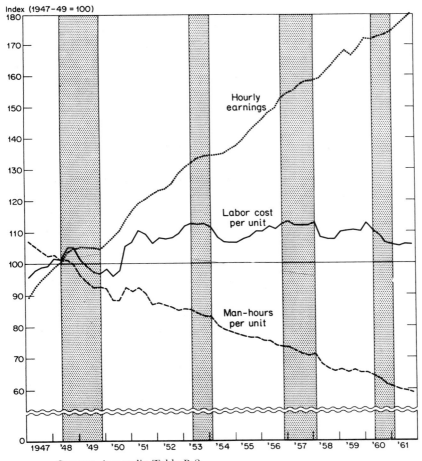

SOURCE: Appendix Table B-2.
NOTE: Shaded areas are contractions in composite quantity produced.

components based on price deflation make up more than half of the weight assigned to the industry. This leaves nine industries with usable data (Table 19).

Annual figures, even if accurate, tend to minimize cyclical fluctuations. Some fluctuations in quantity that appear in quarterly data do not show up at all in yearly data. When they do, a trough quarter often appears in a trough year and a peak quarter in a peak year. In such instances, the percentage change between the annual peak and trough is smaller than that between the quarterly peak and trough. When quantity fluctuations are minimized, any tendency for hours per unit and cost to fluctuate inversely with quantity is likewise minimized. The influence of technology on hours per unit can more often preponderate over the influence of falling volume, and the influence of rising hourly earnings on cost can more often preponderate over the influence of falling hours per unit. We have nevertheless computed annual indexes for the nine industries from 1947 to 1961, using the same sources and methods as for quarterly data.

The effect of using annual statistics was explored in my earlier study. Calculations were made both from annual data and from monthly data for the same industries and approximately the same periods of time. The yearly data indicated declines in hours per unit during most contractions as well as most expansions; but the percentage was lower in the former than in the latter (Table 30). The monthly data indicated a rise in most contractions. In the nine industries considered here, the annual data again indicate a fall in most contractions; but again the percentage is smaller than in expansions. It is likely that if quarterly figures based on independent physical measures of output were available for the nine industries, they would show a majority of rises in contraction as well as of declines in expansion. That is what the quarterly data we actually use indicate (Table 21).

In the earlier study, yearly data indicated a slight majority of increases in labor cost during expansions, but a much larger majority during contractions. The monthly data indicated a clear inverse relation. The annual figures for the nine industries also indicate a slight majority of rises in expansion, but again the percentage is much smaller than in contraction. It is likely that quarterly indexes based on physical measures of output would reveal a majority of declines in expansion as well as of rises during contraction, as the actually available quarterly indexes do (Table 26).

Only thirteen of the expansions and seven of the contractions in the nine industries lasted more than one year. Rises in hours per unit and labor cost were more numerous in the last than in the first year of expansions, and in the first than in the last year of contractions (Table 31). Although the data are skimpy, they agree with our previous finding, based on the available quarterly data, that rises are more numerous around quantity peaks than around

TABLE 30

*Hours and Labor Cost Per Unit: Frequency of Net Rises and Falls
in Phases of Quantity, Monthly Compared with Annual Data*

	EXPANSIONS			CONTRACTIONS		
	Number of Observations	Percentage		Number of Observations	Percentage	
		Rising	Falling		Rising	Falling
	HOURS PER UNIT					
Earlier study[a]						
Production workers, monthly	90	8	92	99	71[c]	28[c]
Production workers, annual	87	11	89	94	40	60
Present study[b]						
Production workers, annual	25	4	96	28	29	71
All workers, annual	25	0	100	28	46	54
	LABOR COST PER UNIT					
Earlier study[a]						
Production workers, monthly	90	38	62	99	91	9
Production workers, annual	87	51	49	94	68	32
Present study[b]						
Production workers, annual	25	52	48	28	64	36
All workers, annual[d]	25	56	44	28	86	14

[a]Hultgren, *Changes in Labor Cost*, pp. 9, 26, 35, 39.

[b]Nine industries.

[c]One observation showed no change.

[d]Based on Department of Commerce annual data for compensation of all employees.

TABLE 31

Hours and Labor Cost Per Unit: Number of Rises and Falls During
First and Last Year of Expansions and Contractions in Quantity
Produced, Nine Manufacturing Industries, 1947−61

	Expansions		Contractions	
	Production Workers	All Workers	Production Workers	All Workers
HOURS PER UNIT				
First year				
Rises	0	0	5	5
Falls	13	13	2	2
Last year				
Rises	3	2	3	3
Falls	10	11	4	4
LABOR COST PER UNIT				
First year				
Rises	3	4	7	7
Falls	10	9	0	0
Last year				
Rises	11	11	4	5
Falls	2	2	3	2

troughs, and that declines are most common in early expansion.[10]

Other Kinds of Cost

For an individual enterprise or industry, expenditures on commodities and services purchased from other business enterprises

[10]Sho-Chieh Tsiang, in *The Variations of Real Wages and Profit Margins in Relation to the Trade Cycle*, London, 1947, studied productivity (the reciprocal of hours per unit) in cotton textiles, paper, steel, and all manufacturing, using annual data. His findings (pp. 65, 94, 101, 108) in terms of the relation of production-worker hours per unit to quantity, may be compared with ours as follows. The blurring effects of annual data and broad aggregation account for Tsiang's finding little relation between productivity and quantity.

	Tsiang (annual data)	*Earlier Study* (monthly data)	*Present Study* (quarterly data)
Cotton textiles	None	Inverse	None[a]
Paper	None	Inverse	Inverse
Steel	Inverse	Inverse	Inverse[b]
All manufacturing	None	None[c]	None[c]

[a]All textiles.
[b]Primary metals.
[c]Composite of fifteen industries (different list in the two studies).

are often comparable in size with labor expenses. Like labor cost, materials cost has a physical and a price component — materials used per unit of product and their prices. There is very little information on how the input of materials per unit of product changes during output cycles, but it probably does not fluctuate inversely with output as input of labor per unit does. It may even vary directly with volume to some extent, because of greater spoilage and resort to inferior materials in busy times. It seems likely, however, that fluctuations in materials cost are similar to those in prices of materials.

We have not ventured to construct indexes of prices paid for materials by individual industries. However, a weighted general index of BLS prices of materials used by manufacturers rose 12.0 per cent in the 1949 – 53 upswing in production and 5.8 per cent in the 1954 – 57 upswing, but fell 0.1 per cent in 1958 – 60 (Table 32). Since some industries had "extra" contractions in quantity sold, with peaks around 1Q 1951 and troughs around 3Q 1951, the table also shows changes during three subphases of the 1949 – 53 upswing. The sharp rise in demand at the Korean outbreak brought a very sharp rise in prices of materials (Chart 5). The subsequent decline continued at a diminished pace in the second expansion subphase.

In contractions, with demand for final products falling, there is no growing eagerness to purchase materials. The index of materials prices fell 9.6 per cent in 1948 – 49 and 4.3 per cent in 1951, rose only 0.8 per cent in 1953 – 54 and 1.5 per cent in 1957 – 58, and fell 0.6 per cent in 1960 – 61.

Changes in materials prices between peaks and troughs in fifteen-industry composite quantity were broadly similar (Chart 5).

Factories buy not only crude materials, such as cotton or coal, but materials which have already been fabricated to some extent by other factories; e.g., steel bars and bolts, plastic materials, parts for assembly. Since 1953 the prices of crude materials have fluctuated inversely rather than positively with fluctuations in output.

These indexes do not include prices of services rendered by other business enterprises; e.g., transportation, supply of electric power, legal services, auditing services, etc. In Chapter 5 it will be shown that prices of railroad service ordinarily have little cyclical

TABLE 32

Wholesale Prices of Materials Used by Manufacturers: Changes
During Cycles in Manufacturing Production, 1947–61

Turns in Federal Reserve Index of Production		ALL MATERIALS PRICES			CRUDE MATERIALS PRICES			MANUFACTURED MATERIALS PRICES		
			Percentage Change			Percentage Change			Percentage Change	
Date	Level	Index (1947–49 = 100)	To Peak from Trough	To Trough from Peak	Index (1947–49 = 100)	To Peak from Trough	To Trough from Peak	Index (1947–49 = 100)	To Peak from Trough	To Trough from Peak
3Q 1948	Peak	107.3	—	—	111.1	—	—	105.2	—	—
2Q 1949	Trough	97.0	—	-9.6	92.7	—	-16.6	99.3	—	-5.6
2Q 1953	Peak	108.6	12.0	—	98.5	6.3	—	114.1	14.9	—
1Q 1954	Trough	109.5	—	0.8	99.7	—	1.2	114.9	—	0.7
1Q 1957	Peak	115.8	5.8	—	95.9	-3.8	—	126.3	9.9	—
2Q 1958	Trough	117.5	—	1.5	99.9	—	4.2	126.8	—	0.4
1Q 1960	Peak	117.4	-0.1	—	93.9	-6.0	—	129.5	2.1	—
1Q 1961	Trough	116.7	—	-0.6	93.6	—	-0.3	128.7	—	-0.6
2Q 1949	Trough	97.0	—	—	92.7	—	—	99.3	—	—
1Q 1951	Quasi-peak	120.7	24.4	—	122.0	31.6	—	120.0	20.8	—
3Q 1951	Quasi-trough	115.5	—	-4.3	113.7	—	-6.8	116.4	-2.0	-3.0
2Q 1953	Peak	108.6	-6.0	—	98.5	-13.4	—	114.1	—	—

fluctuation, and this appears to be true of public utility service also. The price indexes in Table 32, therefore, probably overstate the fluctuation in prices of all privately supplied products and services.

Other costs include such overhead items as interest, depreciation and depletion, and property taxes. In manufacturing we have data only on depreciation and depletion. Aggregate charges of this kind increased somewhat faster than production in the 1949–53 expansion of manufacturing output, and decidedly faster in the 1954–57 expansion (Table 33). In other words, depreciation per unit of product increased. In 1958–60, however, it decreased. Even at the peak in 1960, these charges were only 3.12 per cent of total sales.

CHART 5

Prices Paid by Manufacturers for Crude Materials,
Manufactured Materials, and All Materials, 1947–61

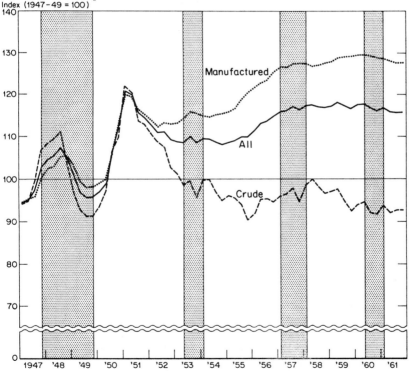

NOTE: Shaded areas are contractions in composite quantity sold (15 industries).

Interest and taxes (other than income taxes) are likewise comparatively unimportant in manufacturing.[11]

TABLE 33

Depreciation and Depletion, All Manufacturing Corporations:
Changes Compared with Changes in Manufacturing Production;
and Ratio of Depreciation and Depletion to Sales

Turns in Federal Reserve Index of Production		Production		Depreciation and Depletion		
Date	Level	Index (1947–49 = 100)	Per-centage Change	Amount (million dollars)	Per-centage Change	Ratio to Sales (per cent)
3Q 1948	Peak	104.0	--	957	--	1.88
2Q 1949	Trough	96.3	−7.4	1,027	7.3	2.20
2Q 1953	Peak	141.3	46.7	1,587	54.5	2.25
1Q 1954	Trough	127.7	−9.6	1,703	7.3	2.64
1Q 1957	Peak	153.3	20.0	2,275	33.6	2.80
2Q 1958	Trough	133.3	−13.0	2,431	6.9	3.31
1Q 1960	Peak	166.3	24.8	2,700	11.1	3.12
1Q 1961	Trough	152.7	−8.2	2,831	4.9	3.40

[11]The tobacco industry, however, pays high excise taxes. Income statements of the five largest companies show that these are included in revenues and in expenses. The taxes are on a so-much-per-unit basis, and are not often changed. Between changes, this kind of cost tends to be constant on a per-unit-of-product-sold basis. Similar remarks apply to the liquor industry, but the latter is only a small part of the FTC-SEC food group.

3

MANUFACTURING: RELATIONS AMONG PROFIT FACTORS DURING CYCLES IN QUANTITY SOLD

Rise in Margins During Expansions and Fall During Contractions

From the preceding chapter it would appear that cost and prices rose in most expansions and contractions of quantity sold, although not in all portions of either. The rises in cost tended to make profit margins narrower, while the rises in prices tended to widen them. It remains to examine the outcome of these often conflicting influences.

There was a net rise in margin during thirty-eight, or 79 per cent, of the quantity expansions in the various industrial groups (Table 34). In contractions of quantity, there was an even stronger predominance of net falls in margins; they declined in fifty-seven, or 95 per cent, of the observations.

Margins therefore varied positively with quantity. How large were the variations? Computing the percentage changes in margins would result in wildly fluctuating figures, since the absolute changes are sometimes large relative to the initial figure. Indeed margins can change from negative to positive; in that case the ratio of the second margin to the first would have a negative sign, which would be confusing since the margin rises algebraically. In fact, none of our fifteen industries had a negative margin at a trough in the relatively prosperous 1947–61 period; but negative margins occured in earlier and more severely disturbed periods, especially around 1932 and 1938. On the other hand, the percentage change in the cost ratio is free of these difficulties.

The median change in the cost ratio during expansions was a

TABLE 34

Margins: Direction of Net Change During Expansions and Contractions
in Quantity Sold, Fifteen Manufacturing Industries, 1947–61

	Number of Quantity Expansions with		Number of Quantity Contractions with	
	Net Rise in Margin	Net Fall In Margin	Net Rise in Margin	Net Fall in Margin
Food and beverages	0	1	0	1
Tobacco	0	1	2	0
Textiles	3	1	0	5
Apparel	2	0	0	3
Lumber and products	3	1	0	5
Paper and products	3	1	0	5
Chemicals	3	1	0	5
Petroleum refining	2	0	1	2
Rubber	2	1	0	4
Leather and products	3	1	0	4
Stone, clay, glass	4	0	0	4
Primary metals	4	0	0	5
Fabricated metals	3	1	0	5
Machinery	3	0	0	4
Electric equipment	3	1	0	5
Total number	38	10	3	57
Percentage of total for expansions or contractions	79	21	5	95

fall of 1.8 per cent (Table 35). The median change in contractions
was a rise of 2.5 per cent. The sharpest falls occurred in the early
Korean expansions, and the sharpest rises in the Korean contractions.

Rising margins were more numerous than falling margins in
every time group of expansions except the late Korean group.
Declining margins were preponderant in every group of contractions.

Rising Margins Most Frequent in Early Expansion

Rising margins outnumbered falling margins in the first three
segments of expansion and were outnumbered in the last three
segments of contraction (Table 36). Rising margins were most
common between stages II and III, falling margins between
stages VII and VIII.

TABLE 35

Cost Ratios: Changes in Successive Groups of Expansions and
Contractions in Quantity Sold,
Fifteen Manufacturing Industries, 1947–61

Group of Phases	Number of Observations	Number of Net Rises	Median Percentage Change
Expansions			
Early Korean	9	0	-7.6
Late Korean	9	6	0.7
1949–53	4	2	-0.7
1954–57	13	2	-1.9
1958–60	13	0	-1.7
Total	48	10	-1.8
Contractions			
1948–49	10	9	3.0
Korean	9	9	4.1
1953–54	15	14	2.5
1957–58	13	13	2.5
1960–61	13	12	1.5
Total	60	57	2.5

During expansions of quantity sold, the most frequent pattern of change was a rise turning into a fall, which occurred in fifteen, or 31 per cent, of the observations (Table 37). A continuous rise was the next most common, occurring in ten instances. In contractions the most common pattern was a continuous decline, found in seventeen, or 28 per cent; a rise-fall occurred in fourteen, or 23 per cent.

In the nine "long" expansions with a continuous rise, the margins of course were highest in the last stage. In some other expansions, an early or intermediate fall was more than offset by a later rise. The margin was highest at stage V in sixteen phases altogether, or 35 per cent of the observations with five stages. This was smaller than the number with a rise from IV to V (twenty-two) which means that in some cases an early or intermediate fall had been partly but not wholly recovered. Stage I was highest in five expansions, II in two, III in fourteen, and IV in nine.

The margin was lowest at stage IX in twenty-five, or 62 per cent, of the forty "long" contractions. Stage V was lowest in two, VI in one, VII in three, and VIII in nine.

The actual peak quarter in the margin preceded the corresponding peak in quantity sold somewhat more often than it

TABLE 36

Margins: Direction of Change from Stage to Stage of Cycles in
Quantity Sold, Fifteen Manufacturing Industries, 1947–61

From Stage	To Stage	Number of Observations			Percentage	
		With Rise	With Fall	Total	Rising	Falling
I	II	30	16	46	65	35
II	III	37	9	46	80	20
III	IV	26	20	46	57	43
IV	V	23	23	46	50	50
V	VI	22	18	40	55	45
VI	VII	8	32	40	20	80
VII	VIII	7	33	40	18	82
VIII	IX	12	28	40	30	70
I	V	38	10	48[a]	79	21
V	IX	3	57	60[a]	5	95

[a]Includes phases too short for division into five stages.

TABLE 37

Margins: Patterns of Change During Expansions and Contractions
in Quantity Sold, Fifteen Manufacturing Industries, 1947–61
(number of phases)

Pattern	Expansions			Contractions		
	Long Phases	Short Phases[a]	Total	Long Phases	Short Phases[a]	Total
Continuous rise	9	1	10	0	0	0
Rise, fall	15	0	15	12	2	14
Rise, fall, rise	5	1	6	8	1	9
Rise, fall, rise, fall	1	--	1	2	--	2
Continuous fall	0	0	0	6	11	17
Fall, rise	9	0	9	3	5	8
Fall, rise, fall	7	0	7	8	1	9
Fall, rise, fall, rise	0	--	0	1	--	1
Total	46	2	48	40	20	60

[a]Too short for division into five stages.

followed the quantity peak. Margin peak led quantity peak in 26 instances, coincided with it in 5, followed it in 20. At troughs the margin lagged more often than not: it led quantity 17 times, coincided 18 times, lagged 23 times. In a few cases there was no turn in margin corresponding to the turn in quantity.

In the forty-six observations of change in the cost ratio from stage I to II, the median change was a fall of 1.0 per cent. In other segments of expansion the figures are, successively, −1.0, −0.2, and 0.0. For segments of contraction they are, −0.2, 0.8, 1.4, 0.6. Declines in cost ratios tended to be larger in early expansion, and rises larger in mid-contraction.

Profits More Closely Related than Margin to Quantity Sold

When an industrial group expands the quantity it sells, the dollar value of its sales will also expand if the prices it receives are stable. If prices go up, value of sales must rise faster than quantity. Aggregate profits equal the product of the profit margin and the dollar value of sales. The rise in sales will assure a rise in profits if the margin rises or does not change; if sales rise enough, profits can increase even if the margin declines. Consequently one should expect profits to increase in more expansions than profit margins. This was true not only of expansions as a whole, but in every segment of expansion. For example, while margins rose in only 50 per cent of the fourth segments observed, profits rose in 74 per cent (Table 38).

Conversely, when the quantity sold by an industrial group is contracting, one would certainly expect profits to decline when the margin declines, as it so often does, and in some cases one would expect the decline in sales to more than offset a rise in margin, producing a fall in profit. Declines in profits might be expected to be even more numerous than declines in margin. However, there was a net rise in margins during only three contractions, and in these the fall in sales was not great enough to offset the wider margin; profits rose also.

In first, third, and fourth segments of contractions in quantity sold, however, declines in profit were more numerous than declines in margin. The second segment figures look peculiar; the

TABLE 38

Profits Before Taxes: Direction of Change from Stage to Stage of
Cycles in Quantity Sold,
Fifteen Manufacturing Industries, 1947–61

From Stage	To Stage	Profits: Number of Observations			Profits: Per Cent		Margins[a]: Per Cent	
		With Rise	With Fall	Total	Rising	Falling	Rising	Falling
I	II	35	11	46	76	24	65	35
II	III	41	5	46	89	11	80	20
III	IV	35	11	46	76	24	57	43
IV	V	34	12	46	74	26	50	50
V	VI	21	19	40	52	48	55	45
VI	VII	9	31	40	22	78	20	80
VII	VIII	6	34	40	15	85	18	82
VIII	IX	8	32	40	20	80	30	70
I	V	46	2	48[b]	96	4	79	21
V	IX	3	57	60[b]	5	95	5	95

[a]From Table 36.
[b]Includes phases too short for division into five stages.

percentage with falling profits is slightly smaller than the percentage with falling margins. The difference is accounted for by an irregularity in one contraction of quantity sold. Quantity, and also the value of sales, rose a little from stage VI to stage VII of that contraction. Consequently it was possible for total profits to rise although the margin declined.

Instances of rising profit greatly outnumbered instances of falling profit in every segment of quantity expansions. Falls were somewhat less frequent than rises in the first segment of quantity contractions, but thereafter greatly outnumbered rises. The percentage of observations with rising profits is highest in the second segment of expansion; thereafter it falls continuously to the third segment of contraction, after which it rises. The upturn of quantity brings a sharp rise in frequencies, from 20 to 76 per cent. A continuous rise was the most common pattern of change during expansions, and a continuous fall was most common in contractions (Table 39).

Because of rising sales, continuous rises in profits from stage to stage were more frequent during quantity expansions than con-

TABLE 39

Profits Before Taxes: Patterns of Change During Expansions and
Contractions in Quantity Sold,
Fifteen Manufacturing Industries, 1947–61
(number of phases)

	Expansions			Contractions		
Pattern	Long Phases	Short Phases[a]	Total	Long Phases	Short Phases[a]	Total
Continuous rise	19	2	21	0	1	1
Rise, fall	10	0	10	14	3	17
Rise, fall, rise	6	0	6	6	0	6
Rise, fall, rise, fall	0	--	0	1	--	1
Continuous fall	0	0	0	8	11	19
Fall, rise	8	0	8	2	4	6
Fall, rise, fall	2	0	2	9	1	10
Fall, rise, fall, rise	1	--	1	0	--	0
Total	46	2	48	40	20	60

[a]Too short for division into five stages.

tinuous rises in margins. There were twenty-one of the former
(Table 39) and only ten of the latter (Table 37); in quantity contractions, there were nineteen continuous declines in profits and
seventeen in margins.

In twenty-eight expansions, profits were highest in the last stage
(V). The corresponding figures for other stages are: I, two; II,
zero; III, ten; and IV, six. In twenty-nine contractions, profits
were at their lowest in the last stage (IX). Figures for other stages
are: V, two; VI, one; VII, three; and VIII, five. In a majority of
instances, therefore, profits were highest at the top of expansions
in quantity and lowest at the bottom of contractions in quantity.

Profits did not turn upward or downward consistently earlier,
or consistently later, than quantity sold. The actual peak quarter
in profits preceded the corresponding peak in quantity eighteen
times, coincided with it sixteen times, and lagged behind it
twenty-three times. The trough quarter in profits preceded the
trough in quantity thirteen times, coincided twenty-eight times,
and lagged nineteen times. In six instances, there was no turn in
profits corresponding to the turn in quantity. Most of the leads
and lags were only one quarter long.

Reflection of Cost in Prices

Changes in cost were usually reflected in prices; changes in the latter were most often in the same direction as those in cost, although not necessarily proportionate. Most net increases in cost during a full upswing or downswing in quantity sold were accompanied by a net rise in the corresponding price index (Table 40). Indeed, even from stage to stage, most increases in one were accompanied by increases in the other, except from stages VIII to IX. Falling prices were associated with most net declines in cost over a full phase. Declines in cost were rare in some segments, and segment-by-segment comparisons with prices yield erratic results. Altogether, however, there were ninety-one declines in cost from one expansion stage to the next, and forty-six from one contraction stage to the next; prices fell in most cases. In every segment of expansion or contraction, the percentage of observations with rising prices is higher for those with rising cost than for those with falling cost.

On the other hand, the state of the market affected prices independently of cost. Of the net rises in cost during expansion, 93 per cent were accompanied by rising prices; but only 78 per

TABLE 40

*Cost Per Unit: Changes Classified According to Change in Price
Between Stages of Cycles in Quantity Sold,
Fifteen Manufacturing Industries, 1947–61*

| | | | OBSERVATIONS WITH COST RISING | | | OBSERVATIONS WITH COST FALLING | | |
| | | | With Price Rising | | | With Price Rising | |
From Stage	To Stage	Total Number	Number	Per Cent	Total Number	Number	Per Cent
I	II	10	7	70	36	12	33
II	III	18	15	83	28	14	50
III	IV	31	30	97	15	4	27
IV	V	34	31	91	12	6	50
V	VI	34	32	94	6	2	33
VI	VII	36	28	78	4	3	75
VII	VIII	26	18	69	14	0	0
VIII	IX	18	9	50	22	5	23
I	V	27	25	93	21	10	48
V	IX	54	42	78	6	0	0

cent of the net rises during contraction were so accompanied. Of the observations with net falling cost, 48 per cent of those for expansions, but none of those for contractions, showed rising prices. Higher prices accompanied 40 per cent of the ninety-one stage-to-stage declines in cost during expansion, but only 22 per cent of the forty-six stage-to-stage declines during contraction.

Rising prices were more frequently associated with rising cost in the second half of expansion than in the first, and in the first half of contraction than in the second. In other words, an industry's chance of recovering at least some part of an increase in cost is greater when the market for its products is active than when the market is dull.

Proximate Causes of Changes in Margins

The characteristic widening of margins during expansion could be caused by a fall in cost, a rise in prices received, or both. On balance over the expansion as a whole, cost fell in a minority of the instances in which the margin rose (Table 41). Prices, on the other hand, rose in 82 per cent. Price was a more frequent contributor than cost to the characteristic change.

The typical net narrowing of margins during contraction might be explained by rising cost, falling price, or both. Cost rose in 89 per cent of the observations; prices received fell in only 32 per cent. Cost was a more frequent contributor than price to the net fall.

The relative importance of price and cost changes between early and late expansion. Cost fell in almost all first segments; the percentage of margin rises in which cost was a factor diminishes steadily thereafter. The percentage in which price was a factor increases, although irregularly. Falling cost contributed to more than half of the rises in margin during the first two segments, to less than half during the last two. Rising prices contributed to more than half of the margin rises during all segments of expansion.

The percentage of declines in margins in which rising cost is a factor is high in all segments of contraction but shows a downward trend after the second. The percentage in which falling

price is a factor is low at first but increases continuously and in the
last segment is well over 50.

Contracyclical net changes in margins over entire expansions or
contractions are too few for analysis. Declines in margin during
early expansion were caused mainly by declines in price, while
those in late expansion were caused mainly by rises in cost. Margins rose in the first segment of contraction in a fair number of

TABLE 41

*Changes in Margin Classified According to Change in Cost Per Unit
and Change in Price Between Stages of Cycles in Quantity Sold,
Fifteen Manufacturing Industries, 1947−61*

| From Stage | To Stage | Total Number | A. OBSERVATIONS WITH MARGINS RISING | | | |
| | | | With Cost Falling | | With Price Rising | |
			Number	Per Cent	Number	Per Cent
I	II	30	25	83	17	57
II	III	37	24	65	27	73
III	IV	26	12	46	18	69
IV	V	23	8	35	21	91
V	VI	22	4	18	20	91
VI	VII	8	3	38	8	100
VII	VIII	7	5	71	2	29
VIII	IX	12	12	100	5	42
I	V	38	17	45	31	82
V	IX	3	0	0	3	100

| From Stage | To Stage | Total Number | B. OBSERVATIONS WITH MARGINS FALLING | | | |
| | | | With Cost Rising | | With Price Falling | |
			Number	Per Cent	Number	Per Cent
I	II	16	5	31	14	88
II	III	9	5	56	7	78
II	IV	20	17	85	4	20
IV	V	23	19	82	7	30
V	VI	18	16	89	4	22
VI	VII	32	31	97	9	28
VII	VIII	33	24	73	17	52
VIII	IX	28	18	64	19	68
I	V	10	6	60	6	60
V	IX	57	51	89	18	32

observations; rising price rather than falling cost was the main explanation. Rising margins were rare after the first segment.

Costs and Profits of Individual Industries

Hitherto we have not discussed the various manufacturing industries separately in describing the relations among cost, prices, margins, profits, and quantity. Often we do not have enough information for a single industry. If we assume that statistics for eight or more phases (expansions or contractions) afford a broad enough foundation on which to erect a conclusion, we have enough statistics for each of nine industries.

In any one industry, the change in cost, prices, or margin is not always consistent from one cycle to the next. Cost may rise in some expansions and fall in some contractions of quantity, suggesting that cost is positively related to quantity; but it may also fall in other expansions and rise in other contractions, suggesting that it is inversely related to quantity. One way of judging such conflicting evidence is to count the number of phases that suggest a positive relation and the number that suggest an inverse relation; give a plus sign to the first number and a minus sign to the second; compute the net or algebraic total, and express the latter as a percentage of the absolute number. A large positive percentage indicates a strong tendency of cost to rise and fall with quantity; a large negative percentage indicates a strong tendency for cost to change in the opposite direction from quantity. Such a "conformity index" has been computed for cost and other variables in the nine industries (Table 42). An index numerically equal to or less than twenty-five can hardly be regarded as indicating any consistent relation.

Production-worker hours per unit, labor cost per unit, all-worker hours per unit, and total cost (including materials, etc.) varied inversely with quantity in most industries. Hourly earnings were not related to quantity in any industry; they tend to rise in quantity expansions and quantity contractions alike. Prices received were positively related in three industries, inversely related in three, and unrelated in three. Both profit margins and profits tended to rise and fall with quantity in all industries.

TABLE 42

Profit Variables and Profits: Conformity Indexes Measuring Relation to Quantity Produced or Sold, Nine Manufacturing Industries, 1947–61

	Production Workers			All Workers, Hours Per Unit	All Cost	Prices Received	Profit Margin	Aggregate Profits
	Hours Per Unit	Hourly Earnings	Labor Cost					
Textiles	-11	11	-56	-11	-78	56	78	78
Lumber and products	-33	-11	-78	-78	56	78	78	78
Paper and products	-56	-11	-78	-78	-33	11	78	100
Chemicals	a	a	a	a	-78	-33	b	100
Rubber	-33	-11	-11	-56	b	b	b	b
Leather and products	-100	0	-75	-100	0	25	75	100
Stone, clay, glass	-56	-11	-78	-56	-25	25	100	100
Primary metals	-100	11	-78	-100	-56	33	100	100
Fabricated metals	-33	-11	-33	-56	-33	-33	78	100
Electric equipment	-11	-11	11	-78	-33	-33	78	100

a Less than eight phases in quantity produced.
b Less than eight phases in quantity sold.

Quantities and Margins of Industries Diverge as Aggregate Quantity Approaches a Peak or Trough

Although most industries have a trough in quantity sold somewhere near a trough in the composite quantity sold by all industries, or in economic activity at large, revival comes to some industries before it come to others. From its lowest point, the number with rising quantity gradually increases. At first the increases in the reviving industries are not large enough to offset the continuing decreases in others, and aggregate quantity continues to decline. But eventually the rise in quantity in the growing number of reviving industries becomes greater than the fall in quantity in the dwindling number of industries that continue to contract. Conversely, recession comes at first to a few industries, then to more and more. Eventually the receding quantity in a growing number of industries outweighs the expanding quantity in a diminishing number of others; total quantity reaches a peak and begins to decline.

These tendencies are very clear in the 1954–58 cycle of composite quantity (Chart 6). In the fourth quarter of 1953, only one industry sold more goods than in the third. From the fourth of 1953 to the first of 1954 (the trough in composite output), three had rising quantity. From 1Q 1954 to 2Q 1954, eleven had rising quantity, and this was enough to turn the balance; composite quantity rose. As it continued to grow, participation continued to widen, until all had rises in quantity from 4Q 1954 to 1Q 1955. Thereafter, although aggregate quantity continued to increase, the number of manufacturing groups participating in the increase declined.

In the 1949–53 expansion, the sequence of participation is more complicated because of the Korean episode. However, the number of industries with rising quantity began to increase long before the trough in aggregate quantity sold, and began to decrease before the peak in aggregate quantity. Complete participation in the growth of quantity was reached in the second quarter of 1950, in which the first Korean alarm was sounded. Participation remained at 93 per cent in the third quarter but fell to 33 per cent in the fourth. On the second alarm it shot up to 93 per cent

CHART 6

Percentage of Industries with Quantity, Cost, Prices, Margins, or
Profits Higher Than in Preceding Quarter,
Fifteen Manufacturing Industries, 1947–61

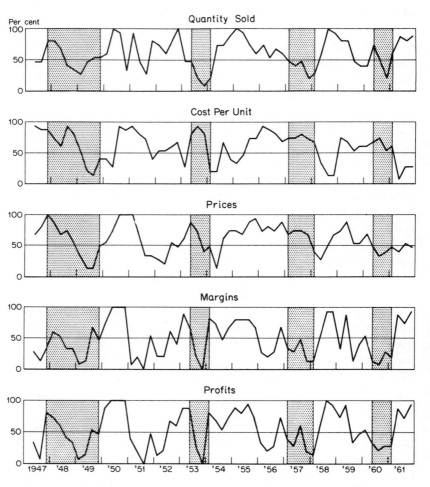

NOTE: Shaded areas are contractions in composite quantity sold.

in 1Q 1951, but fell to 47 per cent in the second quarter, and 29 per cent in the third.

Participation began to decline fairly early in the 1958–60 expansion, although the rebound after the steel strike in the last half of 1959 temporarily raised the percentage.

In every expansion, the point of time at which the smallest number of industries had rising cost preceded the peak in composite quantity sold. The point at which the largest number had rising cost preceded the trough in quantity during all four contractions. It is harder to generalize about prices. The period in which rising margins are most common precedes the peak in composite quantity, and the period in which falling margins are most common precedes the trough with one partial exception. The increasing frequency of falling margins late in composite expansions is associated with the increasing frequency, among individual industries, of declining output and rising cost; and the spread of rising margins late in contractions of quantity is associated with the increase in the number of industries that have begun to expand their quantity and lower their unit costs. Changes in the frequency of rising profits are similar.

On the other hand, there were numerous instances in which an industry's margin fell during the later stages of a rise in its quantity, although these instances did not amount to a majority of the observations (Table 36). Some part of the fall in composite margins late in expansions of composite quantity is accounted for by such industries. Rises in margin during the later stages of an industry's contraction were far less frequent; industries with falling output but rising margins can account for only a small part of such rises in composite margin as occurred late in composite expansions.

A word of caution as to the interpretation of Chart 6, and similar charts, may be helpful. A fall in one of the curves does not mean that the variable depicted is typically declining in the several industries. For example, the margin curve falls from 87 per cent in 1Q 1953 to 67 per cent in 2Q 1953. This means that 87 per cent of the industries had margins rising to 1Q 1953 from the preceding quarter, while only 67 per cent had margins rising from 1Q 1953 to 2Q 1953. Rising margins predominated in both cases; but the predominance was smaller in the second instance. Whenever the curve lies above the 50 per cent line, regardless of its slope, the number of industries in which the variable depicted rises is greater than the number in which it falls.

The curves are highly erratic. A change of direction in just one industry will produce a jump of 7 percentage points. If the data for manufacturing were more finely subdivided—if there were figures for 100 industries instead of fifteen—the changes in the curves would be smoother and might appear more systematic.

Rising Cost Most Often Recouped
in Early or Middle Prosperity

From foregoing sections it is evident that manufacturers with rising cost are sometimes able to increase their prices by a greater percentage, and therefore to reduce their cost ratios and widen their profit margins in spite of the rise in cost. They are more successful in this respect during some parts of the economic cycle than during others.

Chart 7 illustrates these differences. "Rising" and "falling" mean higher or lower than in the preceding quarter. From the first to the second quarter of 1947, for example, fourteen industries had a rise in cost per unit. Of these, four or 28 per cent nevertheless had a falling cost ratio, i.e., a rising margin. In the chart, 28 per cent is therefore shown for the second quarter of 1947.

CHART 7

Number of Manufacturing Industries with Rising Cost but Falling
Cost Ratio, as Percentage of Industries with Rising Cost,
Fifteen Manufacturing Industries, 1947–61

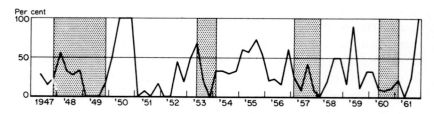

NOTE: Shaded areas are contractions in composite quantity sold.

The statistical foundation for these ratios is at times rather slim. Whenever the percentage of industries with rising costs (Chart 6, cost panel) is less than 50, the number of groups with rising costs is seven or less. Nevertheless, the results of the computations have a somewhat systematic appearance. In the 1954–57 and 1958–60 general expansions, the percentage reached a peak long before the end, and fell irregularly but substantially thereafter. The data suggest that rising costs are very seldom recouped out of higher prices when business activity at large is declining.

The 1949–53 general expansion was, of course, peculiar. At

CHART 8

Cost Per Unit and Price Index,
Composite of Fifteen Manufacturing Industries, 1947–61

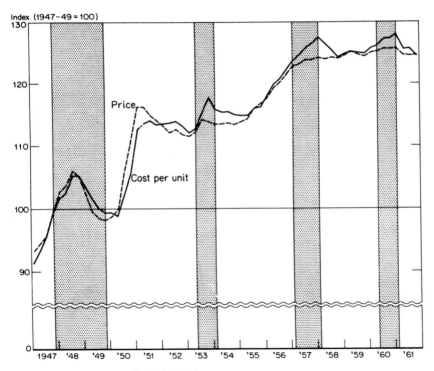

SOURCE: Appendix Table B-1.
NOTE: Shaded areas are contractions in composite quantity sold.

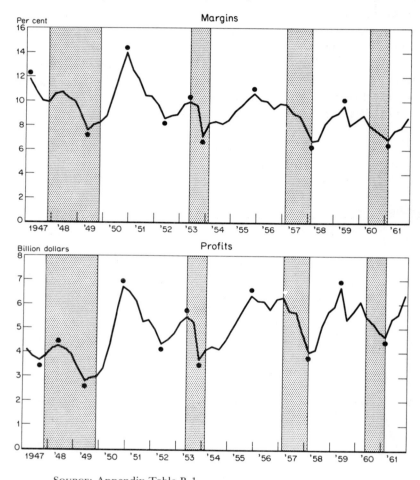

CHART 9
Profit Margins and Profits,
Composite of Fifteen Manufacturing Industries, 1947–61

SOURCE: Appendix Table B-1.
NOTE: Shaded areas are contractions in composite quantity sold.
Dots are at peaks and troughs in margins or profits.

the height of the Korean alarm, all industries with rising costs
were able to raise prices by a greater percentage. Then the situation changed abruptly; during much of 1951 and 1952, few or no

industries with rising costs were able to raise their prices enough to preserve their profit margins.

Costs, Margins, and Profits of Industry Composite

We have divided an index of the combined expenses of the fifteen industries by the index of composite quantity sold to get an index of composite cost per unit. We have also computed a composite margin by totaling their profits and dividing by their total sales. Averages have been calculated for the various stages of the composite quantity cycles. The patterns of cost per unit, margins, and profits are too diverse, however, to permit generalization from so few instances. The net changes during expansions and contractions are more systematic. Cost rose in the two expansions in which prices of materials rose substantially (Chart 8), but fell in 1958–60 when prices of materials were stable. It rose in all contractions, except 1947–49 when prices of materials declined appreciably. The data suggest that if prices of materials were stable, cost per unit would be related inversely to quantity. Profit margins and profits rose in every expansion and fell in every contraction (Chart 9).

4

MANUFACTURING: RELATIONS AMONG PROFIT FACTORS DURING CYCLES IN SALES REVENUE

For some industries and many individual companies there are quarterly figures on sales (i.e., the value of the goods sold) and on margins, but no data on quantity sold. In such industries we cannot tell what happened to costs, prices, and margins during cycles in quantity, but we can tell what happened to margins during sales cycles. In the fifteen industries studied in the last chapter, however, we can compare what happened in cycles of quantity sold with what happened in cycles of sales. The comparison should contribute toward a better understanding of the more abundantly available sales and margin data.

In many instances, an expansion in the sales of an industrial group coincided in time with an expansion in the quantity it sold; a contraction in sales coincided with a contraction in quantity. In many other instances, an upswing or downswing in sales corresponded approximately to a similar fluctuation in quantity, but the troughs, the peaks, or both, did not occur in exactly the same quarter. There were a few phases in sales with no close equivalent in quantity, and vice versa.

Prices Rose and Fell More Often With Sales Than With Quantity

When sales revenue expands but quantity contracts, prices received must be rising; otherwise the revenue would fall with the quantity. Periods of opposite movement associated with rising prices are included in sales but not in quantity expansions. Consequently prices tend to rise more of the time in sales expansions than in quantity expansions. Conversely, when sales contract but quantity expands, prices must be falling. Consequently, prices tend to fall more of the time during sales contractions than during quantity contractions. These differences are observable in almost every segment of expansions and contractions (Table 43).

Cost Rose and Fell More Often With Sales Than With Quantity

Cost falls more often when quantity is rising than when it is falling (Table 43). Consequently, cost tends to rise more of the time during sales expansions, which includes some periods of falling quantity, than during quantity expansions. Conversely, cost tends to fall more of the time during sales contractions, which include some periods of rising quantity, than during quantity contractions. These differences are very consistent from segment to segment.

Margin Changes in Sales Cycles Similar to Those in Quantity Cycles

The greater frequency of price rises during sales expansions than during quantity expansions tends to produce more numerous rises in margins during sales expansions. On the other hand, the greater frequency of rising costs makes for fewer rises in margins during sales expansions. Likewise in contraction, the difference in prices tends to offset the difference in cost. The upshot is that the two kinds of cycles do not differ from each other very consistently with respect to margins. The figure for percentage rising or falling in the sales columns of Table 43 is sometimes higher, sometimes lower, than the corresponding figure in the quantity columns. Each column suggests a somewhat irregular cycle, with the highest frequency early in expansion and the lowest somewhere in contraction. In both, the margin at the peak is usually higher than at the preceding trough; it is almost always lower at the trough than at the preceding peak.

TABLE 43

Sales Cycles and Quantity Cycles Compared: Direction of Change in Three Profit Variables, Fifteen Manufacturing Industries, 1947–61

		Number of Observations		Price Indexes		Cost Per Unit		Margins	
From Stage	To Stage	Sales Cycles	Quantity Cycles	Sales Cycles	Quantity Cycles	Sales Cycles	Quantity Cycles	Sales Cycles	Quantity Cycles
I	II	43	46	63	41	28	22	84	65
II	III	43	46	74	63	51	39	81	80
III	IV	43	46	86	74	79	67	58	57
IV	V	43	46	79	80	81	74	42	50
V	VI	37[b]	40	59	85	43	85	30	55
VI	VII	37[b]	40	49	78	65	90	27	20
VII	VIII	37[b]	40	30	45	49	65	16	18
VIII	IX	37[b]	40	24	35	41	45	14	30
I	V	46[c]	48[c]	85	73	72	56	83	79
I	IX	59[c]	60[c]	42	70	69	90	2	5

PER CENT OF OBSERVATIONS INDICATING RISE[a]

[a] All other observations indicate declines except as noted.

[b] One observation indicates no change in price.

[c] Includes phases too short for division into five stages.

Margins Rise When Sales Expand,
Fall When Sales Contract

Although we have quantity, price, and cost estimates for only fifteen industries, there are data on margins for twenty-two FTC-SEC groups. Our further discussion of margins and profits will be founded on this larger body of information. There is no longer any reason to merge the two primary metals industries; we prefer the greater refinement and diversity obtainable from including them separately. We include furniture, although the portion of the industry included varies, because the sales data are comparable with the margin data. In the twenty-two industries, there were sixty-seven sales expansions (Table 44). In fifty-seven of these, there was a net rise in margin. When the sales expansions are arranged in successive groups by the methods explained in Chapter 2, rising margins are found to preponderate in all. We have data on eighty-five contractions. In these, there was an even stronger preponderance of declines; in eighty-two the margin was lower at the end than at the beginning of the sales contraction. In a broad sense, sales and margins rise and fall together.

Before 1947 we have no comprehensive quarterly data on sales and profits for any major manufacturing group or for manufacturing in the aggregate.[1] We do have annual data derived from a publication of the Bureau of Internal Revenue, *Statistics of Income.* Although we show ratios for these data up to the latest date for which they are available in Chart 10, we regard the quarterly data from 1947 onward as superior for cyclical analysis. These, however, do not cover the full expansion in sales that ended in 1948. Consequently, we shall use the annual data to learn something about 1946–48 as well as earlier expansions and contractions.

The annual figures give us data on five additional full expansions in sales: 1921–23, 1924–29, 1932–37, 1938–44, and 1946–48. In every one, the ratio of profits to sales was higher at the peak than at the trough. They also give us data on five addi-

---

[1]Data on profits only are discussed in my *Cyclical Diversities in the Fortunes of Industrial Corporations,* New York, NBER, OP 32, 1950.

82   COST, PRICES, AND PROFITS

tional contractions: 1920–21, 1923–24, 1929–32, 1937–38, and
1944–46. In every one, the profit ratios were smaller at the
trough than at the peak. The experience over the period from
1920 to 1948 was similar, therefore, to the experience from 1948
onward.

Corresponding data for the twenty-two statistical subdivisions of
manufacturing are not available. We can, however, assemble
separate figures for durable and nondurable manufactures over
the whole period (Chart 11). Between 1920 and 1948, sales of
durables had five expansions and five contractions; the profit
ratios had a net rise in all of the former and a net fall in all of the
latter. Sales of nondurables had four expansions and four contractions before 1948; profit margins again rose and fell with

TABLE 44

*Margins: Direction of Net Change During Sales Expansions and Contractions,
Twenty-Two Manufacturing Industries, 1947–61*

Industry	Number of Sales Expansions with		Number of Sales Contractions with	
	Net Rise in Margin	Net Fall in Margin	Net Rise in Margin	Net Fall in Margin
Food and beverages	0	1	1	1
Tobacco	1	0	0	2
Textiles	4	0	0	5
Apparel	2	0	0	3
Lumber and products	3	1	0	5
Furniture and fixtures	4	0	0	5
Paper and products	3	1	0	5
Printing and publishing	1	0	0	2
Chemicals	4	0	0	5
Petroleum refining	1	0	0	2
Rubber	2	1	0	3
Leather and products	2	1	0	3
Stone, clay, glass	4	0	0	5
Primary iron and steel	4	0	0	5
Primary nonferrous metals	4	0	0	4
Fabricated metals	3	1	0	5
Machinery	3	0	0	4
Electric equipment	2	2	0	5
Motor vehicles	5	0	0	6
Other transportation equipment	1	1	1	2
Instruments	1	1	1	2
Miscellaneous	3	0	0	3
Total number	57	10	3	82
Percentage of total for ex-pansions or contractions	85	15	4	96

CHART 10

Margin, Before and After Taxes: All Manufacturing Corporations,
1919–61

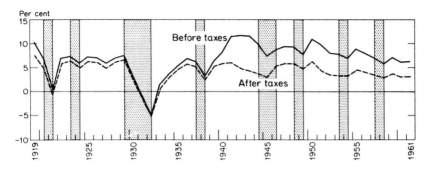

NOTE: Shaded areas are contractions in sales of all manufacturing
corporations.

sales. One of the expansions was somewhat long for comparison
with the kind of expansions we deal with in this study; annual
sales increased continuously from 1938 to 1948.

For reasons explained in Chapter 1, the foregoing discussion
pertains to margins before, rather than after, taxes. The substantial difference between the two that has developed since the beginning of World War II, however, should not be ignored. We
therefore show on the charts the ratio of profits after taxes to
sales as well as the before-tax margin.

With few exceptions, however, the direction of year-to-year
change is the same in both ratios. From 1936 to 1937 the pre-tax
margin for durables increased slightly while the post-tax margin
decreased slightly. Because of steeper wartime taxation, margin
before taxes increased, while margin after taxes decreased, for the
durables group from 1940 to 1941, for all manufacturing and the
nondurables group from 1941 to 1942, and for the nondurables
group from 1942 to 1943. Although the pre-tax margin of the
durables group fell from 1945 to 1946 and from 1953 to 1954,
removal of the excess profits tax and perhaps other tax changes
permitted the post-tax margin to rise on both occasions.

Corporations derive income from other sources as well as the
commodities and services they sell. They have income from rent,

royalties, investments in stocks and bonds, and interest on money
in the bank. Most of these other kinds of income involve little
expense; the gross income from them is almost the same as the
net. (This, however, is not true in many cases of income from
rents and royalties.) We subtracted total deductions allowed by the
income tax laws from sales, including "gross revenue from operations," to get what we call profits from sales. It is eqt al to total net
profit from all sources less gross income from other sources than
sales. The ratio to sales of profits from sales is lower than the
pre-tax curves on the charts. Although they differ in level, the
two ratios invariably move in the same direction from year to year.

There are no quarterly data on margins for groups of manu-

CHART 11
Margin, Before and After Taxes: Corporations Manufacturing
Durables and Nondurables, 1919 – 61

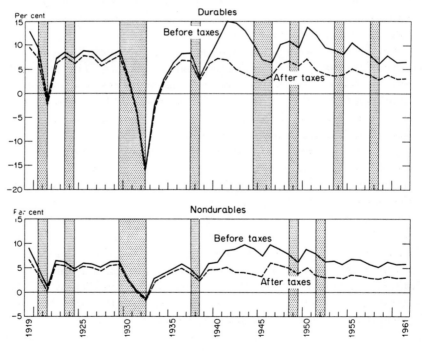

NOTE: Shaded areas are contractions in sales.

facturing industries before 1947, but many large companies published quarterly income statements reporting their own sales and profits. We have tried to exploit such material as a subsidiary source of information. The history of profits during the war was somewhat peculiar because of price fixing by the government, renegotiation of contracts, emergency amortization of facilities, and so forth. In view of the effort that would be required, and the peculiarities of the period, we have collected no systematic data on profits of individual companies during the war. We did look at all individual industrial corporations with assets of more than $50 million at the end of 1941, to see whether they published quarterly statements; and for those who did, we traced the records backward in time as far as they went. It is a comparatively new practice, however, for companies to report sales as well as earnings quarterly; so, as we went farther and farther back, more and more corporations dropped out of our list. We found only twenty-two with satisfactory records covering even one full business cycle, 1933–38. For some, however, we were able to trace the record back farther, in a few cases to 1919. (For companies and time periods, see the appendix.)

The sales and profit margin of each company were charted; and peaks and troughs were determined in the same manner as for industrial groups after the war. In the sales of one company or another, at one time or another, there were thirty-seven expansions and forty-six contractions. The margin was higher at the peak than at the trough in thirty-four of the expansions, and lower at the trough than at the peak in all of the contractions. The prewar experience of these companies was therefore similar to the postwar experience of industrial groups: the margin rose and fell with sales.

MARGINS RISE MOST FREQUENTLY IN
EARLY EXPANSION

In postwar manufacturing, rising margins outnumbered falling margins in all segments of expansion (Table 45), except fourth segments, in which declines were somewhat more frequent than rises. The percentage of observations with rising margins diminishes steadily from eighty-three for first segments to forty-six for fourth segments. Falling margins outnumbered rising margins heavily in every portion of contractions.

In the observations for individual companies between wars, rising margins predominate in every segment of expansion (Table 45). The percentage of rising margins is highest in the first segment of expansion, and falls with some irregularity to the fourth. Falling margins predominate in every segment of contraction.

During upswings in the sales of manufacturing industries, the most common pattern of change was an initial rise and later fall (Table 46). It occurred during twenty-nine, or 43 per cent, of the upswings. During downswings, the most common pattern was a straight fall; this pattern occurred during thirty-three, or 39 per cent, of the downswings.

TABLE 45
Margins: Direction of Change from Stage to Stage of Sales Cycles

From Stage	To Stage	Number of Observations			Percentage	
		With Rise	With Fall	Total	Rising	Falling
		22 MANUFACTURING INDUSTRIES, 1947–61				
I	II	52	11	63	83	17
II	III	47	16	63	75	25
III	IV	37	26	63	59	41
IV	V	29	34	63	46	54
V	VI	15	38	53	28	72
VI	VII	14	39	53	26	74
VII	VIII	14	39	53	26	74
VIII	IX	10	43	53	19	81
I	V	57	10	67[a]	85	15
V	IX	3	82	85[a]	4	96
		22 COMPANIES, 1919–41				
I	II	30	5	35	86	14
II	III	27	8	35	77	23
III	IV	28	7	35	80	20
IV	V	22	13	35	63	37
V	VI	5	30	35	14	86
VI	VII	3	32	35	9	91
VII	VIII	9	26	35	26	74
VIII	IX	12	23	35	34	66
I	V	34	3	37[a]	92	8
V	IX	0	46	46[a]	0	100

[a]Includes phases too short for division into five stages.

In the sales expansions of individual companies, the rise-fall pattern is slightly less common than the continuous rise pattern (Table 46). In their sales contractions, as in those of the postwar industries, a continuous fall was most common, occurring in nineteen, or 41 per cent.

Profit margins for all manufacturing fell during the last year of three sales expansions, 1932–37, 1938–44, and 1946–48 (Chart 10). The margin continued to rise in the last year of 1921–23, although at a diminished rate. In 1924–29 it fell in the middle, then rose again. It is possible that quarterly data for this period would show a sales contraction in the middle, corresponding to the 1926–27 business contraction; consequently the fall in margin is difficult to interpret. Only two sales contractions lasted more

TABLE 46

Margins: Patterns of Change During
Expansions and Contractions of Sales

Pattern	Expansions			Contractions		
	Long Phases	Short Phases[a]	Total	Long Phases	Short Phases[a]	Total
	22 MANUFACTURING INDUSTRIES, 1947–61					
Continuous rise	9	2	11	0	0	0
Rise, fall	28	1	29	11	2	13
Rise, fall, rise	13	0	13	2	0	2
Rise, fall, rise, fall	2	--	2	2	--	2
Continuous fall	0	0	0	15	18	33
Fall, rise	7	1	8	6	10	16
Fall, rise, fall	4	0	4	15	2	17
Fall, rise, fall, rise	0	--	0	2	--	2
Total	63	4	67	53	32	85
	22 COMPANIES, 1919–41					
Continuous rise	11	1	12	0	0	0
Rise, fall	11	0	11	1	4	5
Rise, fall, rise	7	1	8	2	0	2
Rise, fall, rise, fall	1	--	1	2	--	2
Continuous fall	0	0	0	15	4	19
Fall, rise	4	0	4	9	3	12
Fall, rise, fall	1	0	1	5	0	5
Fall, rise, fall, rise	0	--	0	1	--	1
Total	35	2	37	35	11	46

[a]Too short for division into five stages.

than a year; in one of them, 1929–32, the margin fell throughout; in 1944–46, however, it turned up in the second year. Annual
figures for the three one-year contractions tell us nothing about
the time-pattern within a contraction.

Annual profit margins of corporations making durable goods
diminished during the later years of the war expansion, 1938–44,
but not toward the end of any of the other four complete expansions in the 1920–48 period (Chart 11). Two of the contractions,
1929–32 and 1944–46, lasted more than one year; the profit
ratios fell throughout those contractions.

Profit ratios of corporations making nondurables fell in the last
year of all four complete expansions before 1948. Only one contraction, 1929–32, lasted more than one year; ratios fell throughout (Chart 11).

In general the annual data suggest rise-fall sequences during
expansions, like the quarterly data, but are inadequate as to contractions.

Profits More Closely Related Than Margins to Sales

Profits equal the product of sales and margins. When sales are
expanding, profits can rise even though margins fall, provided
sales expand fast enough. When sales are contracting, profits can
fall even if margins are rising, provided sales fall fast enough.
Profits therefore tend to rise even more often than margins during expansions, and to fall even more often than margins during
contractions.

In most cases, profits rise more often than margins in expansions and segments of expansions, and less often than margins in
contractions and segments of contractions (Table 47). In a few
cases the figures are equal. This is not inconsistent with the reasoning in the preceding paragraph. Although the change in sales
may be large enough to more than offset a contrary change in
margin, and hence to raise profits, it will not necessarily be that
large. The data for twenty-two companies from stage VII to stage
VIII, however, appear to contradict that reasoning, which applies
only if the margin in at least one of the stages is positive. If two
successive margins are −10 and −12 per cent, for example, the

change is counted as a fall in margin. Absolute profits are necessarily negative in both cases. But the algebraically lower margin, in conjunction with smaller sales, may mean a smaller absolute loss; this is counted as a rise in profits. Such a situation occurred in two observations, which explains the apparent paradox.

The most common pattern of change in profits when sales were expanding was a continuous rise, which occurred in twenty-five, or 37 per cent, of the industry expansions and twenty-two, or 59 per cent, of the company expansions (Table 48). The most common pattern when sales were contracting was a continuous fall, which occurred in forty-one, or 48 per cent, of the group con-

TABLE 47

Profits Before Taxes: Direction of Change from
Stage to Stage of Sales Cycles

From Stage	To Stage	Profits: Number of Observations			Profits: Per Cent		Margins:[a] Per Cent	
		With Rise	With Fall	Total	Rising	Falling	Rising	Falling
		22 MANUFACTURING INDUSTRIES, 1947–61						
I	II	56	7	63	89	11	83	17
II	III	56	7	63	89	11	75	25
III	IV	44	19	63	70	30	59	41
IV	V	44	19	63	70	30	46	54
V	VI	10	43	53	19	81	28	72
VI	VII	14	39	53	26	74	26	74
VII	VIII	14	39	53	26	74	26	74
VIII	IX	6	47	53	11	89	19	81
I	V	66	1	67[b]	99	1	85	15
V	IX	1	84	85[b]	1	99	4	96
		22 COMPANIES, 1919–41						
I	II	30	5	35	86	14	86	14
II	III	31	4	35	89	11	77	23
III	IV	29	6	35	83	17	80	20
IV	V	31	4	35	89	11	63	37
V	VI	3	32	35	9	91	14	86
VI	VII	2	33	35	6	94	9	91
VII	VIII	10	25	35	29	71	26	74
VIII	IX	7	28	35	20	80	34	66
I	V	36	1	37[b]	97	3	92	8
V	IX	0	46	46[b]	0	100	0	100

[a]From Table 45.
[b]Includes phases too short for division into five stages.

TABLE 48
Profits Before Taxes: Patterns of Change
During Expansions and Contractions of Sales
(number of phases)

Pattern	Expansions			Contractions		
	Long Phases	Short Phases[a]	Total	Long Phases	Short Phases[a]	Total
22 MANUFACTURING INDUSTRIES, 1947–61						
Continuous rise	23	2	25	0	0	0
Rise, fall	18	1	19	7	2	9
Rise, fall, rise	14	0	14	2	0	2
Rise, fall, rise, fall	1	--	1	1	--	1
Continuous fall	0	0	0	20	21	41
Fall, rise	7	1	8	3	7	10
Fall, rise, fall	0	0	0	19	2	21
Fall, rise, fall, rise	0	--	0	1	--	1
Total	63	4	67	53	32	85
22 COMPANIES, 1919–41						
Continuous rise	21	1	22	0	0	0
Rise, fall	3	0	3	0	2	2
Rise, fall, rise	5	1	6	2	0	2
Rise, fall, rise, fall	1	--	1	0	--	0
Continuous fall	0	0	0	19	6	25
Fall, rise	4	0	4	5	3	8
Fall, rise, fall	0	0	0	8	0	8
Fall, rise, fall, rise	1	--	1	1	--	1
Total	35	2	37	35	11	46

[a]Too short for division into five stages.

tractions and twenty-five, or 54 per cent, of the company contractions.

Margins and Profits of Individual Industries or Companies

Eleven manufacturing groups and three companies had eight or more expansions and contractions of sales during the periods covered by our statistics. As previously noted, we consider this a long enough record to support generalizations about each. The groups are textiles, lumber, furniture, paper, chemicals, stone, iron and steel, primary nonferrous metals, fabricated metals, electric equipment, and motor vehicles. The companies are Hercules Powder, Skelly Oil, and Studebaker. For each industry or company, there was a net rise in both margin and profits during most upswings in sales and a net fall in both during most downswings in sales. In other words, the margins and profits of these groups and companies conformed positively to sales (conformity was defined and explained in Chapter 3). Conformity scores ranged from +56 to +100.

INDUSTRIES DIVERGE AS AGGREGATE SALES APPROACH A PEAK OR TROUGH

An expansion in sales begins in some industries and spreads to others. At first the rising sales in a few industries are outweighed by the continuing declines in most, and aggregate sales of all industries continue to fall. Eventually, however, the rises in the growing number of industries whose sales are picking up outweigh the declines in the dwindling number of industries whose sales continue to fall, and aggregate sales increase. Troughs in the number of industries with rising sales therefore tend to precede troughs in aggregate sales, and peaks in the number tend to precede peaks in the aggregate. This order of events can be observed repeatedly from 1947 to 1961 (Chart 12), with an exception in the very short (two-quarter) contraction of 1957–58.

As the speculative demand inspired by the outbreak of the Korean War was gradually satisfied, sales of many industries began to decline, one after another. During the 1949–53 upswing in aggregate sales, therefore, we find two waves instead of one in the curve showing the frequency of participation.

Since the margin earned by an industry has some tendency to fall toward the end of an expansion in the sales of that industry, and usually falls when an industry's sales are falling, one might expect that, when the percentage of industries with rising sales begins to diminish before the composite peak, the percentage with rising margins would also diminish. In fact, the frequency of rising margins did begin to decline at an early date in all three expansions of aggregate sales. Since an industry's margin usually widens when its sales begin to rise, and since the percentage of industries with growing sales begins to increase before the aggregate sales of all industries reach their trough, the percentage of

industries with rising margins should also begin to increase before
that trough. It did begin to increase at an early date in the first
two contractions of aggregate sales. Like the sales percentage, it
did not increase before the end of the 1957–58 contraction.

There are similar waves in the frequency of rising profits. The
sharp dip in all three variables in the last half of 1959 reflects the
steel strike during the first and part of the second quarter.

Similar divergences occurred among companies. (Since we have
data for less than ten companies before 1927, we begin Chart 13
in that year.) Although there are no quarterly figures on the sales
of all manufacturing corporations in the period to which the
company data refer, peaks and troughs in sales probably did not
differ much in time from those in business at large. Rising sales
tended to become more frequent during the later portions of a
business contraction and the earlier portions of an expansion.

CHART 12

Percentage of Industries with Sales, Margins, or Profits
Higher Than in Preceding Quarter,
Twenty-Two Manufacturing Industries, 1947–61

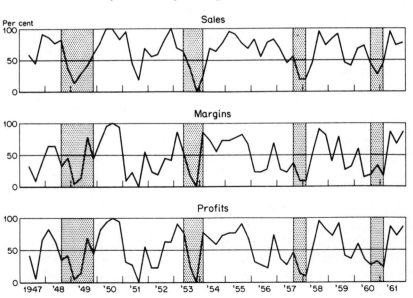

NOTE: Shaded areas are contractions in sales.

They tended to become less frequent during the later portions of an expansion and the earlier portions of a contraction. There was no net rise in frequency, however, during the later quarters of the 1937–38 contraction.

CHART 13

Percentage of Companies with Sales, Margins, or Profits Higher Than in Preceding Quarter, Twenty-Two Companies, 1927–41

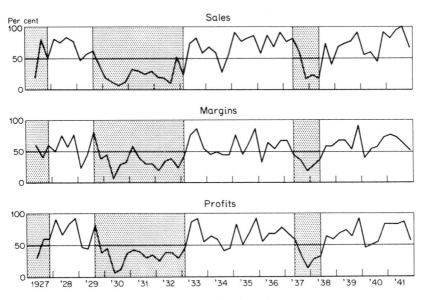

NOTE: Shaded areas are contractions in business.

At the beginning of the 1933–37 upswing, as at a somewhat later stage of the one in 1949–53, there was a special speculative influence at work. Expectations of higher costs and prices as a result of New Deal legislation stimulated sales. Even in the first quarter after the 1933 trough, 82 per cent of the twenty-two companies had rising sales. Probably as a reaction to the initial speculation, the percentage fell in late 1933 and early 1934. The outbreak of World War II caused a temporary drop in the sales of some companies. The fluctuations in sales are reflected broadly in the curves for frequency of rising margins and profits.

SALES, MARGINS, AND PROFITS, ALL MANUFACTURING

Aggregate sales of all manufacturing corporations combined were rising in 1947 when the statistics begin (Chart 14). The expansion reached a peak in the third quarter of 1948. Four full contractions and three full expansions followed. Another expansion began at the trough in the first quarter of 1961 and was still in progress during the last quarter covered by our statistics at the time of writing.

At each peak in sales the profit margin was higher than at the preceding sales trough; at each sales trough the margin was lower

TABLE 49

Sales, Margins, and Profits: Averages for Stages of Sales Cycles, All Manufacturing Industries, 1947 – 61

Stage of Cycle in Sales	First Quarter Included	Sales (million dollars)	Margins (per cent of sales)	Profits (million dollars)
V	3Q 1948	50,346	10.0	5,035
VI	4Q 1948	49,799	9.9	4,930
VII	1Q 1949	47,202	8.2	3,875
VIII	3Q 1949	46,444	8.5	3,948
IX / I	4Q 1949	44,664	8.3	3,707
II	1Q 1950	54,399	11.6	6,390
III	1Q 1951	63,558	10.9	6,919
IV	2Q 1952	66,312	9.2	6,073
V	2Q 1953	70,446	10.0	7,045
a	3Q 1953	70,334	9.7	6,822
a	4Q 1953	65,823	7.1	4,673
IX / I	1Q 1954	63,942	8.2	5,243
II	2Q 1954	65,670	8.8	5,806
III	2Q 1955	74,169	10.3	7,654
IV	3Q 1956	79,038	9.4	7,431
V	3Q 1957	82,084	8.7	7,141
a	4Q 1957	77,803	7.6	5,913
IX / I	1Q 1958	73,071	6.5	4,750
II	2Q 1958	77,096	7.7	5,930
III	1Q 1959	84,741	9.1	7,746
IV	4Q 1959	85,580	8.3	7,108
V	3Q 1960	87,478	7.7	6,736
a	4Q 1960	84,785	7.0	5,935
IX	1Q 1961	83,258	6.6	5,495

[a]Contraction too short for division into five stages. Full quarterly detail shown instead.

CHART 14
Sales, Margins, and Profits: All Manufacturing Industries, 1947–61

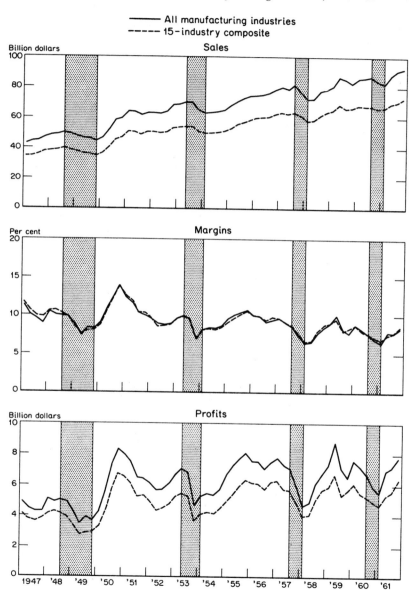

SOURCE: Appendix Table B-1.
NOTE: Shaded areas are contractions in sales.

than at the preceding sales peak (Table 49). There was a net rise in the margin during each expansion in sales for which we have a complete record, a net fall in each complete contraction.

In the 1949–53 expansion of sales, the margin followed a rise-fall-rise pattern from stage to stage. In the 1954–57 and 1958–60 expansions it followed a rise-fall pattern, the most common pattern in sales expansions of the separate industries (Table 46). In the contraction of 1948–49 there was a fall-rise-

TABLE 50
Sales, Margins, and Profits: Averages for Stages of Business Cycles,
All Manufacturing Industries, 1947–61

Stage of Business Cycle	First Quarter Included	Sales (million dollars)	Margins (per cent of sales)	Profits (million dollars)
V	4Q 1948	49,799	9.9	4,930
VI	1Q 1949	47,879	8.9	4,261
VII	2Q 1949	46,524	7.5	3,489
VIII	3Q 1949	46,444	8.5	3,948
IX / I	4Q 1949	44,664	8.3	3,707
II	1Q 1950	54,399	11.6	6,390
III	1Q 1951	63,558	10.9	6,919
IV	2Q 1952	66,312	9.2	6,073
V	2Q 1953	70,44	10.0	7,045
VI	3Q 1953	70,334	9.7	6,822
VII	4Q 1953	64,882	7.6	4,958
VIII	2Q 1954	63,970	8.5	5,437
IX / I	3Q 1954	64,174	8.4	5,391
II	4Q 1954	69,871	9.8	6,850
III	4Q 1955	75,299	10.3	7,754
IV	3Q 1956	79,038	9.4	7,431
V	3Q 1957	82,084	8.7	7,141
a	4Q 1957	77,803	7.6	5,913
a	1Q 1958	73,071	6.5	4,750
IX / I	2Q 1958	73,328	6.7	4,913
II	3Q 1958	78,980	8.2	6,439
III	1Q 1959	84,741	9.1	7,746
IV	4Q 1959	84,976	8.3	7,060
V	2Q 1960	86,790	8.3[b]	7,204
a	3Q 1960	87,478	7.7	6,736
a	4Q 1960	84,785	7.0	5,935
IX	1Q 1961	83,258	6.6	5,495

[a]Contraction too short for division into five stages. Full quarterly detail shown instead.

[b]Higher than preceding stage before rounding.

fall; a fall-rise in 1953–54, and a fall in 1957–58 and 1960–61. These were the three most common patterns in sales contractions of individual industries (Table 46). The patterns in composite profits were the same as those in margins.

The early declines in the sales of some industries, accompanied by declines in their margins, help to explain why the all-manufacturing margin fell during the last two segments of the 1954–57 and 1958–60 expansions of all-manufacturing sales. These falling margins were earned, to a large extent, by industries whose own sales were already falling.

Cycles in total manufacturing sales correspond to those in the National Bureau chronology of business cycles, although the dates of peaks and troughs differ somewhat. There was a net rise in the margin and profits during each business expansion, and a net fall during each contraction (Table 50).

The fluctuations in the composite of fifteen industries for which we have quantity data were similar to those in all manufacturing (Chart 14).

5

RAILROADS

The statistical record of monthly railroad revenues and expenses is much longer than the quarterly record for manufacturing. It gives us an adequate basis for separate generalizations about the railroad industry such as we are not prepared to venture for many of the twenty-two manufacturing industries.

For railways we have an approximate measure of the physical volume of "production," namely traffic units. It consists of ton-miles plus 2.4 times passenger-miles. The 2.4 factor is the average ratio of revenue per passenger-mile to revenue per ton-mile over a long period of years. Traffic units are therefore a roughly price-weighted composite of the two main kinds of railway service. Having this measure, we prefer to study the relation of margins, prices, and costs to cycles in traffic rather than to cycles in railroad revenues. In some respects, the following discussion will bring up to date the findings in my monograph, *American Transportation in Prosperity and Depression* (New York, NBER, 1948). Margins, however, were not discussed in that work; instead, attention was focused on profits per unit.

Traffic Cycles Since 1938

Cycles in traffic correspond broadly to those in the economy at large (Chart 15).[1] Railway passenger traffic, however, had been greatly swollen during World War II because of large military movement and because civilians could not buy new cars and could buy gasoline only for "necessary" motor travel. Rail travel, therefore, declined not only in the immediate postwar business contraction but throughout the following expansion and into the next contraction. The decline was so severe that the composite of

[1]For a similar chart, 1907–38, see *American Transportation*, p. 76.

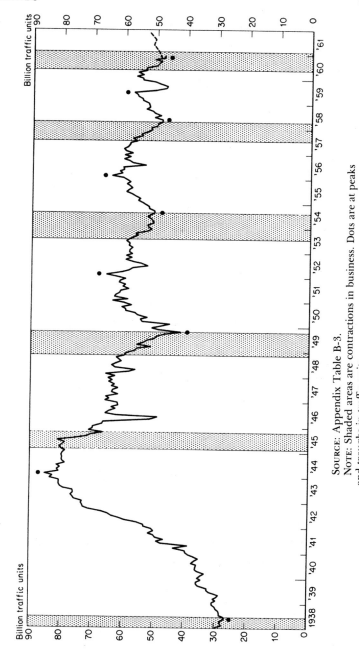

CHART 15
Traffic Units, 1938–61

SOURCE: Appendix Table B-3.
NOTE: Shaded areas are contractions in business. Dots are at peaks and troughs in traffic units.

freight and passenger movement also declined through all three phases. Competition for freight traffic from motor and other means of transport also became more formidable after the war; partly at least for this reason, composite traffic ceased to expand and began to contract early in the 1949–53, 1954–57, and 1958–60 business expansions.

As in other industries, we shall be interested to learn not only what net changes occur in costs, prices, margins, and profits during an upswing or downswing of traffic, but whether the changes are dissimilar in the earlier and later portions of the traffic fluctuations. A cycle in traffic can be divided into stages, and therefore segments, as cycles in quantity sold or sales were divided in preceding chapters. With monthly data, we divide the months between a peak and a trough month into three successive stages (stages II, III, IV or VI, VII, VIII), covering as nearly as possible the same length of time, and strike a monthly average of whatever variable is being studied, for each stage. We prefer to base the figure for a peak stage (V) or a trough stage (IX, I) not only on data for the peak or trough month but also on data for the preceding and following month.[2] For example, the operating ratio (a ratio explained in a later section) for January 1956 is used to compute the average ratio for stage V as well as for stage IV, and the ratio for March 1956 enters the average both for stage V and stage VI (Table 51).

Cost Inversely Related to Traffic

The cost experience of railroads was quite different from that of manufacturing companies after the war. In all but two of the twelve traffic expansions for which we have monthly data, there was a net decline in operating expense per traffic unit. In every one of the twelve contractions there was a net rise (Table 52). Railroads are not immune to the rises in prices of materials and wage rates, to which other industries are subjected in expansions. Fluctuations in traffic do not differ greatly from those in manu-

---

[2]The traffic peak in June 1959, however, was followed by the steel strike, which sharply reduced traffic and distorted the profit variables. Averages for this peak are, therefore, based on figures for May and June only.

TABLE 51
Illustrative Division into Stages of a Cycle in Traffic Units, 1954–58[a]

Stage	Months Included				Operating Ratio (per cent)
	First		Last		Number	
I	July	1954	September	1954	3	79.7
II	September	1954	February	1955	6	76.6
III	March	1955	July	1955	5	75.0
IV	August	1955	January	1956	6	76.5
V	January	1956	March	1956	3	76.1
VI	March	1956	November	1956	9	77.2
VII	December	1956	July	1957	8	77.6
VIII	August	1957	April	1958	9	80.2
IX	April	1958	June	1958	3	81.0

[a]Trough, August 1954; peak, February 1956; trough, May 1958.

facturing production. We must conclude that increases in the volume of business have a stronger tendency to reduce costs on railroads than in factories, and declines in the volume of business have a stronger tendency to raise them on railroads.

INVERSE RELATION MORE CONSISTENT AT BEGINNING OF SWINGS IN TRAFFIC

Even on railroads there is some tendency for cost to rise as traffic approaches its peak, and a decided tendency for it to fall as traffic approaches its trough. Cost fell in all except one of the first segments of the twelve expansions (Table 53). In later segments, falls were less frequent. Cost rose in all first segments of contraction, in all but one of the second and third segments, and in seven of the fourth segments. Rises were therefore more frequent than falls in all segments, but the majority was close at the end.

Cost fell continuously from stage to stage in only three expansions (Table 54). In four, it fell at the beginning but rose after the second, third, or fourth stage. It rose continuously in five contractions, and rose at first but declined later in another five.

Cost was lowest in the last stage of only five expansions. It was highest in the last stage of five contractions, and in the fourth stage of five others.

TURN IN COST OFTEN PRECEDED TURN IN TRAFFIC

The foregoing data lead one to expect that a turn in cost often should precede a turn of the opposite character in traffic. Troughs in cost occurred before six of twelve traffic peaks. Peaks in cost occurred before ten of twelve traffic troughs (Table 55).

In the 1932–37 expansion there are two "extra" turns in cost. After declining as usual in the early months, cost began to rise after July 1933, reaching a peak in July 1935; they cannot be matched with turns in traffic. Restoration of wage levels helps to account for this extra movement in cost. Wages had been cut 10

TABLE 52
Cost (Railway Operating Expenses) Per Traffic Unit at Peaks and Troughs in Traffic, 1907–61

Turn in Traffic		Cost Per Unit[a] (cents)	Change in Cost Per Unit	
Date	Level		To Peak from Trough	To Trough from Peak
June 1908	Trough	.5391	--	--
Apr. 1910	Peak	.5664	.0273	--
Mar. 1911	Trough	.5782	--	.0118
Feb. 1913	Peak	.5556	−.0226	--
Dec. 1914	Trough	.5885	--	.0329
May 1918	Peak	.6746	.0861	--
Mar. 1919	Trough	.9765	--	.3019
Feb. 1920	Peak	.9702	−.0063	--
July 1921	Trough	1.1830	--	.2128
Apr. 1923	Peak	.9319	−.2511	--
June 1924	Trough	.9849	--	.0530
July 1926	Peak	.8789	−.1060	--
Dec. 1927	Trough	.9212	--	.0423
Aug. 1929	Peak	.8694	−.0518	--
Aug. 1932	Trough	.8827	--	.0133
Mar. 1937	Peak	.6975	−.1852	--
May 1938	Trough	.8113	--	.1138
Feb. 1944	Peak	.6203	−.1910	--
Oct. 1949	Trough	1.1615	--	.5412
Feb. 1952	Peak	1.0940	−.0675	--
Aug. 1954	Trough	1.2080	--	.1140
Feb. 1956	Peak	1.0932	−.1148	--
May 1958	Trough	1.2625	--	.1693
June 1959	Peak	1.1760	−.0865	--
2Q 1959	Peak	1.1796	--	--
4Q 1960	Trough	1.2286	--	.0490

[a]Three-month averages.

TABLE 53

Cost Per Traffic Unit: Direction of Change from Stage to Stage of Traffic Cycles, 1907–61

From Stage	To Stage	Number of Observations		
		With Rise	With Fall	Total
I	II	1	11	12
II	III	3	9	12
III	IV	6	6	12
IV	V	4	8	12
V	VI	12	0	12
VI	VII	11	1	12
VII	VIII	11	1	12
VIII	IX	7	5	12
I	V	2	10	12
V	IX	12	0	12

TABLE 54

Cost and Revenue Per Traffic Unit, Operating Ratio, and Profit: Patterns of Change During Expansions and Contractions in Traffic, 1907–61

(number of phases)

Pattern	Cost Per Unit		Revenue Per Unit		Operating Ratio		Net Operating Revenue	
	Expan- sions	Contrac- tions	Expan- sions	Contrac- tions	Expan- sions	Contrac- tions	Expan- sions	Contrac- tions
Continuous rise	0	5	2	3	0	2	7	0
Rise, fall	1	5	0	3	0	3	1	1
Rise, fall, rise	0	2	2	2	1	5	3	0
Rise, fall, rise, fall	0	0	0	0	0	1	1	0
Continuous fall	3	0	3	1	2	0	0	4
Fall, rise	4	0	0	1	4	1	0	3
Fall, rise, fall	4	0	5	2	5	0	0	4
Fall, rise, fall, rise	0	0	0	0	0	0	0	0

per cent late in the preceding contraction. 2.5 points were restored to the workers on July 1, 1934, another 2.5 on January 1, 1935, and the remaining 5 on April 1, 1935. [3]

[3]See my *American Transportation*, p. 250.

TABLE 55
Traffic and Cost Per Unit: Turning Points Compared, 1907–61

Turn in Traffic		Turn in Cost		Lead or Lag[a] of Cost at	
Level	Date	Level	Date	Traffic Peak	Traffic Trough
Trough	June 1908	Peak	Oct. 1907	--	-8
Peak	Apr. 1910	Trough	Aug. 1909	-8	--
Trough	Mar. 1911	Peak	Oct. 1912	--	+19
Peak	Feb. 1913	Trough	Feb. 1913	0	--
Trough	Dec. 1914	Peak	May 1914	--	-7
Peak	May 1918	Trough	Dec. 1915	-29	--
Trough	Mar. 1919	Peak	Apr. 1919	--	+1
Peak	Feb. 1920	Trough	Aug. 1919	-6	--
Trough	July 1921	Peak	May 1921	--	-2
Peak	Apr. 1923	Trough	Apr. 1923	0	--
Trough	June 1924	Peak	Oct. 1923	--	-8
Peak	July 1926	Trough	July 1926	0	--
Trough	Dec. 1927	Peak	July 1927	--	-5
Peak	Aug. 1929	Trough	Feb. 1929	-6	--
Trough	Aug. 1932	Peak	June 1932	--	-2
------	---------	Trough	July 1933	--	--
------	---------	Peak	July 1935	--	--
Peak	Mar. 1937	Trough	Mar. 1937	0	--
Trough	May 1938	Peak	Feb. 1938	--	-3
Peak	Feb. 1944	Trough	Oct. 1942	-16	--
Trough	Oct. 1949	Peak	Oct. 1949	--	0
Peak	Feb. 1952	Trough	Oct. 1950	-16	--
Trough	Aug. 1954	Peak	Dec. 1953	--	-8
Peak	Feb. 1956	Trough	Feb. 1956	0	--
Trough	May 1958	Peak	Apr. 1958	--	-1
Peak	June 1959	Trough	June 1959	0	--
Trough	4Q 1960	Peak	3Q 1960	--	-3

SUMMARY

Number of peaks in traffic with:
    Earlier trough in cost   6
    Coinciding trough in cost   6
    Later trough in cost   0

Number of troughs in traffic with:
    Earlier peak in cost   10
    Coinciding peak in cost   1
    Later peak in cost   2

    Total   25

[a]Number of months by which turn in cost preceded (-) or followed (+) turn of opposite character in traffic units.

Hours Per Unit and Labor Cost
Inversely Related to Traffic

Monthly figures on man-hours and compensation of railroad workers are available for eight traffic expansions and contractions, beginning in 1921. There was a net fall in man-hours per traffic unit in all expansions, and a net rise in most contractions (Table 56). Hourly earnings, on the other hand, rose in all but one of the expansions and contractions. But in the upswings, the rise in earnings was not large enough to offset the fall in hours per unit: labor cost per traffic unit fell in all of them. In the downswings, of course, the rise in hourly pay reinforced the effect of rising hours per unit on cost.

TABLE 56

Man-Hours Per Traffic Unit, Hourly Earnings, and Labor Cost Per Traffic Unit: Direction of Change from Stage to Stage of Traffic Cycles, 1921–61

| From Stage | To Stage | Number of Observations with | | | | | |
		Rise in Hours Per Unit	Fall in Hours Per Unit	Rise in Earnings	Fall in Earnings	Rise in Cost	Fall in Cost
I	II	0	8	5	3	0	8
II	III	0	8	6	2	1	7
III	IV	1	7	6	2	3	5
IV	V	1	7	4	4	3	5
V	VI	8	0	7	1	8	0
VI	VII	3	5	8	0	7	1
VII	VIII	6	2	7	1	7	1
VIII	IX	2	6	6	2	6	2
I	V	0	8	7	1	0	8
V	IX	5	3	7	1	7	1

The inverse relation between hours per unit or labor cost and traffic is strongest at the beginning of an upswing or downswing in traffic. Hours per unit fell in a majority of the second and fourth segments of traffic contractions. Labor cost rose in most cases in all segments, but less frequently in the last segment of traffic declines than in the first.

Hours per unit fell continuously from stage to stage in six of the eight traffic expansions (Table 57). Hourly earnings rose

106 COST, PRICES, AND PROFITS

continuously in five of the eight traffic contractions. Labor cost
had a continuous fall in three expansions, and a fall-rise pattern
in three; it had a continuous rise in four contractions.

TABLE 57
Man-Hours Per Traffic Unit, Hourly Earnings, and Labor Cost Per
Traffic Unit: Patterns of Change During
Expansions and Contractions in Traffic, 1921–61
(number of phases)

Pattern	Hours Per Unit		Hourly Earnings		Cost Per Unit	
	Expansions	Contractions	Expansions	Contractions	Expansions	Contractions
Continuous rise	0	0	1	5	0	4
Rise, fall	0	3	2	2	0	2
Rise, fall, rise	0	2	1	0	0	2
Rise, fall, rise, fall	0	3	1	0	0	0
Continuous fall	6	0	0	0	3	0
Fall, rise	1	0	2	1	3	0
Fall, rise, fall	1	0	1	0	2	0
Fall, rise, fall, rise	0	0	0	0	0	0

Direction of Change Same in Labor and Total Cost

Total operating cost per traffic unit changed in the same direction
as labor cost per traffic unit in all eight traffic expansions, and in
all contractions except 1929–32. From the 1929 peak stage to the
1932 trough stage, labor cost declined a little (2.2 per cent) while
total cost increased a little (1.5 per cent). These are net changes.
Between successive stages of this contraction (from V to VI, VI to
VII, etc.) the directions do not differ. Both labor and total cost
rose in the first three segments of the contraction, and fell in the
fourth. The decline in labor cost in the fourth segment was more
than sufficient to offset the previous rises; the decline in total cost
was insufficient. Data for all cycles make possible sixty-four comparisons of changes during segments of cycles. The direction of
change in labor and total cost is similar in all but one. From the
fourth to the fifth stages of the 1954–56 traffic expansion, labor
cost rose 2.1 per cent while total cost fell 2.2 per cent.

Little or Inverse Relation Between Rate Level and Traffic

Railroads provide an almost infinite variety of services, each of which has its price. They carry nearly every commodity and they carry each between various pairs of places. They carry passengers and mail, and collect minor portions of their revenue from still other sources. Although much is done to simplify matters by grouping commodities, origins, and destinations, the prices of railway services form a complex system; and no really precise index describing percentage changes in the average level of the whole system over short periods of time has ever been constructed. I have elsewhere argued, however, that a rough substitute, revenue per traffic unit, is useful in analyzing cyclical changes.[4]

Revenue per traffic unit, unlike prices in manufacturing, has shown no tendency to rise and fall with the volume of business done (Table 58). It rose in four of the twelve traffic expansions for which we have monthly data, but fell in the other eight. It fell in only three of the traffic contractions, and rose in the other nine.

Many of the net changes were slight, and might be accounted for by changes in the composition of traffic. The larger increases in contractions are accounted for by general changes in the level of rates authorized in proceedings before the Interstate Commerce Commission.[5] During the World War II expansion, traffic increased so greatly, and the effect of increased volume on costs was so favorable, that railroads were able to operate profitably at prewar freight rates (passenger fares were increased a little).

After the war, however, railroads suffered not only from the brief postwar recession, but from the loss of abnormal wartime traffic and the diversion of peacetime traffic to other means of transport, as well as from rising wage rates and prices of materials. Falling volume and inflation threatened them with insolvency; they asked for, and the Interstate Commerce Commission authorized, a series of general increases in freight rates (Table 59). In the prolonged 1944–49 contraction, freight rates were in-

[4]*American Transportation*, pp. 231–235.
[5]The general rate increases before 1940 are described in *American Transportation*, pp. 246–248.

TABLE 58
Revenue Per Traffic Unit at Peaks and Troughs in Traffic, 1907–61

Turn in Traffic		Revenue Per Unit[a] (cents)	Change in Revenue Per Unit	
Date	Level		To Peak from Trough	To Trough from Peak
June 1908	Trough	.7987	--	--
Apr. 1910	Peak	.8409	.0422	--
Mar. 1911	Trough	.8410	--	.0001
Feb. 1913	Peak	.7924	-.0486	--
Dec. 1914	Trough	.8160	--	.0236
May 1918	Peak	.8821	.0661	--
Mar. 1919	Trough	1.1251	--	.2430
Feb. 1920	Peak	1.1455	.0204	--
July 1921	Trough	1.4401	--	.2946
Apr. 1923	Peak	1.2320	-.2081	--
June 1924	Trough	1.2669	--	.0349
July 1926	Peak	1.2237	-.0432	--
Dec. 1927	Trough	1.2090	--	-.0147
Aug. 1929	Peak	1.2238	.0148	--
Aug. 1932	Trough	1.1299	--	-.0939
Mar. 1937	Peak	.9862	-.1437	--
May 1938	Trough	1.0450	--	.0588
Feb. 1944	Peak	.9516	-.0934	--
Oct. 1949	Trough	1.4430	--	.4914
Feb. 1952	Peak	1.4418	-.0012	--
Aug. 1954	Trough	1.5161	--	.0743
Feb. 1956	Peak	1.4364	-.0797	--
May 1958	Trough	1.5577	--	.1213
June 1959	Peak	1.5482	-.0095	--
2Q 1959	Peak	1.5527	--	--
4Q 1960	Trough	1.5324	--	-.0203

[a]Three-month averages.

creased about 57 per cent over the rates in effect on June 30, 1946 (substantially the prewar rates). Other general postwar increases also occurred, mostly during traffic contractions. In consequence of these general increases, the curve of revenue per traffic unit rises very steeply in the 1946–49 portion of the postwar traffic contraction and in the 1956–58 contraction (Chart 16).[6]

The rises in Table 59 are somewhat exaggerated because state railroad commissions may not have allowed them to become fully effective on intrastate traffic and because the railroads cut many rates to meet competition of other forms of transport. The pattern of step-by-step rises suggested by the precise dates does not show up in the chart of revenue per unit because there were also

[6]For charts of unit revenue and cost from 1907 to 1938, see *American Transportation*, pp. 234, 275.

TABLE 59

General Increases in Freight Rates, 1944–59

Effective Date of Rate Increases	Percentage Increase over June 30, 1946	
	Cumulated	Decumulated
During traffic contraction, Feb. 1944 to Oct. 1949		
July 1, 1946	6.5	6.5
January 1, 1947	17.6	11.1
October 13, 1947	28.1	10.5
January 5, 1948	37.8	9.7
May 6, 1948	42.8	5.0
August 21, 1948	44.2	1.4
January 11, 1949	51.7	7.5
September 1, 1949	57.3	5.6
Total		57.3
During traffic expansion, Oct. 1949 to Feb. 1952		
April 4, 1951	61.1	3.8
August 28, 1951	67.6	6.5
Total		10.3
During traffic contraction, Feb. 1952 to Aug. 1954		
May 2, 1952	78.9	11.3
During traffic contraction, Feb. 1956 to May 1958		
March 7, 1956	88.8	9.9
December 28, 1956 or Feb. 23, 1957	98.2	9.4
August 26, 1957	107.7	9.5
Total		28.8
During traffic expansion, May 1958 to June 1959		
September 15, 1958	112.1	4.4

rises in passenger fares, and because of changes in the composition of traffic.

A coal strike in April and May 1946 provided a salient instance of such a change in composition. Revenue per ton-mile from this commodity is low compared with the average received for the movement of other commodities. When a large part of this traffic disappeared, over-all revenue per traffic unit showed a sharp temporary rise (Chart 16).

Changes in the general level of railway rates, fares, and charges are small except in times of inflation or intensifying competition from other means of transport. Serious inflation occurred only in postwar periods. Competition from other means of transport has been more influential in some cycles than in others. It had no noticeable influence on general rate levels before, say, 1928, and none during the World War II expansion; its effects are quite noticeable in the 1954–56 expansion. There is no systematic difference

CHART 16

Railway Operating Revenues and Expenses Per Traffic Unit,
1938–61

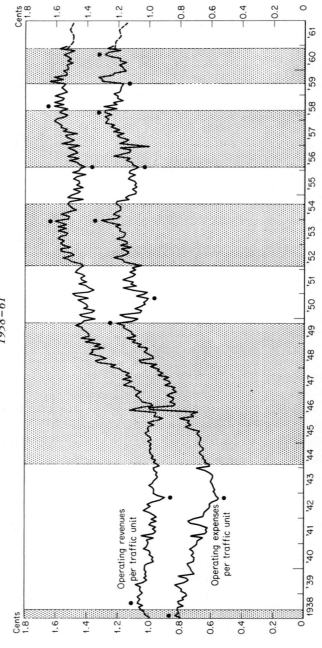

SOURCE: Appendix Tables B-4, B-5.
NOTE: Shaded areas are contractions in traffic units. Dots are at peaks and troughs in the charted variable.

in frequency of change between early and late expansion or contraction (Table 60). Revenue per unit has not followed any simple
and consistent pattern in successive segments of traffic cycles
(Table 54).

TABLE 60
Revenue Per Traffic Unit (Price): Direction of Change from
Stage to Stage of Traffic Cycles, 1907 – 61

From Stage	To Stage	Number of Observations		
		With Rise	With Fall	Total
I	II	4	8	12
II	III	4	8	12
III	IV	7	5	12
IV	V	4	8	12
V	VI	8	4	12
VI	VII	9	3	12
VII	VIII	7	5	12
VIII	IX	6	6	12
I	V	4	8	12
V	IX	9	3	12

Operating Margin Usually Rises
and Falls With Traffic

In proportion to their revenues, railroads own much more property than most other industries. To provide the money to build
their properties, they relied largely on long-term borrowing.
Present operating railroad companies have taken over properties
formerly operated independently by other companies, paying
fixed rents for the use of these properties. Consequently, in this
industry an unusually large proportion of revenue goes to pay
interest, rent, and property taxes. In the aggregate, these outlays
fluctuate very little with fluctuations in traffic. In railway statistics,
operating expenses – mainly labor and materials – have long been
shown separately from taxes and fixed charges. Analysts of railway finances have been accustomed to use the operating ratio
– the percentage ratio of operating expenses to operating revenues – as a key figure. To distinguish the more from the less
variable deductions from revenue, it would be more logical to
exclude depreciation from operating expenses and to include

TABLE 61

Railway Operating Ratio at Peaks and Troughs in Traffic, 1907–61

Turn in Traffic		Operating Ratio[a] (per cent)	Change in Operating Ratio	
Date	Level		To Peak from Trough	To Trough from Peak
June 1908	Trough	67.5	--	--
Apr. 1910	Peak	67.3	-0.2	--
Mar. 1911	Trough	68.8	--	1.5
Feb. 1913	Peak	70.1	1.3	--
Dec. 1914	Trough	72.2	--	2.1
May 1918	Peak	87.1	14.9	--
Mar. 1919	Trough	86.8	--	-0.3
Feb. 1920	Peak	85.0	-1.8	--
July 1921	Trough	82.1	--	-2.9
Apr. 1923	Peak	75.6	-6.5	--
June 1924	Trough	77.7	--	2.1
July 1926	Peak	71.8	-5.9	--
Dec. 1927	Trough	76.2	--	4.4
Aug. 1929	Peak	71.0	-5.2	--
Aug. 1932	Trough	78.5	--	7.5
Mar. 1937	Peak	70.9	-7.6	--
May 1938	Trough	77.4	--	6.5
Feb. 1944	Peak	65.2	-12.2	--
Oct. 1949	Trough	80.5	--	15.3
Feb. 1952	Peak	75.9	-4.6	--
Aug. 1954	Trough	79.7	--	3.8
Feb. 1956	Peak	76.1	-3.6	--
May 1958	Trough	81.0	--	4.9
June 1959	Peak	76.0	-5.0	--
2Q 1959	Peak	76.0	--	--
4Q 1960	Trough	80.1	--	4.1

[a]Three-month averages.

payroll taxes, which vary with labor expense. These adjustments are not customary, however, and we shall follow the custom.

In ten of twelve expansions in traffic since 1908, the operating ratio fell from the initial trough in traffic to the peak. In ten of twelve contractions, it rose from the peak to the terminal trough (Table 61). One may call the difference between 100 and the operating ratio the operating margin; obviously, it rises and falls with traffic.

MARGIN OFTEN MOVES CONTRARY TO TRAFFIC IN LATE EXPANSION OR CONTRACTION

The operating ratio rose only once during the first segment of an expansion (Table 62). Rises were slightly more frequent in the second segment, and more frequent in the third and fourth segments. The ratio rose in all but one of the first segments of contractions; this is the period when a rising operating ratio is most common. Rises are less frequent thereafter. They outnumbered declines, however, in all four segments.

TABLE 62

Railway Operating Ratio: Direction of Change from Stage to Stage of Traffic Cycles, 1907–61

From Stage	To Stage	Number of Observations		
		With Rise	With Fall	Total
I	II	1	11	12
II	III	2	10	12
III	IV	7	5	12
IV	V	5	7	12
V	VI	11	1	12
VI	VII	8	4	12
VII	VIII	7	5	12
VIII	IX	8	4	12
I	V	2	10	12
V	IX	10	2	12

Translating these findings into terms of the operating margin, it appears that the latter almost always widens in the first segment of an upswing in traffic, but rises become less frequent thereafter. It very seldom rises in the first segment of a contraction, but rises are not uncommon in the last three segments.

TURNS IN MARGIN OFTEN LEAD TURNS IN TRAFFIC

In most cases there was a peak in the operating ratio near each trough in traffic, and a trough in the operating ratio near each peak in traffic (Chart 17). As one might expect from the foregoing sections, where turns can be paired, the turn in the ratio often precedes the turn of opposite character in traffic. Troughs in the ratio preceded traffic peaks in six of nine pairs of turns (Table 63). Peaks in the ratio preceded traffic troughs in eight of ten pairs.

Every peak in the operating ratio is a trough in the operating margin, and vice versa. The operating margin, therefore, often reached a peak before the peak in traffic, and a trough before the trough in traffic.

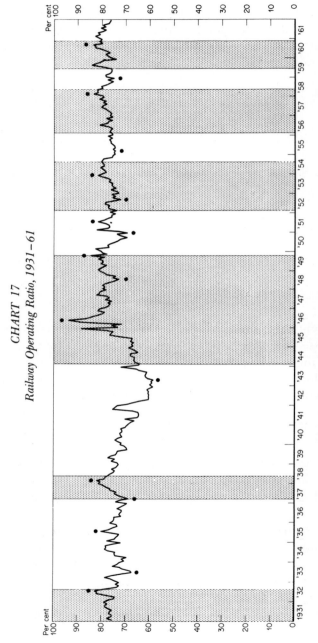

CHART 17
Railway Operating Ratio, 1931–61

SOURCE: Appendix Table B-6.
NOTE: Shaded areas are contractions in traffic units. Dots are at
peaks and troughs in the operating ratio.

TABLE 63

Traffic and Operating Ratio: Turning Points Compared, 1907 – 61

Turn in Traffic		Turn in Operating Ratio		Lead or Lag[a] of Ratio at	
Level	Date	Level	Date	Traffic Peak	Traffic Trough
Trough	June 1908	Peak	Nov. 1907	--	-7
Peak	Apr. 1910	Trough	Nov. 1909	-5	--
Trough	Mar. 1911	------	---------	--	--
Peak	Feb. 1913	------	---------	--	--
Trough	Dec. 1914	Peak	Feb. 1914	--	-10
Peak	May 1918	Trough	Dec. 1915	-29	--
Trough	Mar. 1919	------	---------	--	--
Peak	Feb. 1920	------	---------	--	--
Trough	July 1921	Peak	Aug. 1920	--	-11
Peak	Apr. 1923	------	---------		--
Trough	June 1924	------	---------		
Peak	July 1926	Trough	July 1926	0	--
Trough	Dec. 1927	Peak	Dec. 1927	--	0
Peak	Aug. 1929	Trough	Dec. 1928	-8	--
Trough	Aug. 1932	Peak	July 1932	--	-1
------	---------	Trough	June 1933		
------	---------	Peak	July 1935		
Peak	Mar. 1937	Trough	Mar. 1937	0	--
Trough	May 1938	Peak	Feb. 1938	--	-3
Peak	Feb. 1944	Trough	Apr. 1943	-10	--
------	---------	Peak	May 1946	--	--
------	---------	Trough	July 1948	--	--
Trough	Oct. 1949	Peak	Oct. 1949	--	0
------	---------	Trough	Dec. 1950	--	--
------	---------	Peak	July 1951	--	--
Peak	Feb. 1952	Trough	Sep. 1952	7	--
Trough	Aug. 1954	Peak	Dec. 1953	--	-8
Peak	Feb. 1956	Trough	Mar. 1955	-11	--
Trough	May 1958	Peak	Feb. 1958	--	-3
Peak	June 1959	Trough	Dec. 1958	-6	--
Trough	4Q 1960	Peak	3Q 1960	--	-3

SUMMARY

Number of peaks in traffic with:
  Earlier trough in ratio 6
  Coinciding trough in ratio 2
  Later trough in ratio 1
  No trough in ratio
    Ratio rising 2
    Ratio falling 1

Number of troughs in traffic with:
  Earlier peak in ratio 8
  Coinciding peak in ratio 2
  Later peak in ratio 0
  No peak in ratio
    Ratio rising 2
    Ratio falling 1

Total 25

[a]Number of months by which turn in ratio preceded (-) or followed (+) turn of opposite kind in traffic.

Cost Factor Usually Dominates
Operating Ratio and Margin

In seven of the twelve expansions, prices received (revenue per traffic unit) fell, but cost per traffic unit fell by a greater percentage (Table 64). Lower cost rather than higher prices, therefore, account for half of the declines in the operating ratio. In two other cases, cost fell and price rose. Falling cost was therefore the sole factor in the operating-ratio decline in seven instances and a contributing factor in two. A rise in price was the sole factor in only one instance.

In seven of the twelve contractions, the operating ratio rose in spite of rising prices; cost per traffic unit rose by a greater percentage. In three, prices fell and cost rose. No rise in the ratio was caused by a fall in prices received accompanied by a smaller fall in cost.

Similar conclusions result if the data are examined segment by segment in every cycle of traffic. With six possible combinations of change and only twelve observations for each segment, an attempt to discuss progressive changes from segment to segment in the comparative frequency of the various combinations would not be justified. It is fair, however, to count their frequency in all segments (Table 64). A rise in cost, accompanied by some, but not an offsetting, rise in price, accounts for most stage-to-stage rises in the operating ratio. A fall in cost, accompanied by some, but not an offsetting, fall in price, accounts for most stage-to-stage declines in the ratio.

The dominating influence of cost is perhaps more clearly illustrated if we leave changes in unit revenue out of account (Table 65). Thirty of the thirty-four stage-to-stage declines in cost during expansions were reflected in the operating ratio. Thirty-one of the forty-one rises in cost during contractions were reflected in the ratio. Cost and the ratio move together, both up or both down, in seventy-six of the ninety-six stage-to-stage observations in the table.

At least four of the thirteen instances in which cost rose but the operating ratio fell are accounted for by general increases in rates. If we turn aside from the stage analysis and look at the graphs

TABLE 64

Operating Ratio: Changes Classified According to Combinations of Change in Price and Cost, 1907–61

From Stage	To Stage	Rise in Operating Ratio				Fall in Operating Ratio			
		Rise in Price, Larger Percentage Rise in Cost	Fall in Price, Rise in Cost	Fall in Price, Smaller Percentage Fall in Cost	Total	Rise in Price, Smaller Percentage Rise in Cost	Rise in Price, Fall in Cost	Fall in Price, Larger Percentage Fall in Cost	Total
I	II	0	1	0	1	0	4	7	11
II	III	0	2	0	2	1	3	6	10
III	IV	5	0	2	7	1	1	3	5
IV	V	2	1	2	5	1	1	5	7
Total		7	4	4	15	3	9	21	33
V	VI	7	4	0	11	1	0	0	1
VI	VII	6	2	0	8	3	0	1	4
VII	VIII	3	4	0	7	4	0	1	5
VIII	IX	3	2	3	8	2	1	1	4
Total		19	12	3	34	10	1	3	14
I	V	1	0	1	2	1	2	7	10
V	IX	7	3	0	10	2	0	0	2

TABLE 65
*Cost Per Unit: Changes Classified According to Changes in
Operating Ratio, 1907 – 61*

From Stage	To Stage	Rise in Cost			Fall in Cost		
		With Rise in Ratio	With Fall in Ratio	Total	With Rise in Ratio	With Fall in Ratio	Total
I	II	1	0	1	0	11	11
II	III	2	1	3	0	9	9
III	IV	5	1	6	2	4	6
IV	V	3	1	4	2	6	8
Total		11	3	14	4	30	34
V	VI	11	1	12	0	0	0
VI	VII	8	3	11	0	1	1
VII	VIII	7	4	11	0	1	1
VIII	IX	5	2	7	3	2	5
Total		31	10	41	3	4	7
I	V	1	1	2	1	9	10
V	IX	10	2	12	0	0	0

(Charts 16 and 17)[7], it appears that the broad movements of cost and the ratio are similar. During the twenty-six months from May 1946 to July 1948, the fourteen months from July 1951 to September 1952, and the nine months from August 1920 to May 1921, however, the general drift of cost per unit was upward, but that of the ratio was downward. These are the longest periods with cost rising but the ratio falling. In each of the three periods, general rate increases were made.

From the foregoing, it appears that rises in cost per traffic unit have usually been accompanied by declines in the operating profit margin, and vice versa. Cost has never risen for a considerable period without producing a decline in margin, except when the rise in cost was so great that general increases in the rate level were deemed necessary.

*Pre-Tax Margin Fluctuates More
Than Operating Margin*

The profit margin as we defined it in Chapter 1 differs from the operating margin that we have discussed in this chapter. Pre-tax income (j) equals net operating revenue (c) plus miscellaneous

[7]See also my *American Transportation*, Chart 95.

income (g) minus net rents (d), tax accruals (e and f), fixed charges
(h), and other deductions (i) in Table 66. Miscellaneous income,
net rents, and payroll tax accruals tend to fluctuate, in the aggregate, with traffic or business conditions. Fixed charges, tax
accruals other than payroll and U.S. income taxes, and other deductions, on the other hand, tend to change very slowly, in the
aggregate. Consequently one might expect the net change in the
pre-tax margin during an upswing or downswing of traffic to be
wider than the net change in the operating margin, and so it was
in eight of the ten comparisons we can make (Table 67 — monthly
data on the final margin begin in 1931).

The first of the two exceptions occurred in the 1944–49 contraction of traffic. During these years, eighteen Class I railways
emerged from receivership or trusteeship. For one, the end meant
sale of its assets to another road; for a second, it meant the aban-
donment of operations. Reorganization reduced the long-term
debt of the other sixteen from $2,424 million shortly before the
end of the receivership or trusteeship to $1,255 million shortly
after. Elimination of debt reduced aggregate interest charges.
Roads that were not in the wringer, moreover, were able to refund
old obligations at lower rates of interest. On December 31, 1943
the average rate of interest on all outstanding long-term debt was
4.15 per cent; by December 31, 1949, it had fallen to 3.68 per cent.

The other exception occurred in the expansion of 1954–56,
when the final margin increased by a somewhat smaller increment
than the operating margin. Without seasonally adjusting the intermediate items, which would be laborious, it is impossible to explain
this exception.

Although the final margin tends to fluctuate more widely than
the operating margin, the direction of change is similar. All the
net changes over traffic phases are in the same direction (Table 67).
All troughs in the operating ratio can be matched with nearby
peaks in the final margin, and vice versa (Chart 17 and Chart
18). In eight of seventeen pairs, the dates of opposite turns coincide. In most of the others, the interval between the earlier and
later turn is short, one or two months. The directions of change
from one stage of a traffic cycle to the next are opposite in thirty-
five of the forty comparisons we can make. Consistently opposite

TABLE 66
Railway Income Account, 1957
(million dollars)

a.	Railway operating revenues	10,491
b.	Railway operating expenses[a]	8,227
c.	Net revenue from railway operations, a-b	2,264
d.	Rents for equipment and joint facilities[b]	273
e.	Railway tax accruals: payroll	342
f.	Railway tax accruals: other (except U.S. income taxes)	407
g.	Miscellaneous income[c]	234
h.	Fixed charges (rent for leased roads, fixed interest, etc.)	369
i.	Other deductions (contingent interest, etc.)	50
j.	Net income before U.S. income taxes, (c+g) - (d+e+f+h+i)	1,057
k.	U.S. income taxes	320
l.	Net income	737
m.	Operating ratio, 100 x b/a	78.4
n.	Operating margin, 100 x c/a	21.6
o.	Margin, 100 x j/a	10.1

[a]Includes depreciation, $581 million.

[b]Payments by all roads minus receipts of all.

[c]"Other" income minus miscellaneous deductions.

TABLE 67
Railway Profit Margin at Peaks and Troughs in Traffic, 1931 – 61

Turn in Traffic		Pre-Tax Margin[a] (per cent)	Change From Preceding Turn in Traffic		
Date	Level		Pre-Tax Margin	Operating Ratio	Operating Margin
Aug. 1932	Trough	-7.5	--	--	--
Mar. 1937	Peak	7.6	15.1	-7.6	7.6
May 1938	Trough	-5.1	-12.7	6.5	-6.5
Feb. 1944	Peak	21.6	26.7	-12.2	12.2
Oct. 1949	Trough	7.0	-14.6	15.3	-15.3
Feb. 1952	Peak	14.6	7.6	-4.6	4.6
Aug. 1954	Trough	9.0	-5.6	3.8	-3.8
Feb. 1956	Peak	12.2	3.2	-3.6	3.6
May 1958	Trough	5.9	-6.3	4.9	-4.9
June 1959	Peak	11.2	5.3	-5.0	5.0
2Q 1959	Peak	11.6	--	--	--
4Q 1960	Trough	3.8	-7.8	4.1	-4.1

[a]Three-month averages.

change in operating ratio and final margin, of course, means consistently similar change in the operating margin and final margin.

Profits More Closely Related Than Margins to Traffic

Rising traffic, accompanied by rising revenue, can sometimes cause profits to rise even though the aggregate margin declines. The operating margin rose in eleven of twelve first segments of expansion; net operating revenue rose in all twelve (Table 68). For other segments the corresponding figures are, respectively, second segments, ten, ten; third segments, five, nine; fourth segments, seven, ten. There was a net rise in operating margin during ten expansions, and in operating profit during eleven.

Falling traffic, usually accompanied by falling revenue, sometimes results in falling profits even when margins are rising. The number of first and second segments of contraction with a fall in operating margin, however, was the same as the number with a fall in operating profit. But the margin declined in only seven third segments and eight fourth, while profits fell in nine. The number of net declines over a contraction as a whole was the same for operating profits as for operating margins.

TABLE 68

Operating Profits (Net Operating Revenue): Direction of Change from Stage to Stage of Traffic Cycles, 1907–61

From Stage	To Stage	Number of Observations		
		With Rise	With Fall	Total
I	II	12	0	12
II	III	10	2	12
III	IV	9	3	12
IV	V	10	2	12
V	VI	1	11	12
VI	VII	4	8	12
VII	VIII	3	9	12
VIII	IX	3	9	12
I	V	11	1	12
V	IX	2	10	12

CHART 18
Railway Pre-Tax Margin, 1931–61

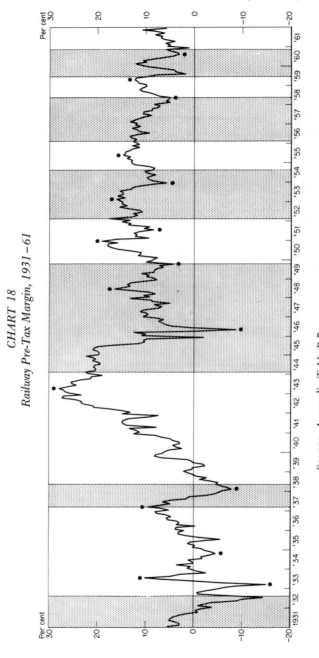

SOURCE: Appendix Table B-7.
NOTE: Shaded areas are contractions in traffic units. Dots are at peaks and troughs in margin.

In thirty-seven of the forty comparisons we can make, the direction of stage-to-stage change in net income before taxes was the same as in net railway operating revenue. The net changes over a traffic expansion or contraction as a whole were in the same direction in all ten instances.

6

PUBLIC UTILITIES, CONSTRUCTION, AND TRADE

The margin and related figures for manufacturing and railroads are more detailed and instructive than the available statistics for most other divisions of economic activity. Too often the data for other parts of the economy pertain to a minor industry, or a hodge-podge of industries, cover too short a stretch of time, are not comparable from one interval to the next, or are published in annual form only. For the large and homogeneous telephone and electric utilities, however, there are monthly figures over a fairly long period. Trade and construction are such important sectors that even the annual figures deserve some examination.

Telephone Companies

The telephone industry has been almost free of those contractions in the physical and dollar volume of sales that occur more or less concurrently in so many other industries. Monthly physical measures of sales—the number of local and toll calls—begin with January 1948. We see no contraction in local calls (Chart 19). Annual statistics on local calls, 1920–48, show a decline from 1930 to 1933. Customers of the A and B (i.e., all but the smallest) phone companies made 30,028 million local calls in the earlier and 25,860 million in the later year. This decline of 13.9 per cent was a loss of business much smaller than that experienced by most other industries in the Great Depression. There was also a very slight decline (0.2 per cent) from 1943 to 1944.

The monthly figures for toll calls show a small decline from November 1949 to April 1951. Beginning in 1950, however, the telephone companies enlarged local dialing areas considerably, and many calls that would formerly have been counted as toll were now counted as local. The decline is probably just a statistical illusion. Annual data indicate real declines from 1929 to 1933 (37.3 per cent), and from 1937 to 1938 (1.7 per cent).

Toll calls appear to have been somewhat more sensitive than local calls to business conditions. The first decline in the former began a year earlier than the corresponding decline in the latter, and was much larger percentagewise. Only toll messages declined in 1937–38.

Although diminishing prosperity seldom caused people to curtail their use of telephones, it nevertheless retarded the growth of the service (Tables 69 and 70). The number of local calls, for example, increased at the rate of 35.6 million per month in the

CHART 19

Telephone Companies: Local and Toll Calls, 1948–61

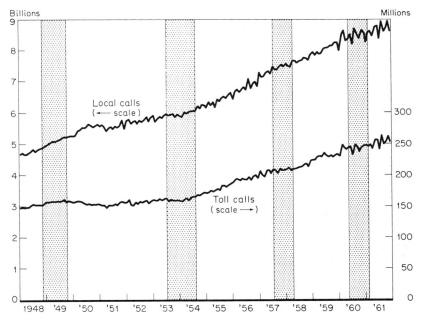

SOURCE: Appendix Table B-11.
NOTE: Shaded areas are contractions in business.

1954–57 business expansion, but only 24.2 million in the following contraction. The number of toll calls increased by 1,120,000 per month in the former, but only 310,000 in the latter.

Even retardation did not always occur. We can, however, measure the regularity of its occurrence, which turns out to be quite high. If the number of messages increased in an expansion but fell in an adjacent contraction, or increased in both but more rapidly in the expansion, we may say that the rate of change "conformed positively" to business. If the direction of change in messages was opposite to that in business or if the growth was faster in the contraction, we may say that the rate of change "conformed inversely." Using both monthly and annual data, and comparing each phase with the preceding one, we find fourteen cases of positive and four of inverse conformity in the rate of growth for local calls (Tables 69 and 70). The difference, ten, is

TABLE 69

Telephone Calls, Local and Toll: Change and Rate of Change
During Business Expansions and Contractions, 1948–61

				CHANGE FROM PRECEDING DATE			
Turn in Business		Months from Preced- ing Date	Number of Calls[a] (millions)		Per Month		Conformity of Rate of Change[b]
Date	Level			Total	To Peak from Trough	To Trough from Peak	
			LOCAL CALLS				
Nov. 1948	Peak	--	4,890	--	--	--	--
Oct. 1949	Trough	11	5,244	354	--	32.2	--
July 1953	Peak	45	5,919	675	15.0	--	Inverse
Aug. 1954	Trough	13	6,113	194	--	14.9	Positive
July 1957	Peak	35	7,360	1,247	35.6	--	Positive
Apr. 1958	Trough	9	7,578	218	--	24.2	Positive
May 1960	Peak	25	8,385	807	32.3	--	Positive
Feb. 1961	Trough	9	8,491	106	--	11.8	Positive
			TOLL CALLS				
Nov. 1948	Peak	--	153.6	--	--	--	--
Oct. 1949	Trough	11	159.2	5.6	--	.51	--
July 1953	Peak	45	160.3	1.1	.02	--	Inverse
Aug. 1954	Trough	13	166.4	6.1	--	.47	Inverse
July 1957	Peak	35	205.6	39.2	1.12	--	Positive
Apr. 1958	Trough	9	208.4	2.8	--	.31	Positive
May 1960	Peak	25	242.6	34.2	1.37	--	Positive
Feb. 1961	Trough	9	247.0	4.4	--	.49	Positive

[a]Three-month averages.

[b]Based on comparison with preceding line, alternate column.

TABLE 70
Telephone Calls, Local and Toll: Change and Rate of Change During Business Expansions and Contractions, 1920–49

Turn in Business Date	Level	Years from Preceding Date	Number of Calls[a] (millions)	Change from Preceding Date Total	Per Year To Peak from Trough	Per Year To Trough from Peak	Conformity of Rate of Change[b]
			LOCAL CALLS				
1920	Peak	--	11,652	--	--	--	--
1921	Trough	1	12,290	638	--	638	--
1923	Peak	2	15,005	2,715	1,358	--	Positive
1924	Trough	1	16,097	1,092	--	1,092	Positive
1926	Peak	2	18,243	2,146	1,073	--	Inverse
1927	Trough	1	19,192	949	--	949	Positive
1926	Peak	--	25,706	--	--	--	--
1927	Trough	1	26,417	711	--	711	--
1929	Peak	2	30,029	3,612	1,806	--	Positive
1932	Trough	3	27,887	-2,142	--	-714	Positive
1929	Peak	--	29,916	--	--	--	--
1932	Trough	3	27,588	-2,328	--	-776	--
1937	Peak	5	29,258	1,670	334	--	Positive
1938	Trough	1	29,868	610	--	610	Inverse
1937	Peak	--	29,255	--	--	--	--
1938	Trough	1	29,920	665	--	665	--
1944	Peak	6	38,675	8,755	1,459	--	Positive
1946	Trough	2	48,125	9,450	--	4,725	Inverse
1948	Peak	2	58,005	9,880	4,940	--	Positive
1949	Trough	1	61,022	3,017	--	3,017	Positive
			TOLL CALLS				
1920	Peak	--	486	--	--	--	--
1921	Trough	1	495	9	--	9	--
1923	Peak	2	614	119	60	--	Positive
1924	Trough	1	672	58	--	58	Positive
1926	Peak	2	867	195	98	--	Positive
1927	Trough	1	954	87	--	87	Positive
1926	Peak	--	952	--	--	--	--
1927	Trough	1	1,032	80	--	80	--
1929	Peak	2	1,237	205	102	--	Positive
1932	Trough	3	851	-386	--	-129	Positive
1929	Peak	--	1,224	--	--	--	--
1932	Trough	3	842	-382	--	-127	--
1937	Peak	5	892	50	10	--	Positive
1938	Trough	1	877	-15	--	-15	Positive
1937	Peak	--	890	--	--	--	--
1938	Trough	1	877	-13	--	-13	--
1944	Peak	6	1,589	712	119	--	Positive
1946	Trough	2	2,054	465	--	232	Inverse
1948	Peak	2	2,188	134	67	--	Inverse
1949	Trough	1	2,151	-37	--	-37	Positive

[a] 1920-27 segment: Bell system. 1926-32: Class A, B, and C companies. 1929-38: Class A and B companies. 1937-49: Class A companies.
[b] Based on comparison with preceding line, alternate column.

56 per cent of the observations. We call this percentage an index of conformity. For toll calls, the corresponding index also is 56.

One of the exceptions, in both kinds of calls, is found when we compare the postwar contraction, 1944–46, with the wartime expansion, 1938–44. Defense regulations greatly restricted the growth of telephone plant and of the number of phones in service during the war. After hostilities ended, the phone companies hastened to accommodate their waiting customers by installing many more phones. This particular comparison is not a real exception to the rule that business contraction at least retards the growth of service.

Telephone revenue has had even less actual decline than the number of calls. Monthly figures on operating revenue are available from October 1915 to date. In that long period we can see only one contraction in sales; they fell from May 1930 to March 1933. Averages for the usual three-month periods are $100.0 million and $77.7 million, indicating a decline of 22.3 per cent.

Developing depression, however, retarded the growth of revenue a little more consistently than the growth of telephone conversation. Twenty comparisons of adjoining phases can be made (Table 71). Only three fail to indicate decline or retardation in contraction. The rate-of-change conformity score is therefore 70.

In the telephone industry, as in the railroad industry, the investment in plant and equipment is large relative to sales. The kinds of costs that are associated with fixed physical investment—depreciation, property taxes, interest on long-term obligations—make up a high proportion of all cost (Table 72).

Unfortunately, property taxes are not segregated from other taxes, such as payroll taxes, which fluctuate more or less like labor and material expense; we are obliged to use the data with this defect.

We can compute profits before all three plant-associated deductions. Since this is not usually done, we had to invent a name for the resulting figure: operating profit (line k of Table 72). We call its percentage ratio to operating revenue (line a) the operating margin.

A figure regularly computed in the official statistics is net operating income (line f). It is equivalent to profits after deducting

TABLE 71
Telephone Operating Revenue: Change and Rate of Change During
Business Expansions and Contractions, 1918 – 61

Turn in Business		Months from Preced- ing Date	Total Operating Revenue[a] (million dollars)	CHANGE FROM PRECEDING DATE			Conformity of Rate of[b] Change
					Per Month		
Date	Level			Total	To Peak from Trough	To Trough from Peak	
Aug. 1918	Peak	--	28.9	--	--	--	--
Mar. 1919	Trough	7	31.2	2.3	--	.33	--
Jan. 1920	Peak	10	38.1	6.9	.69	--	Positive
July 1921	Trough	18	45.6	7.5	--	.42	Positive
May 1923	Peak	22	53.8	8.2	.37	--	Inverse
July 1924	Trough	14	58.4	4.6	--	.33	Positive
Oct. 1926	Peak	27	75.7	17.3	.64	--	Positive
Nov. 1927	Trough	13	82.3	6.6	--	.51	Positive
Aug. 1929	Peak	21	96.8	14.5	.69	--	Positive
Mar. 1933	Trough	43	77.7	-19.1	--	.44	Positive
Aug. 1929	Peak	--	91.0[c]	--	--	--	--
Mar. 1933	Trough	43	73.5	-17.5	--	-.41	--
May 1937	Peak	50	91.2	17.7	.35	--	Positive
June 1938	Trough	13	90.6	-0.6	--	-.05	Positive
Feb. 1945	Peak	80	162.4	71.8	.90	--	Positive
Oct. 1945	Trough	8	172.0	9.6	--	1.20	Inverse
Nov. 1948	Peak	37	238.2	66.2	1.79	--	Positive
Oct. 1949	Trough	11	264.0	25.8	--	2.35	Inverse
July 1953	Peak	45	387.5	123.5	2.74	--	Positive
Aug. 1954	Trough	13	422.3	34.8	--	2.68	Positive
July 1957	Peak	35	556.1	133.8	3.82	--	Positive
Apr. 1958	Trough	9	581.1	25.0	--	2.78	Positive
May 1960	Peak	25	692.6	111.5	4.46	--	Positive
Feb. 1961	Trough	9	722.4	29.8	--	3.31	Positive

[a] Three-month averages. 1918-33 segment based on ICC data; 1933-61 segment based on FCC data.

[b] Based on comparison with preceding line, alternate column.

[c] Estimated FCC basis, see appendix.

TABLE 72
Income Account of Telephone Companies, 1959
(million dollars)

a.	Operating revenues	7,789
b.	Operating expenses (fuel, labor, materials, etc.)	3,734
c.	Depreciation	988
d.	Federal taxes on income	1,106
e.	Other operating taxes	665
f.	Net operating income, a-(b+c+d+e)	1,296
g.	Other income	172
h.	Interest deductions	241
i.	Other deductions	24
j.	Net income, f+g - (h+i)	1,203
k.	Operating profit, a - b	4,055
l.	Net income before taxes on income, d + j	2,309
m.	Operating margin, 100 k/a	52.1
n.	Before-tax margin, 100 l/a	29.6
o.	After-tax margin, 100 f/a	16.6

depreciation and all taxes (including the highly variable income tax) but before deducting interest (and before allowing for income from sources other than operations). We shall call its percentage ratio to revenue the operating income ratio.

Since data on the operating margin begin in 1933, we cannot compare its changes with fluctuations in operating revenue, the

TABLE 73

Telephone Companies, Operating Margin (1933–61), Before-Tax Margin, and After-Tax Margin (1948–61):
Change During Business Expansions and Contractions

Turn in Business			Change from Preceding Date	
			To Peak from Trough	To Trough from Peak
Date	Level	Margin[a]		
		OPERATING MARGIN		
Mar. 1933	Trough	46.46	--	--
May 1937	Peak	48.03	1.57	--
June 1938	Trough	46.97	--	-1.06
Feb. 1945	Peak	47.22	0.25	--
Oct. 1945	Trough	42.50	--	-4.72
Nov. 1948	Peak	30.92	-11.58	--
Oct. 1949	Trough	35.71	--	4.79
July 1953	Peak	39.60	3.89	--
Aug. 1954	Trough	41.17	--	1.57
July 1957	Peak	46.33	5.16	--
Apr. 1958	Trough	48.93	--	2.60
May 1960	Peak	52.70	3.77	--
Feb. 1961	Trough	52.63	--	-0.07
		BEFORE-TAX MARGIN		
Nov. 1948	Peak	11.17	--	--
Oct. 1949	Trough	14.31	--	3.14
July 1953	Peak	21.37	7.06	--
Aug. 1954	Trough	22.85	--	1.48
July 1957	Peak	24.86	2.01	--
Apr. 1958	Trough	26.55	--	1.69
May 1960	Peak	29.86	3.31	--
Feb. 1961	Trough	29.57	--	-0.29
		AFTER-TAX MARGIN		
Nov. 1948	Peak	7.70	--	--
Oct. 1949	Trough	9.38	--	1.68
July 1953	Peak	10.90	1.52	--
Aug. 1954	Trough	11.88[b]	--	0.98
July 1957	Peak	13.17	1.29	--
Apr. 1958	Trough	13.84	--	0.67
May 1960	Peak	15.49	1.65	--
Feb. 1961	Trough	15.44	--	-0.05

[a]Three-month averages, except as noted.

[b]Two-month average: July 1954 omitted because of erratic fluctuation.

only contraction in which occurred between May 1930 and March 1933. We can, however, observe how it changed during business cycles (Table 73). Although operating revenue increased more rapidly in business expansions than in business contractions, the operating margin displays no consistent relation to business cycles. It rose in all expansions except one, but it also rose in all contractions except three. The conformity index for its direction of change is only +33.

The record of the operating income ratio is much longer (Table 74). During the one actual downswing in revenue, from May 1930 to March 1933, it fell as we might expect from our experience

TABLE 74

Telephone Companies, Operating Income Ratio:
Change During Business Expansions and Contractions, 1918–61

Turn in Business		Operating Income Ratio[a]	Change from Preceding Date	
Date	Level		To Peak from Trough	To Trough from Peak
Aug. 1918	Peak	20.60	--	--
Mar. 1919	Trough	19.45	--	-1.15
Jan. 1920	Peak	19.65	0.20	--
July 1921	Trough	20.38	--	0.73
May 1923	Peak	21.02	0.64	--
July 1924	Trough	20.76	--	-0.26
Oct. 1926	Peak	24.49	3.73	--
Nov. 1927	Trough	24.09[b]	--	-0.40
Aug. 1929	Peak	23.92	-0.17	--
Mar. 1933	Trough	21.81	--	-2.11
Aug. 1929	Peak	19.61[c]	--	--
Mar. 1933	Trough	17.89	--	-1.72
May 1937	Peak	19.88	1.99	--
June 1938	Trough	18.32	--	-1.56
Feb. 1945	Peak	12.07	-6.25	--
Oct. 1945	Trough	12.20	--	0.13
Nov. 1948	Peak	9.24	-2.96	--
Oct. 1949	Trough	11.86	--	2.62
July 1953	Peak	12.09	0.23	--
Aug. 1954	Trough	13.02[b]	--	0.93
July 1957	Peak	13.89	0.87	--
Apr. 1958	Trough	15.29	--	1.40
May 1960	Peak	16.66	1.37	--
Feb. 1961	Trough	16.86	--	0.20

[a]Three-month averages, except as noted. 1918–33 segment based on ICC data; 1933–61 segment based on FCC data.

[b]Two-month average: December 1927 and July 1954 omitted because of erratic fluctuations.

[c]Estimated FCC basis, see appendix.

with other industries. But the fall was very slight, from 22.65 to 21.81 (three-month averages) or 0.84 points. Its direction of net change during the business cycles from March 1933 onward was the same as the direction of net change in the operating margin, except in three instances. The differences change the direction-of-change conformity index for this period from the positive figure, +33, to a small inverse figure, −17.

Net declines in the operating income ratio during business contractions, however, were the rule rather than the exception up to March 1933. Taking the period since 1918 as a whole, the direction-of-change score is +14.

A more logical point at which to break the history of the ratio might be the trough in June 1938. Until then, all but one of the changes in the operating income ratio during contractions are declines. Thereafter, they are all rises. The direction-of-change score for the period ending with that trough is +64; for the period since then, it is −40.

Before 1933 we are forced to base our impressions of how telephone margins fluctuated on the operating income ratio, because we have no data on other variants of profit. The operating margin, however, gives a better impression of the interplay between prices of telephone service on the one hand, and wages, prices of materials, and physical inputs on the other. Depreciation and property taxes, which do not represent month-to-month variations in physical input, are included in the deductions made to arrive at the net operating income ratio; while taxes on income, which in the short run depend on profits and which are subject to changes in tax rates, are also included in those deductions.

Probably these differences in components of the ratio do not cause a decisive difference in the shape of the margin curve up to 1938. During the war and postwar periods, however, changes in the system of taxes do create important differences. The operating margin had a slight net rise in the 1938–45 business expansion. During the course of that expansion, however, the tax rates on corporate income were drastically increased, and the excess profits tax was imposed (and telephone companies did have "excess" profits). Consequently the operating income ratio fell from 18.32 to 12.07. In the brief 1945 contraction, the operating margin fell 4.72 percentage points, but along with the fall came a reduction in income tax liability accrued, and the operating income ratio rose by 0.13 percentage points. In the 1945–48 expansion, the operating margin fell 11.58 points, but the operating income ratio fell only 2.96 points.

We are unable to account for the fall in the operating margin during the 1945 contraction. The tremendous fall in 1945–48, however, reflects inflation. The telephone companies were caught in a price squeeze. Wage rates and prices of materials rose rapidly, as in other industries. Telephone workers received 91.6 cents per hour around February 1945, 97.8 cents around October 1945, and 128.5 cents around November 1948 (three-month averages). The increase between the last two dates is 31 per cent. Telephone companies began to ask utility commissions for higher rates late in 1946. By 1948 the commissions had approved increases amounting, for the Bell system, to $178 million per annum. By 1949 the figure was about $364 million or 14 per cent of Bell system operating revenue in 1948.

The before-tax margin is available only for the business expansions and contractions after 1948 (Table 73). Like the after-tax margin, it rose in both kinds of phases, except in 1960–61.

As in other industries, growth of revenue in the telephone industry can result in rising profit even if the profit margin declines. Operating profit rose in all of the six business expansions since 1933, and in four of the six contractions; it declined in 1937–38 and 1945 (Table 75). Its direction-of-change conformity score is +33. Net operating income fell only in 1937–38; in 1945 the decline in operating profit was more than offset by a decline in federal income tax accruals. The conformity score is +17. Net operating income also rose in all business expansions and contractions between 1918 and 1933, except the 1929–33 contraction. For the whole period 1918–61, the conformity score is only +14. Like these two variants, net income both before and after taxes has increased in all phases since the 1948 business peak.

In the expansion of 1945–48, when inflation sharply reduced the operating margin and the operating income ratio, profits increased very little; operating profit rose from $73.03 million to $73.62 million, net operating income from $20.98 million to $21.98 million.

TABLE 75

Telephone Profits at Business Peaks and Troughs, 1918–61[a]

(million dollars)

| Turn in Business | | Net Operating Income (old accounting definition) | Turn in Business | | Operating Profit | Net Operating Income | Net Income Before Taxes[b] | Net Income After Taxes[b] |
Date	Level		Date	Level				
Aug. 1918	Peak	5.96	Mar. 1933	Trough	34.35	13.15		
Mar. 1919	Trough	6.07	May 1937	Peak	43.78	18.12		
Jan. 1920	Peak	7.49	June 1938	Trough	42.57	16.61		
July 1921	Trough	9.29	Feb. 1945	Peak	76.67	19.59		
May 1923	Peak	11.30	Oct. 1945	Trough	73.03	20.98		
July 1924	Trough	12.13	Nov. 1948	Peak	73.62	21.98	26.58	18.32
Oct. 1926	Peak	18.54	Oct. 1949	Trough	94.29	31.30	37.78	24.78
Nov. 1927	Trough	19.72[c]	July 1953	Peak	153.41	46.85	82.78	42.21[c]
Aug. 1929	Peak	23.14	Aug. 1954	Trough	173.86	55.24[c]	96.46	50.37[c]
Mar. 1933	Trough	16.95	July 1957	Peak	257.61	77.22	138.21	73.24
			Apr. 1958	Trough	284.36	88.89	154.32	80.43
			May 1960	Peak	364.98	115.39	206.80	107.25
			Feb. 1961	Trough	380.21	121.83	213.60	111.56

[a] Three-month averages, except as noted.

[b] No data for earlier turns.

[c] Two-month average: December 1927 and July 1954 omitted because of erratic fluctuations.

Electric Utilities

The electric light and power industry has been somewhat more sensitive to business fluctuations than the telephone industry. Its customers have reduced their purchases of kilowatt-hours on five occasions since the end of World War II, and the periods during which they did so correspond roughly to the contractions in business at large, although the dates differ (Chart 20). Earlier figures on kilowatt-hours generated show that production of power fell off in the vicinity of every business contraction after 1919 (when the data begin) except 1926–27. In general, however, the declines in kilowatt-hours have been small in comparison with

CHART 20
Electric Utilities: Kilowatt-Hours Sold, 1944–61

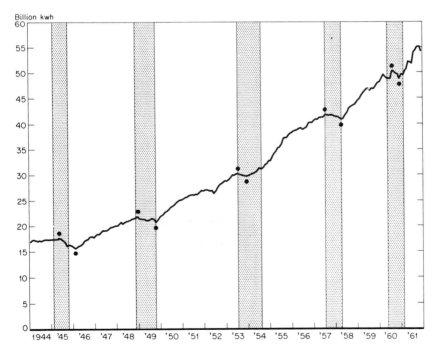

SOURCE: Appendix Table B-21.
NOTE: Shaded areas are contractions in business. Dots are at peaks and troughs in kwh.

either the intervening rises or declines in the output of other industries.

Since World War II, revenue from the sale of electricity, unlike kilowatt-hours, has seldom declined, but has continued to rise even when fewer kilowatt-hours were being sold. There was a net rise in revenue during every contraction in kilowatt-hours sold except that of 1945–46 (Table 76). Earlier figures on revenue, beginning with 1913, indicate declines in the neighborhood of every business contraction except 1913–14 and 1926–27. They were all, however, quite mild.

In the postwar period, rising wage rates and prices of fuel and other commodities used by power companies eventually forced the utility commissions to allow increases in prices for electric service. Some of these doubtless became effective when consumption of energy was falling.

Even if the rate schedules do not change, however, one should not expect electric operating revenue to fall in proportion to the quantity of current sold. The rate schedules are designed to reflect economies of large-scale consumption. Commercial and industrial users pay less per kilowatt-hour than householders. When business declines they are likely to reduce their consump-

TABLE 76
Electric Utilities, Electric Operating Revenue:
Change and Rate of Change During Expansions and Contractions
in Kilowatt-Hours Sold, 1945–61

Turn in kwh Sold		Months from Preceding Date	Electric Operating Revenue[a] (million dollars)	CHANGE FROM PRECEDING DATE		
					Per Month	
Date	Level			Total	To Peak from Trough	To Trough from Peak
May 1945	Peak	--	265.3	--	--	--
Feb. 1946	Trough	9	265.1	-.2	--	-.02
Dec. 1948	Peak	34	361.0	95.9	2.82	--
Oct. 1949	Trough	10	365.2	4.2	--	.42
July 1953	Peak	45	517.4	152.2	3.38	--
Dec. 1953	Trough	5	522.5	5.1	--	1.02
July 1957	Peak	43	697.5	175.0	4.07	--
Apr. 1958	Trough	9	712.0	14.5	--	1.61
Aug. 1960	Peak	28	848.6	136.6	4.88	--
Dec. 1960	Trough	4	849.8	1.2	--	0.30

[a]Three-month averages.

tion by a greater percentage than householders do. A larger portion of the power sold therefore yields the higher residential rates. The schedules usually embody a block system, with a lower charge per kilowatt-hour for each additional block. Even if a householder reduces his consumption, he cuts back on the electricity that costs him least, and his average payment per kilowatt-hour rises.

Although the last three contractions in electricity sold were not accompanied by declines in revenue, they did reduce the rate of growth in the latter. Revenue in each contraction increased less rapidly than in the neighboring expansions (Table 76).

Power is another industry in which labor and materials currently consumed account for a comparatively small part of revenues and total costs, while costs related to capital expenditure account for a comparatively large part (Table 77).

The reported figures make it possible to compute profits before depreciation, all taxes, and interest. As this figure is not given a name in the usual statistics, we shall call it operating profit, as we

TABLE 77
Income Account of Electric Utility Companies, 1957
(million dollars)

		Electric Department	All Departments
a.	Operating revenues	8,308	9,670
b.	Operating expenses (fuel, labor, materials, etc.)	3,937	4,875
c.	Depreciation and amortization	826	907
d.	Federal taxes on income	1,066	1,163
e.	Other taxes	774	876
f.	Net operating revenues, a-(b+c+d+e)	1,705	1,849
g.	Other income (including income from plant leased to others)	3	67
h.	Interest on long-term debt	--	524
i.	Other deductions (net)	--	-21
j.	Net income, f+g - (h+i)	--	1,413
k.	Operating profit, a-b	4,371	4,795
l.	Net income before taxes on income, d+j	--	2,576
m.	Operating margin, 100 k/a	52.6	49.6
n.	Before-tax margin, 100 l/a	--	26.6
o.	Net revenue ratio, 100 f/a	20.5	19.1
p.	After-tax margin, 100 j/a	--	14.6

did in the telephone industry, and shall call its percentage ratio to operating revenue (sales), the operating margin.

Instead of this ratio, the Federal Power Commission statisticians compute and publish "net operating revenues," i.e., sales minus not only labor, materials, etc. but depreciation and all taxes (even federal income taxes), but before deducting interest, etc. It is similar to "net operating income" in the telephone statistics. We shall call its percentage ratio to sales the net revenue ratio.

Many power companies also sell gas or receive revenues from still other utility services. The monthly FPC statistics, however, do not show revenue from other utility sales, but only the net earnings from them. Consequently, it is not possible to compute the operating profit or net revenue from all sales month by month, and we must confine our discussion of monthly fluctuations to the *electric* operating margin or net revenue ratio. Annual figures on total revenue, however, are published.

The statistics do not segregate interest paid and the related "other deductions" between electric and other services. We can therefore compute the final before-tax (or after-tax) margin only year by year and only for all services combined.

The earliest monthy statistics on electric profits are those for December 1941, and the earliest comparable statistics on kilowatt-hours sold are those for January 1944. Conclusions about earlier fluctuations in margins and their relation to energy sold must therefore rest on annual data, which start in1926.

The experience of power companies with respect to margins, like that of telephone companies, has differed from that of manufacturing corporations or railroads. The electric operating margin fell during three of six expansions in kilowatt-hours sold, and rose in six of seven contractions (Table 78). The electric net revenue ratio fell in four of seven expansions, and rose in four of six contractions. The operating margin was inversely rather than positively related to fluctuations in the physical volume of sales, and the net revenue ratio had no relation to physical volume.

Annual data on electricity sales indicate only two contractions between 1926 and 1944: from $1,894 million in 1930 to $1,640 million in 1933, and from $2,031 million in 1937 to $2,018 million in 1938. The operating margin increased in the two contractions, and fell in the expansion; the net revenue ratio fell in all three phases (Table 79).

The relation of operating margins and net revenue ratios to cycles in business at large was similar to their relation to cycles in the power industry. Before we consider the former relation, however, we ought to note that, even when the consumption of electricity declines in the vicinity of a business contraction, it may show a net rise from the business peak to the business trough, because of differences between the dates of turning points in the power and in the business cycles. In fact, sales of energy increased in one of the four postwar contractions (Table 80). Kilowatt-hours sold also increased in 1926–27, but less rapidly than in 1927–29. Declining business retarded the growth of power consumption. From 1929 to 1946, peaks and troughs in annual power sold coincided with those in business.

Electric operating revenue declined in only three of eight business contractions for which data are available (Table 81). Growth was more rapid in 1926–27 than in 1927–29; otherwise, contracting business retarded the growth of revenue.

The rapid growth of revenue in most expansions did not assure a widening of the operating margin. On the contrary, the latter fell in four of seven expansions, and rose in all but one of eight contractions (Table 82). The net revenue ratio fell in five of seven expansions, and rose in five of eight contractions.

As previously noted, we can compute the before-tax margin only from annual data and only from combined electric and non-electric operations. For comparison we have also computed the operating margin on this basis. Both fell in two of five expansions. The operating margin rose in five, and the pre-tax margin in three, of the six contractions (Table 83). The annual margins had little relation to business (conformity index: operating margin, −27; pre-tax margin, −9).

Electric utilities, like telephone companies, were squeezed in the postwar inflation. The electric operating margin fell 6.55 points from the kilowatt-hour trough in February 1946 to the peak in December 1948 (Table 78). From the business trough in October 1945 to the business peak in November 1948, it fell 9.38 points (Table 82). From 1946 to 1948, the over-all operating margin fell

TABLE 78

Electric Operating Margin and Net Revenue Ratio: Change During
Expansions and Contractions in Kilowatt-Hours Sold, 1929 – 61

Turn in kwh Sold		Operating Margin[a]	Net Revenue Ratio[a]	CHANGE FROM PRECEDING DATE			
				Operating Margin		Net Revenue Ratio	
Date	Level			To Peak from Trough	To Trough from Peak	To Peak from Trough	To Trough from Peak
1929	Peak	60.98	42.93	--	--	--	--
1932	Trough	63.92	42.79	--	2.94	--	-0.14
1937	Peak	61.55	35.75	-2.37	--	-7.04	--
1938	Trough	62.24	35.03	--	0.69	--	-0.72
1944	Peak	58.54	24.84	-3.70	--	-10.19	--
May 1945	Peak	53.99	23.38	--	--	--	--
Feb. 1946	Trough	54.07	25.09	--	0.08	--	1.71
Dec. 1948	Peak	47.52	19.13	-6.55	--	-5.96	--
Oct. 1949	Trough	48.26	20.93	--	0.74	--	1.80
July 1953	Peak	50.17	19.64	1.91	--	-1.29	--
Dec. 1953	Trough	50.94	20.04	--	0.77	--	0.40
July 1957	Peak	52.65	20.59	1.71	--	0.55	--
Apr. 1958	Trough	53.61	21.27	--	0.96	--	0.68
Aug. 1960	Peak	55.54	22.00	1.93	--	0.73	--
Dec. 1960	Trough	54.95	21.96	--	-0.59	--	-0.04

[a]Annual data are twelve-month averages; monthly data are three-month averages.

TABLE 79

Electric Operating Margin and Net Revenue Ratio: Change During
Expansions and Contractions in Operating Revenues, 1930 – 38

Turn in Operating Revenue		Operating Margin	Net Revenue Ratio	Change from Preceding Date	
				Operating Margin	Net Revenue Ratio
Date	Level				
1930	Peak	61.83	43.56	--	--
1933	Trough	63.41	40.37	1.58	-3.19
1937	Peak	61.55	35.75	-1.86	-4.62
1938	Trough	62.24	35.03	0.69	-0.72

7.76 points. These are the largest falls in our record for any phase of kilowatt-hours sold or of business. Electric utility workers received 112.0 cents per hour around February 1945, 114.6 cents around October 1945, and 150.8 cents around November 1948. Electric utility companies paid $4.45 for a ton of coal in 1945, $4.89 in 1946, $5.60 in 1947, and $6.69 in 1948. Prices of electric serv;ce, meanwhile, did not increase. Average rates for the various classes of customers and for the several quantities of kilowatt-hours consumed per month are available for January 1 of each year. Residential and commercial rates were generally lower on January 1, 1949 than on January 1, 1945. Rates for industrial service rose between the same dates, but not very much; the percentage increases for three quantity ranges are 5.9, 7.2, and 8.4.

Since operating revenues increased almost continuously after 1938, the occasional declines in profit ratios were not necessarily accompanied by declines in profits. Operating profit declined only in the 1929–32 and 1960 contractions of kilowatt-hours (Table 84). Net operating revenues declined in those contractions and in 1937–38. A large rise in depreciation and taxes resulted in a small net decline in the 1932–37 expansion also. With these exceptions, both kinds of profit increased in expansions and contractions alike.

TABLE 80

Kilowatt-Hours Sold: Change and Rate of Change During
Business Expansions and Contractions, 1945–61

Turn in Business		Months from Preceding Date	Kilowatt-Hours [a] (millions)	CHANGE FROM PRECEDING DATE		
					Per Month	
Date	Level			Total	To Peak from Trough	To Trough from Peak
Feb. 1945	Peak	--	17,459	--	--	--
Oct. 1945	Trough	8	16,229	-1,230	--	-153.8
Nov. 1948	Peak	37	21,602	5,373	145.2	--
Oct. 1949	Trough	11	21,033	-569	--	-51.7
July 1953	Peak	45	30,255	9,222	204.9	--
Aug. 1954	Trough	13	31,402	1,147	--	88.2
July 1957	Peak	35	41,642	10,240	292.6	--
Apr. 1958	Trough	9	41,013	-629	--	-69.9
May 1960	Peak	25	49,066	8,053	322.1	--
Feb. 1961	Trough	9	49,832	766	--	85.1

[a]Three-month averages.

TABLE 81
Electric Operating Revenue: Change and Rate of Change During Business Expansions and Contractions, 1926–61

Turn in Business		Years or Months from Preceding Date	Revenue[a] (million dollars)	CHANGE FROM PRECEDING DATE			Conformity of Rate of Change[b]
					Per Year or Month		
Date	Level			Total	To Peak from Trough	To Trough from Peak	
		YEARS			PER YEAR		
1926	Peak	--	1,415	--	--	--	--
1927	Trough	1	1,567	152	--	152	--
1929	Peak	2	1,817	250	125	--	Inverse
1932	Trough	3	1,713	-104	--	-35	Positive
1937	Peak	5	2,031	318	64	--	Positive
1938	Trough	1	2,018	-13	--	-13	Positive
1944	Peak	6	2,955	937	156	--	Positive
1946	Trough	2	3,127	172	--	86	Positive
		MONTHS			PER MONTH		
Feb. 1945	Peak	--	264.4	--	--	--	--
Oct. 1945	Trough	8	260.0	-4.4	--	-.6	--
Nov. 1948	Peak	37	360.7	100.7	2.7	--	Positive
Oct. 1949	Trough	11	365.2	4.5	--	.4	Positive
July 1953	Peak	45	517.4	152.2	3.4	--	Positive
Aug. 1954	Trough	13	550.4	33.0	--	2.5	Positive
July 1957	Peak	35	697.5	147.1	4.2	--	Positive
Apr. 1958	Trough	9	712.0	14.5	--	1.6	Positive
May 1960	Peak	25	834.6	122.6	4.9	--	Positive
Feb. 1961	Trough	9	856.1	21.5	--	2.4	Positive

[a] Annual totals or three-month averages.
[b] Based on comparison with preceding line, alternate column.

TABLE 82
Electric Operating Margin and Net Revenue Ratio: Change During Business Expansions and Contractions, 1926–61

Turn in Business		Operating Margin[a]	Net Revenue Ratio[a]	CHANGE FROM PRECEDING DATE			
				Operating Margin		Net Revenue Ratio	
Date	Level			To Peak from Trough	To Trough from Peak	To Peak from Trough	To Trough from Peak
1926	Peak	56.96	39.01	--	--	--	--
1927	Trough	58.33	40.65	--	1.37	--	1.64
1929	Peak	60.98	42.93	2.65	--	2.28	--
1932	Trough	63.92	42.79	--	2.94	--	-0.14
1937	Peak	61.55	35.75	-2.37	--	-7.04	--
1938	Trough	62.24	35.03	--	0.69	--	-0.72
1944	Peak	58.54	24.84	-3.70	--	-10.19	--
Feb. 1945	Peak	54.08	21.83	--	--	--	--
Oct. 1945	Trough	54.55	24.84	--	0.47	--	3.01
Nov. 1948	Peak	45.17	18.86	-9.38	--	-5.98	--
Oct. 1949	Trough	48.26	20.93	--	3.09	--	2.07
July 1953	Peak	50.17	19.64	1.91	--	-1.29	--
Aug. 1954	Trough	52.70	21.14	--	2.53	--	1.50
July 1957	Peak	52.65	20.59	-0.05	--	-0.55	--
Apr. 1958	Trough	53.61	21.27	--	0.96	--	0.68
May 1960	Peak	55.52	22.03	1.91	--	0.76	--
Feb. 1961	Trough	54.86	21.83	--	-0.66	--	-0.20

[a] Annual data are twelve-month averages; monthly data are three-month averages.

TABLE 83

Electric Utilities: Change in Operating Margin and Pre-Tax Margin
During Business Expansions and Contractions, 1937 – 61

Turn in Business		Margin[a]		CHANGE FROM PRECEDING DATE			
				Operating Margin		Pre-Tax Margin	
Date	Level	Operating	Pre-Tax	To Peak from Trough	To Trough from Peak	To Peak from Trough	To Trough from Peak
1937	Peak	53.12	22.31	--	--	--	--
1938	Trough	53.83	21.58	--	0.71	--	-0.73
1944	Peak	51.84	24.40	-1.99	--	2.82	--
1946	Trough	49.25	24.77	--	-2.59	--	0.37
1948	Peak	41.49	20.35	-7.76	--	-4.42	--
1949	Trough	44.35	22.27	--	2.86	--	1.92
1953	Peak	47.67	26.56	3.32	--	4.29	--
1954	Trough	49.09	27.00	--	1.42	--	0.44
1957	Peak	49.59	26.64	0.50	--	-0.36	--
1958	Trough	50.60	26.59	--	1.01	--	-0.05
1960	Peak	51.53	26.79	0.93	--	0.20	--
1961	Trough	52.02	26.52	--	0.49	--	-0.27

[a]Includes income from other operations as well as electric operations.

TABLE 84

Electric Operating Profit and Net Revenue at Peaks or Troughs in
Kilowatt-Hours Sold, 1929 – 61
(million dollars)

Turn in kwh Sold		Operating Profit[a]	Net Operating Revenue[a]
Date	Level		
1929	Peak	1,108	780
1932	Trough	1,095	733
1937	Peak	1,250	726
1938	Trough	1,256	707
1944	Peak	1,730	734
May 1945	Peak	143.3	62.0
Feb. 1946	Trough	143.3[b]	66.5
Dec. 1948	Peak	171.5	69.0
Oct. 1949	Trough	176.3	76.4
July 1953	Peak	259.6	101.6
Dec. 1953	Trough	266.2	104.7
July 1957	Peak	367.2	143.6
Apr. 1958	Trough	381.7	151.4
Aug. 1960	Peak	471.2	186.7
Dec. 1960	Trough	466.9	186.6

[a]Annual totals or three-month averages.

[b]Before rounding, slightly higher than May 1945.

The annual dates of turns in kilowatt-hours are also dates of annual peaks and troughs in business at large. Both kinds of profit increased in the business contraction of 1926–27 and the expansion of 1927–29. Monthly data after 1944 indicate a net rise in both kinds of profit in every business expansion or contraction, except for a slight decline in operating profit from $143.0 million around February 1945 to $141.8 million around October. Actual cyclical declines in profits have therefore been a rarity in this rapidly growing industry.

Gas Utilities

Separate annual figures on sales and profits of the gas industry are available, beginning in 1937. They include gas operations of electric utilities as well as those of companies engaged in the gas business only. The quantity of gas (measured in therms) sold to ultimate consumers (industrial or household), and the revenue derived from it, fell slightly from 1937 to 1938, but rose steadily thereafter. Growth was especially rapid after the war, when long-distance pipelines were constructed and began to carry natural gas from the southwestern fields to eastern, northern, and Pacific coast markets.

Without exception, however, the quantity sold increased faster in each business expansion than during its neighboring contraction (Table 85). With two exceptions, revenue also increased more rapidly during the expansions.

The income account of gas companies can be arranged in the same categories as for electric companies, and we define the operating margin in the same way. In general, the operating margin was not consistently related to fluctuations in business (Table 86). It changed in the same direction as business five times, and in the opposite direction six times.

The pre-tax margin followed business somewhat more closely. It changed in the same direction eight times, and the opposite direction only three. In the 1948–49 business contraction, more rapid growth in capital charges than in revenue converted a rising operating margin into a falling pre-tax margin. In the 1949–53 and 1954–57 expansions, slower growth in capital charges than in sales turned a slight decline in the operating margin into a small rise in the final margin.

Like the profit ratios, aggregate operating profits, and also pre-tax profits, fell in 1937–38. Operating profits, but not pre-tax profits, fell in 1944–46. Other declines in the ratios were not reflected in profits; with the three exceptions just noted, both kinds of profit increased in every business expansion and contraction after 1937.

TABLE 85

Gas Utilities[a]: Change and Rate of Change in Quantity Sold and Revenue During Business Expansions and Contractions, 1937–61

Turn in Business		Years from Preceding Date	Quantity Sold or Revenue[b]	CHANGE FROM PRECEDING DATE		
					Per Year	
Date	Level			Total	To Peak from Trough	To Trough from Peak
QUANTITY (billion therms)						
1937	Peak	--	15.8	--	--	--
1938	Trough	1	14.7	-1.1	--	-1.1
1944	Peak	6	25.1	10.4	1.7	--
1946	Trough	2	26.4	1.3	--	0.6
1948	Peak	2	33.9	7.5	3.8	--
1949	Trough	1	35.8	1.9	--	1.9
1953	Peak	4	56.1	20.3	5.1	--
1954	Trough	1	61.0	4.9	--	4.9
1957	Peak	3	77.0	16.0	5.3	--
1958	Trough	1	80.3	3.3	--	3.3
1960	Peak	2	92.9	12.6	6.3	--
1961	Trough	1	95.9	3.0	--	3.0
REVENUE (million dollars)						
1937	Peak	--	802	--	--	--
1938	Trough	1	777	-25	--	-25
1944	Peak	6	1,108	331	55	--
1946	Trough	2	1,213	105	--	52
1948	Peak	2	1,579	366	183	--
1949	Trough	1	1,689	110	--	110
1953	Peak	4	2,716	1,027	257	--
1954	Trough	1	3,049	333	--	333
1957	Peak	3	4,134	1,085	362	--
1958	Trough	1	4,568	434	--	434
1960	Peak	2	5,617	1,049	524	--
1961	Trough	1	5,993	376	--	376

[a]Includes publicly owned gas utilities.

[b]Does not include gas sold for resale (e.g., by a pipeline company to a local gas company) or revenue from such sales.

TABLE 86

Investor-Owned Gas Utilities: Change in Operating Margin and Pre-Tax Margin During Business Expansions and Contractions, 1937–61

Turn in Business		Margin				CHANGE FROM PRECEDING DATE			
						Operating Margin		Pre-Tax Margin	
Date	Level	Operating	Before All Taxes	Before Federal Income Taxes	Before Federal and State Income Taxes	To Peak from Trough	To Trough from Peak	To Peak from Trough	To Trough from Peak
1937	Peak	39.70	22.61			—	—	—	—
1938	Trough	39.73	21.78			—	0.03	—	-0.83
1944	Peak	43.50	28.06			3.77	—	6.28	—
1946	Trough	38.02	26.89	19.80		—	-5.48	—	-1.17
1948	Peak	32.75		17.09		-5.27	—	-2.71	—
1949	Trough	33.11		16.91	17.24	—	0.36	—	-0.18
1953	Peak	32.94			17.28	-0.17	—	0.04	—
1954	Trough	32.42			17.33	—	-0.52	—	0.05
1957	Peak	32.40			17.58	-0.02	—	0.25	—
1958	Trough	32.04			17.04	—	-0.36	—	-0.54
1960	Peak	31.57			16.93	-0.47	—	-0.11	—
1961	Trough	31.44			16.10	—	-0.13	—	-0.83

Construction

As explained in the appendix, usable statistics on profits of construction industry corporations start in 1932. Sales reached a trough in 1933 (Chart 21). Thereafter they followed the business cycle until 1942, rising to a peak in 1937 and falling to a trough in 1938. During the war the government severely restricted construction that served no military purpose. War construction apparently reached a peak in 1942, for total sales of the corporate construction industry declined thereafter until 1945. From that year onward, they increased year by year without regard to the business cycle, at least through 1961. During most of the period covered by our data, therefore, the construction business has not been related very directly to business at large. (In 1948–49, 1953–54, and 1957–58, however, the annual increases were not as large as in the adjoining business expansions.)

Because of the long-sustained growth after 1945, our data include only two complete cycles in construction revenues, those between 1933 and 1945. The margin rose in both expansions, and fell in both contractions (Chart 21). In the long upswing, however, the margin rose continuously for only three years, declining thereafter except in two years, and was lower in 1961 than in 1945.

Since there are few turning points in the industry's revenue, it may once more be of some interest to note how the margin changes between turning points in business at large. Between the 1932 business trough and 1960, the margin had a net rise in the first three business expansions, and fell in the last three. It fell in four of six business contractions, rising only in 1944–46 (during the postwar shortage of housing) and in 1960–61. Margin changes in the same direction as those in business outnumbered changes in the opposite direction by two, or 17 per cent of the twelve observations.

Aggregate profits, like the margin, rose and fell with sales from 1933 to 1945 (Chart 21). During the long subsequent expansion of sales, they fluctuated irregularly. They fell in the business contractions of 1948–49 and 1957–58; a decline from 1952 to 1955 overlaps the 1953–54 business contraction at both ends.

CHART 21

Construction Corporations: Sales, Margins, and Profits, 1932–61

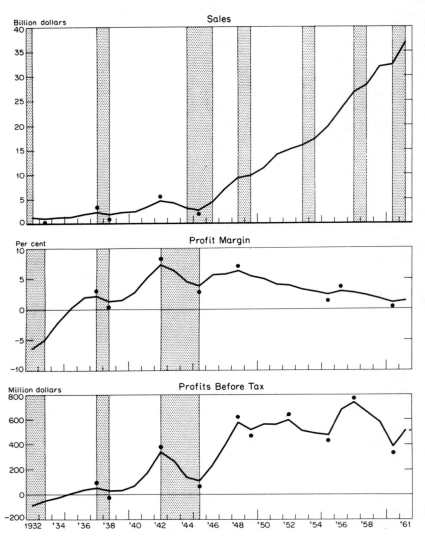

SOURCE: Appendix Table B-30.
NOTE: In upper panel, shaded areas are contractions in business; in others, in sales. Dots are at peaks and troughs in the charted variable.

The industry achieved an increase in sales during these periods of recession, but at the price of a decline in profit. For the whole 1932–61 period, the index of conformity of profits to business is +33.

Trade

According to annual figures, four expansions and five contractions in the sales of trade corporations began and ended between 1920 and 1958 (Chart 22).

The slight decline from 1941 to 1942 was confined to traders whose supplies of merchandise were curtailed by wartime regulations. [1]

If this untypical contraction is ignored, and sales are regarded as expanding from 1938 to 1948, there was a net rise in margin during every sales expansion except 1949–57, and a net decline in every sales contraction (Chart 22).

The annual figures show no declines in sales during the business contractions of 1923–24, 1926–27, 1944–46, 1953–54, and 1960–61. In 1926–27 and 1953–54, however, the increase was smaller than the average annual increase in either the preceding or the following business expansion. In 1944–46 the increase was less rapid than in 1946–48 but more rapid than in 1938–44. In 1960–61, the increase was less rapid than in 1958–60. In 1923–24, sales increased more rapidly than in either of the neighboring business expansions; the direction-of-change conformity score is + 50.

The release of demand from wartime restrictions, with the related upswing in prices, resulted in an extremely rapid rise in sales from 1945 to 1946.

The trade margin, although it bore a high positive relation to cycles in sales (78), was poorly related to cycles in business. It changed in the same direction as business during three expansions and eight contractions in the latter. It changed in the opposite direction during seven expansions and two contractions. These figures yield a conformity index of only +10.

---

[1]Automotive dealers lost 69 per cent of their 1941 sales, filling stations lost 16 per cent, furniture dealers 14 per cent, and vendors of building materials 2 per cent.

CHART 22
Trade Corporations: Sales, Margins, and Profits, 1919–61

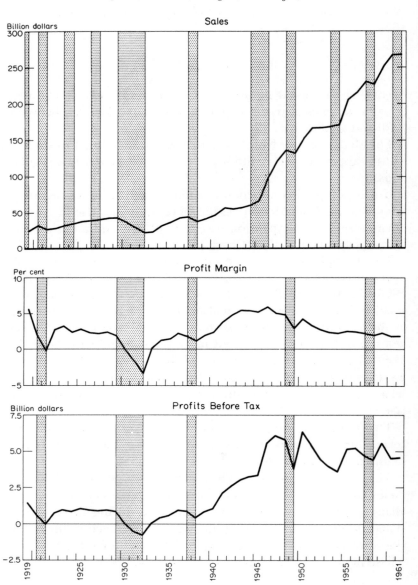

SOURCE: Appendix Table B-31.
NOTE: In upper panel, shaded areas are contractions in business; in others, in sales.

The inflationary postwar increase in demand brought a sharp rise in the already high margin from 1945 to 1946. The sudden Korean burst of demand in the last half of 1950 brought an even sharper rise from 1949 to that year. The margin declined in at least the last year of all the expansions in sales. The fall may have been general, or it may have been concentrated in those enterprises or lines of trade whose sales had begun to fall, moving contrary to the total for all trade.

Aggregate profits, like the margin, had a net rise in every sales expansion, and a net fall in every contraction, again ignoring 1941–42 (Chart 22). The upswing in sales and widening of margins immediately after the war, and again in the Korean crisis, resulted in remarkable upsurges in profits. After the all-time 1950 peak, however, they fell off year by year through 1954. Profits, like the margin, fell off moderately in the last year of every sales expansion.

Because sales frequently, and the margin sometimes, rose and fell with business, profits were more closely related than either profit factor to business. The profit conformity score is +60.

7

COMPARISONS AND
INTERPRETATIONS

Preceding chapters contain findings about seven related variables in a variety of industries: man-hours per unit of product, hourly earnings, labor cost, total cost, prices received, profit margins, and aggregate profits. In some divisions of manufacturing and in the railroad industry, it was possible to explore the relations between each of the seven variables and fluctuations in the quantity of goods or services sold. In other industries, it was possible only to explore the relation between margins and profits on the one hand and fluctuations in sales (revenue) on the other. In still others, quantity and revenue tended to rise without serious interruption over long periods; the only cyclical relations that could be investigated were those between the last two variables and cycles in business at large. The charts and tables in this chapter summarize many of the findings. For the reasons just indicated, the kinds of information assembled differ from industry to industry.

Net Changes During Expansions and Contractions of Quantity: Manufacturing and Railroads

A conformity score, it will be remembered, is a means of comparing the direction of change in two variables. A high positive score means that the two variables tend to rise and fall together. A high negative (inverse) score means that they tend to move in opposite directions. A low score means there is little relation between their directions of movement. Man-hours per unit of output produced by manufacturing industries tended to vary inversely with quantity (Table 87). Hourly earnings, on the other hand, had little relation to quantity; they rose both in expansions and in contractions of the latter. Because hourly earnings rose in expansions and contractions alike, labor cost per unit of product rose more often than hours per unit in both. Labor cost, nevertheless, was also inversely related to quantity. Total cost per unit (including not only labor but materials, interest on borrowed capital, etc.) also fluctuated inversely with quantity, although the score was much lower, since cost often rose in expansions of quantity. The net, full-phase changes in the prices manufacturers received bore little relation to upswings and downswings in the quantity of goods they sold in the mild postwar cycles to which our information pertains; they tended to rise in contractions as well as expansions. (The BLS index of prices of finished products, which begins in 1913, fell in all contractions of business or of manufacturing production between that year and World War II. So did the index of prices of semimanufactures.)

In many postwar expansions, prices rose faster than cost, while in contractions they rose less rapidly than cost. Profit margins therefore had a strong positive relation to cycles in quantity. Profits themselves sometimes rose in an expansion even when the profit margin was declining, and sometimes fell in a contraction

TABLE 87

Manufacturing and Railroads: Profit Variables and Output

	Relation to Manufacturing Quantity Sold, 15 Industries[a]		Relation to Railroad Traffic	
	Conformity Score	Relation Inferred	Conformity Score	Relation Inferred
Hours per unit	-71	Inverse	-62	Inverse
Hourly earnings	-8[b]	None	0	None
Labor cost per unit	-56[b]	Inverse	-88	Inverse
Total cost per unit	-39	Inverse	-83	Inverse
Prices received	-2	None	-42	Inverse
Operating margin[c]	--	--	$+67$	Positive
Operating profits[d]	--	--	$+75$	Positive
Margin before tax	$+76$	Positive	$+100$	Positive
Profits before tax	$+91$	Positive	$+100$	Positive

[a]Each expansion or contraction in each industry is treated separately in computing score.

[b]Production workers only.

[c]Ratio to sales of net revenue from railway operations.

[d]Net revenue from railway operations.

even when the margin was rising. Profits were therefore even more closely related than margins to swings in quantity.

Fluctuations in labor cost on railroads are similar to those in factories. Hours per unit of service rendered to the shipping and traveling public varied inversely with traffic. Hourly earnings tended to rise in both upswings and downswings, with no relation to traffic; but the rise in expansions was not large enough to keep labor cost, as well as hours per unit, from varying inversely. Total cost per unit had a much stronger inverse relation to volume in the railroad industry than in manufacturing. Prices received for railroad services, however, tended to vary inversely with volume, while there was no relation in manufacturing. The inverse fluctuations in cost were larger, percentagewise, than those in railway rates and fares; profit margins, and likewise profits, therefore tended to rise and fall with volume on railroads also.

In spite of partial differences with respect to cost and prices, margins in both manufacturing and the railroad industry usually widened when volume rose, and narrowed when it declined. In manufacturing expansions, the rise in margins was caused mainly by rising prices; in traffic expansions, it was caused mainly by falling cost. In manufacturing contractions since 1947, and in traffic contractions, the fall in margins was caused mainly by rising cost.

Railway rates, fares, and charges were more stable cyclically than prices of manufactured products. The strong inverse relation between unit operating cost and traffic, and the large aggregate size of railway fixed charges, make stable rates compatible with profitability in expansion, and impose obstacles to reduction of rates in contraction. It has been suggested that railway charges should be raised in periods of business expansion, and, more urgently, that they should be reduced in business contraction as a means of controlling the business cycle, just as interest rates supposedly are or can be used for the same purpose. But if this were done, railway profit margins would have to be much higher during peak prosperity than they have been in the past, or else the railroads would be in even more imminent danger of bankruptcy in depressions than they have been. Furthermore, railway charges are an important component in the costs of manufacturers and other businessmen. If they fluctuated in the manner suggested, manufacturing costs would rise more sharply in expansion than they do. Even though prices of manufactured products are only loosely related to cost, it is not clear that rising railway charges would be counter-inflationary.

PATTERNS OF CHANGE DURING EXPANSIONS AND CONTRACTIONS

The foregoing discussion pertains to net changes in profit variables during upswings and downswings in quantity of goods or services sold. Where Table 87 suggests a positive, or inverse, relation, the relation is often more pronounced during some portions of cycles in quantity than during others. For some variables the characteristic direction of change in the earlier portion of expansions or contractions is different from the characteristic direction in the later portion.

When a manufacturing industry begins to expand output, the hours of labor it requires to turn out a unit of product usually decline (Chart 23). Hourly earnings of production workers commonly rise even at this early stage, but the rise is not large enough to offset the fall in hours per unit, and labor cost per unit usually declines. Total cost including labor and other expense also usually falls. In these early stages, the prices the industry receives for its products decline in most cases, although the majority of declines is not large. The net result of changes in cost, prices, and volume is that most profit margins and profits rise.

In later segments of expansion, rises in hours per unit become more and more frequent, except in the last segment, an exception which might disappear if we had more data. Falls, however, outnumber rises in all segments. Hourly earnings in most cases continue to rise. Labor cost rises more and more frequently, with the same exception; it rises in more than half of the third segments, and with more data might be found to rise in most fourth segments. Rises in total cost become steadily more frequent, and predominate in the last half of expansion. Increases in the prices factories receive for their products also become more frequent but do not always offset the increase in cost. Margins do not widen as often in the third segment as in the first two. At least in our

CHART 23

*Percentage Frequency of Rises in Profit Variables During
Successive Segments of Quantity Cycles,
Fifteen Manufacturing Industries, 1947–61*

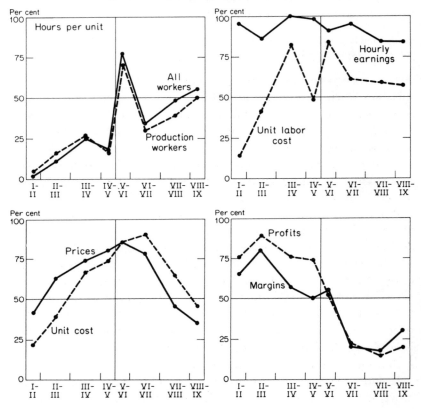

sample of observations, they rise in only half of the fourth segments. Rising profits, however, predominate over falling profits in every segment.

When recession comes to an industry, the initial decline in quantity is usually accompanied by a rise in man-hours and labor cost per unit of product. Increases in total cost are even more numerous than in late expansion. But so are increases in prices received. Margins rose in a small majority of our observations, and profits in a slightly smaller majority.

Rises in hours per unit are less common after the first segment of contraction, although the succession of frequencies is irregular. Hourly earnings and labor cost continued to rise, but the labor cost frequency declined continuously. Even at the end, however, there were more rises than falls; and the percentages would probably be higher if they included nonproduction labor. Increases in total cost likewise become less frequent after the second segment. After the first, rises in prices received become less frequent, and falls predominate in the last half of contraction. Margins and profits fall in most cases after the first segment.

Cycles in sales revenue (rather than in quantity) can be observed in all twenty-two subdivisions of manufacturing. Rising margins and profits were more common in the first than in the second half of upswings in sales (Chart 24). Rises predominate in all segments of expansion, however, (except for margins in the fourth segments) and declines predominate in all segments of contraction. Changes in the margins and profits of twenty-two companies before 1942 were similar, except that margins and profits held up better throughout expansions.

Corresponding curves for the railroad industry look more eccentric, perhaps because of fewer observations. Hours per unit always fall in the first half of traffic expansions (Chart 25). Some rises occur thereafter, but declines predominate throughout. Hourly earnings usually rise in all except fourth segments; they rose in exactly half of those. Rises in labor cost become more frequent, but even in the last segment occur in less than half of the observations. Rises in total cost also become more frequent except in fourth segments. Rises in rates and fares have an irregular curve; but, on the whole, falls predominate. Declines in the operating margin and in net revenue are more numerous in the last half of expansion than in the first. Even in the last half, however, net revenue rises more often than it falls.

When traffic begins to decline, hours per unit, hourly earnings, labor cost, and total cost rise in most cases. Prices received are also likely to rise, but not enough to prevent the operating margin and profit from falling. Rises in the four cost variables are less frequent in later stages. Rises in the operating margin and net revenue become somewhat more frequent; but declines still predominate.

CHART 24

Percentage Frequency of Rises in Margins and Profits During Successive Segments of Sales Cycles

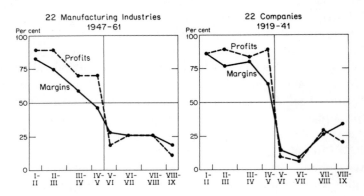

CHART 25

Railroads: Percentage Frequency of Rises in Profit Variables During Successive Segments of Traffic Cycles

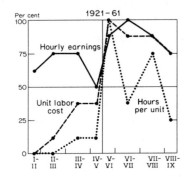

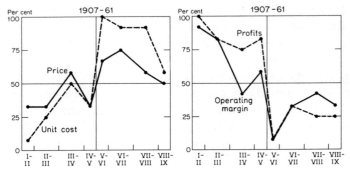

The charts show what happened most often in the same segment of different expansions or contractions. They could, however, give an erroneous impression of the typical sequence of change in a single expansion or contraction. In Chart 23, for example, rises in cost outnumber falls in the first three segments of contractions, but falls are more numerous than rises in the last segment. The impression might result that a manufacturing industry, during a downswing, usually encounters rising cost at first, and falling cost later. In fact, the most common pattern was a continuous rise, which occurred in 38 per cent of the observations. For most profit factors, the commonest pattern occurred in a plurality, but not a majority, of the observations (Table 88).

These percentages may seem low. But if there were no systematic relations among the directions of change in successive segments, each of the sixteen permutations of change described in Chapter 1 (Table 3) should occur approximately as often as any other. A continuous rise should occur in about 1/16, or 6 per cent, of the observations; so should a continuous fall. Since we lump three permutations into "rise, fall," a rise-fall pattern should occur in about 3/16, or 19 per cent; so should a fall-rise. We may call these "neutral" frequencies. The frequencies of the most common patterns in Table 88 are all higher.

Margins in Other Industrial Divisions

We have not ventured to construct measures of quantity sold for the telephone industry, the electric utilities, or for trade or construction corporations. At first thought it might seem that we could use the number of telephone calls in the first case, and kilowatt-hours sold in the second. But telephone subscribers pay for a minimum number of calls whether they use them or not. Is the number of calls, the number of phones, or some weighted average the best measure? The convenience of the telephone has greatly increased with the increase in the number of parties that can be called from any one instrument; subscribers get more and more potential connections for their money. The average distance called on toll calls may fluctuate with business conditions. Kilowatt-hours sold include those sold for low-cost, low-price uses (like

TABLE 88

Profit Factors and Profits: Most Common Pattern of Change During Cycles in
Manufacturing Quantity Sold or Produced and Railroad Traffic

	During Expansions		During Contractions	
	Most Common Pattern	Percentage of Observations	Most Common Pattern	Percentage of Observations
15 MANUFACTURING INDUSTRIES, 1947-61[a]				
Hours per unit				
Production workers	Continuous fall	46	Rise, fall	28
All workers	Continuous fall	52	Rise, fall, rise	31
Hourly earnings	Continuous rise	83	Continuous rise	69
Labor cost per unit	Fall, rise	38	Rise, fall	28
Total cost per unit	Fall, rise	54	Continuous rise	38
Prices received	Fall, rise	44	Rise, fall	47
Margin	Rise, fall	31	Continuous fall	28
Profits	Continuous rise	44	Continuous fall	32
RAILROADS, 1907-61				
Hours per unit[b]	Continuous fall	75	Rise, fall	38
			Rise, fall, rise, fall	38
Hourly earnings[b]	Rise, fall	25	Continuous rise	62
	Fall, rise	25		
Labor cost per unit[b]	Continuous fall	38	Continuous rise	50
	Fall, rise	38		
Total cost per unit	Fall, rise	33	Continuous rise	42
	Fall, rise, fall	33	Rise, fall	42
Prices received	Fall, rise, fall	42	Continuous rise	25
			Rise, fall	25
Operating margin	Rise, fall, rise	42	Fall, rise, fall	42
Operating profits	Continuous rise	58	Continuous fall	33
			Fall, rise, fall	33

[a] Each expansion or contraction in each industry is counted separately in determining frequency of patterns.
[b] 1921-61.

those in industrial processes) and those sold for high-cost, high-price uses (as in private homes); industrial use fluctuates more than household consumption. It would be possible to take care of this difficulty, but another would remain: sales to any one class of user include sales in the high-price initial brackets, and sales in the lower-price later brackets. When the total sales diminish, the percentage of kilowatt-hours in the higher brackets increases.

With no production indexes, we cannot construct indexes of price or cost per unit in these four industries. We do, however, know something about their profit margins. Margins of construction corporations, and somewhat more imperfectly those of trade corporations, appear to rise and fall with sales; probably they also rise and fall with quantity sold. If so, these industries are like manufacturing and railroads.

Although we have no good measure of percentage change in the production of electric utilities, the peaks and troughs in a price-weighted output index would probably not differ greatly from those in kilowatt-hours. Profit margins of electric utilities vary inversely with kilowatt-hours sold; at least, operating profits before fixed charges do so.

The telephone industry has had only one contraction in the number of calls; even if we accept the number of calls as indicating the dates of turning points in the quantity of service, there are virtually no cycles. Nevertheless, the telephone industry increases its service when most other industries are increasing their production, i.e., during the greater part of business expansions. It differs from other industries in that its volume of business rises, although more gradually, when the income of the others is falling. Telephone operating margins, however, show no consistent relation to business cycles (Table 89). If one considers recent cycles only, they show an inverse relation. When both the telephone industry and other industries are expanding, the telephone industry, unlike construction, manufacturing, railroads, or trade has had a falling margin in recent times.

Probably the decline in the electric operating margin, and in the telephone operating margin during recent cycles, has been caused by delays in the adjustment of publicly regulated rates, together with rises in wages and prices of materials during business expan-

TABLE 89
Margins and Profits: Relation to General Business

	Period Covered	Margins		Profits	
		Conformity Score	Relation Inferred	Conformity Score	Relation Inferred
Manufacturing	1919–61	+90	Positive	+90	Positive
Railroads					
Operating profits	1907–61	+77	Positive	+92	Positive
Net income before taxes	1933–61	+100	Positive	+100	Positive
Telephone Industry					
Operating profits	1933–61	+33	Positive	+33	Positive
Net operating income	1933–61	−17	None	+17	None
	1918–61	+14	None	+14	None
	1918–38	+64	Positive	+27	Positive
	1938–61	−40	Inverse	0	None
Electric and Gas Utilities					
Electric operating profits	1926–61	−47	Inverse	+20	None
Electric net operating revenue	1926–61	−33	Inverse	+7	None
Electric utility net income before taxes[a]	1937–61	+9	None	−9	None
Gas operating profits[b]	1937–61	−9	None	+27	Positive
Gas net income before taxes[b]	1937–61	+45	Positive	+9	None
Construction	1932–61	+17	None	+33	Positive
Trade	1919–61	+10	None	+60	Positive

[a] Includes income from nonelectric operations.
[b] Gas companies and gas departments of electric utilities.

sions. Short-run economies associated with larger volume, if they exist, are apparently not sufficient to offset the increases in prices paid.

The telephone and power industries are regulated with a view toward giving the investor a fair return over a period of years, but not necessarily the same rate of return every year, still less every month or quarter. Cyclical fluctuations in operating margin are not incompatible with the regulatory objective. Heavy fixed charges tend to counteract any rise in operating cost during expansion, although investment in plant and equipment has at times increased fast enough to negate the tendency. Except in the inflationary period after the war, the declines in margin during business expansion have not been severe; a margin ample to protect against bankruptcy remains at the business peak. The more rapid growth of telephone or electric service during business expansion tends to offset the mild decline in margin, sometimes producing higher aggregate profits and perhaps even a higher rate of return on investment.

Some Quasi-Margins for All Domestic Business

Profit data for many sections of the economy are inadequate. From estimates that enter into the Department of Commerce national income figures, however, it is possible to construct what may be called a consolidated income account for all domestic business. The details are illustrated in Table 90. The consolidated statement differs from ordinary income statements because sales by one domestic business to another domestic business, charged to cost of sales by the purchaser, are not included in either sales or cost. Sales to domestic business, charged to capital account by the purchaser, are included.

The omissions make it impossible to calculate cost ratios and profit margins analogous to those we have so far considered. The omitted items reduce aggregate sales and aggregate costs by the same amount. We can calculate the ratio of what may be called external costs (cost-type payments to nonbusiness) to external sales (sales to nonbusiness, including sales of business capital equipment, which one may think of as sales to the individuals who own business enterprises). The difference between this external cost ratio and 100 (Chart 26) may be considered a profit margin of a sort.

These are very rough figures. For example, the sales include the gross rental value of homes occupied by their owners, and the costs include expenses associated with home ownership. One does not usually think of one's home as an enterprise conducted for a profit.

Nevertheless, the "margin" looks similar to many other margins we have examined. It narrows in five contractions of sales. It widens at the beginning of all four expansions, and usually narrows later. In two of the four expansions it has a net rise, although it has a net fall in the other two.

TABLE 90

Estimated Income Account of Domestic Business, 1956

(million dollars)

		SALES	
	To "public"		
a.	Consumers		250,515
b.	Federal government		24,487
c.	State and local governments		15,758
d.	Foreigners		20,466
e.	Total, a + b + c + d		311,226
	To domestic business, charged by purchaser to		
f.	Capital expense		69,042
g.	Cost of sales		x
h.	Total, f + g		69,042 + x
i.	Total sales, e + h		380,268 + x
	COST OF SALES		
j.	Compensation of employees		195,476
k.	Indirect tax and non-tax liability		35,000
l.	Transfer payments		1,303
m.	Purchases from foreigners		14,658
n.	Interest		7,322
o.	Rent		10,322
p.	Capital consumption allowances		34,266
q.	Purchases from domestic business		x
r.	Total cost		298,347 + x
	PROFIT[a]		
s.	Before tax, i − r		81,921
t.	Corporate profits tax liability		21,959
u.	After tax		59,962
	COST RATIO		
v.	100 · r (excluding x) ÷ i (excluding x)		78.5

Note: x indicates an unknown amount.

[a]"Profit" is total of **corporate** profit plus income of unincorporated enterprises. The latter includes reward for owners' labor and management as well as for use of their capital.

Concurrent Margin and Profit Changes
in Different Industries

In a way, the rough, general, annual figures in the preceding section round out the picture. More interesting inferences can be drawn, however, from the varied and detailed data for manufacturing industries, to which we revert. In particular, they show that the profit experiences of different industries are more diverse at some times during the general economic cycle than at others.

During the later portion of a contraction in business at large, a growing number of industries expand the quantity of goods they

CHART 26

Ratio of "External" Cost to "External" Sales, All Domestic Business,
1929 – 56

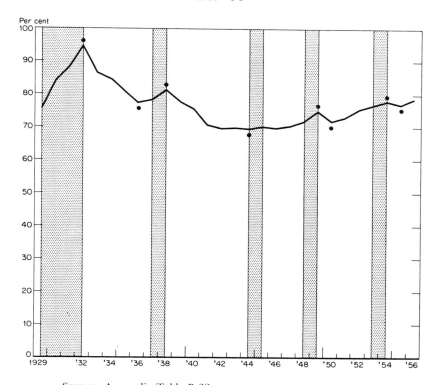

SOURCE: Appendix Table B-32.

NOTE: Shaded areas are contractions in "external" sales. Dots are at peaks and troughs in ratio.

sell. Most of these expanding industries enjoy rising margins and profits. At the same time, a small but increasing percentage of the industries that continue to contract also have rising margins, although not necessarily rising profits.

During the earlier portion of a business expansion, an increasing majority of industries expand. They have rising margins and profits which presently spread over most of the business economy. During the later portion of a business expansion, however, an increasing number of industries contract. Eventually their margins and profits fall. A majority of the still expanding industries continue to have rising margins, but the majority is smaller than before. Falling margins and profits become more prevalent.

In the earlier portion of a business contraction, an increasing majority of industries have a falling physical volume of sales, accompanied sooner or later by falling margins and, even more widely, by falling profits. But as the business contraction wears on, the number of expanding industries eventually begins to rise, and the cyclical sequence just described begins to repeat itself. In one of the three postwar business expansions for which we have data, however, the Korean episode greatly complicated the sequence.

Causes of Rising Cost
in Expansion and in Contraction

The difference between the percentage of contractions in quantity with labor cost rising and that with total cost rising is not as wide as the corresponding difference in expansions. The rises in total cost during contractions, where they are much more frequent than during expansions, are due largely to the rise in labor input per unit of product that is so often associated with diminishing volume. In other words, rising prices of materials and rising wage rates are the main causes of rising cost during expansion; greater input of labor is an important cause during contraction.

When discussing cost in Chapter 2, we noted that the predominance of rises over declines was concentrated in certain time groups of expansions. In the early Korean, 1949–53, and 1954–57 groups, when costs of most industries with expansions approximately covering those periods rose (Table 15), prices of materials rose substantially (Table 32). In the late Korean and 1958–60 groups, on the other hand, when cost fell in most industries, prices of materials either fell or rose very little. The difference among time groups strengthens the conclusion that rising cost during expansions is caused mostly by rising prices.

Why Cost Often Falls in Late Contraction

Although rising cost predominates in contractions in quantity sold, the predominance is not nearly as strong in the last as in the first half of such contractions. Hours per unit and labor cost rise most often during the first segment.

A substantial amount of new equipment, perhaps ordered before the contraction set in, is put into service as a contraction proceeds; new equipment is usually more efficient than old. Whether or not they have recently received equipment, many enterprises have some that is more efficient and some that is less efficient. When the quantity of goods turned out recedes, production can be concentrated on the better facilities.

With a smaller volume of business on hand, management may have more time to devote to more efficient operation of whatever facilities are at hand; i.e., such matters as discipline, scheduling, waste of materials, etc.

As cost falls in some industries, managers of those industries are encouraged to reduce prices. Most reductions in cost during late contraction are translated into price reductions. Insofar as their customers are other industries, their price reductions tend to reduce the costs of those customers. Even industries with rising cost reduce their prices more frequently in late than in early contraction.

Rising Demand Often Makes Higher Cost Compatible with Higher Volume and Profits

There was a net rise in price during thirty-five of the forty-eight expansions in quantity sold (Table 10). Price and quantity both rose. We must conclude that in most expansions demand was higher at the end than at the beginning. Prices also rose in 63 per

cent of the second, 74 per cent of the third, and 80 per cent of the
fourth segments. We must further conclude that demand rose in
a majority of these instances. Prices roses in nineteen, or 41 per
cent of the first segments; these may be regarded as cases of rising
demand. But what of the first segments of the twenty-seven expansions in which prices fell?

A rise in quantity sold, accompanied by a fall in price, might be
interpreted as a response of customers to lower prices, i.e., as a
movement along a fixed demand curve. Or it might be interpreted as evidence also of an upward shift in the curve. But if the rise
in quantity is very large in comparison with the fall in price, it is
difficult to believe that demand has not shifted. If a 2 per cent fall
in price is accompanied by a 20 per cent rise in quantity, one
questions whether so large an increase in quantity can be attrib-
uted entirely or even mainly to so small a reduction in price. In
technical language, such an interpretation implies a "price elasticity" of $20 \div (-2)$ or -10. A figure computed in this way from
observed changes in price and quantity may be called a purported
elasticity. Many economists are skeptical of alleged elasticities
materially larger, numerically, than -1. Confronted with a materially larger figure, they would surmise that something else, as
well as the reduction in price, stimulated customers to increase
their purchases. The demand curve must have risen. Customers
would have increased their purchases to some extent even if the
price had not been cut.

We have computed purported elasticities for each of the
twenty-seven observations. When the change in price is very small,
such computations often yield fantastically high purported elasticities, e.g., -100. In such cases the error in the figures may be
large relative to the change in price, and the extreme ratios
should be disregarded. However, we can arrange the purported
elasticities in the order of size and pick out the median. In this
case the median of the twenty-seven elasticities turns out to be
-2.7, which implies a response to price reduction so large it is
hard to believe. One may conclude that in many of the twenty-
seven observations, rising demand as well as falling price helped
to stimulate sales. Considering these as well as the observations
in which prices went up, demand appears to have risen in most
first as well as most later segments.

In earlier and more severe recessions than those with which we deal here, prices as well as quantities declined; and no doubt demand fell. In forty-two of the sixty postwar contractions of quantity sold for which we have data—mostly mild contractions—there was a net rise in price. Consequently, it is possible on first thought to explain most of the contractions mainly in terms of rising prices. But computation of the elasticities implied by such an explanation again renders this interpretation doubtful. The median is -4.3; demand must have fallen in many of these forty-two contractions.

Prices fell in 55 per cent of the third segments and 65 per cent of the fourth segments of contractions in quantity; in these, therefore, falling demand predominated. Prices rose, however, in thirty-four, or 85 per cent, of the first segments and thirty-one, or 78 per cent, of the second segments. The median purported elasticity for the thirty-four observations is -1.6. In the second segments, nine of the thirty-one rises in prices were accompanied by small increases in quantity, which temporarily interrupted the contractions in the latter. For the remaining twenty-two, the median purported elasticity is -2.0. These figures suggest that demand fell in many instances.

That demand for the products of an industry should be higher at the peak than at the trough of the industry's activity may not seem remarkable, since its own peak will usually occur in the neighborhood of a peak in general business activity. When income is high, consumer spending is large, and industry in general may badly need additional capacity and therefore have a high demand for productive equipment. At such a time almost any industry can sell more goods than it could have sold at the same price when the general level of activity was lower. But this kind of explanation is applicable only to one industry or a narrow group of industries, *given* a rise in demand in most other industries. It does not explain a general rise in demand which appears in most of the diverse branches of manufacturing.

There are influences other than a rise in income, sales, or realized profits that tend to raise demand. They include the development of new commodities and inventions to a point of more widespread practicability, the wearing out of consumer durables and industrial equipment, fear of wars, changes in taxes and governmental spending, changes in the ability and willingness of bankers to expand credit, and other factors. A preponderance of such influences will raise demand, increase quantities sold, and thereby generate additional incon e. The spending of the additional income will, however, tend to spread rising demand over a wider area.

That factors other than the general business situation influence demand is shown by the fact that an increasing number of industries have upturns before the general upturn. Before the business trough in 4Q 1949, for example, one of our fifteen manufacturing industries had a trough in quantity sold in 3Q 1948, three had a trough in 1Q 1949, and four in 2Q 1949. In all, thirty-three of our quantity expansions began before the corresponding business expansion. In ten of these, there was a net rise in price between the industry and business trough, so rising demand was presumably a factor. For the other twenty-three, we have computed the percentage change in output and price for the interval between the two peaks, and the purported elasticity coefficients. The median is −3.9, suggesting rises in demand.

Conversely, consumers can become well stocked in the latest styles of consumer durables, businessmen can become well supplied with the most modern equipment, fear of war may subside, and other influences may tend to reduce demand. A preponderance of such influences may cause a general decline in demand schedules.

Rising demand explains why it was so often possible for a manufacturing group to widen its profit margin during expansions in spite of rising cost. Falling demand, at least in the last half of contractions, explains why even groups that were able to reduce their costs had their margins squeezed.

No Glut Before the Peak

It has sometimes been supposed that, as new plants and equipment are completed and begin to operate during an expansion, a flood of products from the new equipment gluts the markets, causing a fall in price which reveals that much of the increased stock of equipment is unprofitable to operate, at least for the time being. Further investment in new facilities is discouraged, and these developments help to usher in a recession. If this is how expansions meet their end, however, one would expect the statistics to show that prices commonly fall in the last segment of an upswing in quantity sold. Such a conjunction of changes in quantity and price seems to have been rare in the postwar period. Rising prices were more frequent in the last segment than in any other segment of expansions in quantity sold. They occurred in 80 per cent of the observed last segments. Margins rose in 48 per cent, and profits in 74 per cent.

These figures do not make it necessary to reject "excess" capacity as a cause of postwar recessions. While capacity increases, the percentage of capacity actually operated may fall. What the figures do show is that excess capacity, if any, did not often display itself in the form of a price-breaking glut of products actually made and hunting a market.

Rising Margins Imply Barriers to Expansion

A rise in the demand curves for the products of an industry would not, under some circumstances, raise its average margin. If, as the curves rose, the quantity supplied to its customers rose fast enough, prices would remain at their initial level; and if the average cost did not change, the margin would also remain at its initial level. (In Chart 1, if the quantity sold increased from OA to OA', the price would not change.) Since prices did rise in many cases, the quantity sold did not increase fast enough to hold prices at their initial level. What prevented the quantity sold from expanding to that extent?

One explanation might be accentuated differences in cost. Manufacturers of any product may at any time have some minimum price in mind for any volume of that product. It would not be worth their while to sell that quantity at less than that minimum price, which may be called their out-of-pocket cost. If this cost is higher for larger than for smaller quantities, quantity sold will not be expanded to the point at which it would sell at the initial price. Instead, quantity and price will rise to some intermediate position, such as OA'' and $A'' B''$ on the chart.

Different parts of the potential supply may have different out-of-pocket costs. At low levels of demand, only the low-cost sources will actually supply the market. As demand rises, higher-cost sources may come in as rising demand makes it possible for them to charge higher prices. But in a competitive market, the low-cost sources will also get comparable prices, and they will earn higher margins. If the inequality of costs among different sources of supply rises the average margin should rise.

But actually, cost fell during the first half of most expansions. Price also fell in some, but not all, of these instances. Even when prices fell, margins often increased. Changes in cost fail to explain much of the early rise in prices and margins.

Physical limitations on the expansibility of supply may be an alternative explanation. If demand rises rapidly, it may be physically impossible, within a short period, to expand the quantity sold to the amount that buyers would take, if they could get it, at the initial prices. Stocks of the commodity in the hands of vendors may be small, and even a slight rise in sales would exhaust them. Vendors may wish to sell more, but it takes time for them to place orders with their sources of supply, for the latter to carry out the manufacturing or other processes necessary to fill the orders, and for transport agencies to deliver them. Time may also be consumed in making arrangements to finance an enlarged volume of business. If the rise in the demand schedule stops, vendors might soon be able to catch up with it; but if it continues, the physical limitations may also continue to operate indefinitely.

Most vendors will probably sense a situation of this kind when the orders or inquiries they receive begin to increase. Each will realize that he can raise his price without fear of diverting trade to other vendors, since his competitors would also be offered more trade than they could handle if they maintained their initial prices. Or the initiative as to prices may come from buyers; the latter, finding they cannot obtain enlarged quantities at the old price, may bid it up. The price will rise, and the quantity sold per month or quarter will be an amount intermediate between the original quantity and the quantity that could be sold under the new demand conditions at the old price. (Again, in Chart 1, a quantity such as OA'' might sell for $A''\,B''$.) Such a rise in price can occur without any conscious or deliberate collusion among vendors. It could also occur as the result of collusion.

Physical limitations are more likely to operate when rises in the demand for many commodities appear simultaneously than if only one of those rises had occurred. To a large extent, vendors of different commodities make use of the same raw materials and would look for additional employees among the same groups of workers.

Physical limitations in conjunction with rising demand could raise prices in this manner even if out-of-pocket cost remained at levels equal to or below the initially prevailing prices, or if it fell. In such a situation, not only prices but margins would rise. Furthermore, the rise in demand could happen so fast, compared with the capacity of industry to expand, that even margins on the highest-cost portion of a higher-cost quantity sold would rise.

Cost, Profits, and the Generation of Cycles

In this report our principal concern has been to determine what kinds of change in cost and profit accompany fluctuations in quantity sold, sales revenue, or business at large. Profits, which depend among other things on cost, have long been regarded as a part of the economc mechanism by which supply is adjusted to demand. Reversing our approach, can we say anything about the roles cost and profit play in generating business fluctuations?

Cost falls with increasing frequency in the later half of contractions, and also falls in the earlier half of most expansions. Falling cost lowers the floor beneath which business men will not go in naming prices. Most reductions in cost during late contraction and early expansion are reflected in falling prices. Even enterprises with rising cost become increasingly willing to cut prices as contraction proceeds. Price cutting appears first in one industry and then in another, but at low stages of the general economic cycle it is widespread. Do the increasingly prevalent reductions stimulate sales and thereby help to turn the economic tide? One cannot answer this question with much confidence, because the effect of reducing a price on the sale of that product is not the only aspect that needs to be considered. General reductions in price mean that less income is being distributed by business per unit of product sold. Such reductions therefore tend to lower the demand for any specified commodity. In terms of Chart 1, they tend to move the quantity purchased to the right along demand curves, but also tend to lower the demand curves themselves. Conversely, high cost and high prices at high levels of the cycle tend to move quantity purchased to the left along demand curves, but also tend to raise the demand curves. We cannot say with confidence that price increases tend to produce a business recession.

It is evident, on the other hand, that businessmen do respond to shifts in demand, which are linked with changes in margins. Demand usually falls during the later part of contractions and rises during expansions of quantity sold. This is another way of saying that quantity sold is adjusted upward and downward in response to changes in demand. Margins also fall in late contraction and rise in expansion. What part do the margin changes play in the adjustment?

Businessmen are often in a position to increase the quantities they sell without adding to their plant or durable equipment, particularly near the bottom of a depression. The only additional expenditure needed is an increase in outlays for material and labor. Some time must elapse between the additional outlay and the sale of the resulting product; the additional outlay is temporarily an investment. A rise in margin, unless it is accompanied by a substantial lengthening of the production period, means a rise in the rate of return on such investments. If the average interval between outlay and the associated revenue is two months, a rise in the margin amounting to 1 per cent of sales is roughly equivalent to 6 per cent per year on the investment. Experience shows that once margins have begun to rise they often continue to rise for many months. An initial rise can be interpreted as evidence of better things to come. When this kind of investment ceases to yield satisfactory returns it can quickly be halted. The changes in margin that accompany shifting demand do appear to be part of the mechanism of adjustment.

Margins, however, are usually higher when quantity sold begins to contract than when it begins to expand. Furthermore, in most cases they rise for a short while when quantity begins to decline. The foregoing line of analysis does not explain these paradoxes.

Experienced rises in margins probably have less effect on business purchases of plant and durable equipment than on requisitions of materials and labor for use in current production. Such purchases usually require years to pay off. If they are to be made wisely, they must often promise to improve profits over a period considerably longer than most of the upswings studied in this investigation. A cyclical upturn in margins does not provide a basis for projection sufficient to justify such expenditures. If the latter would improve profits by reducing cost, a decline in margins may actually make the investments more attractive, although it may also make them harder to finance.[1]

Recent margins or profits have only a limited effect on quasi-permanent expenditures. Strengthened expectations of long-run economic growth, new commodities that are expected to have wide sales appeal, and improved designs of plant and equipment raise the demand for products of the construction and equipment industries and their suppliers; they help to explain rises in margins. Conversely, gradual satisfaction of the demand for capital equipment inspired by such prospects, and failure of equally potent new prospects to appear, help to explain declines in demand and margins.

---

[1]Some readers may wonder why rates of return on existing investment have not been discussed. Such rates, in quarterly or monthly form, are reported in, or readily computable from, many of our sources of data. The reason they have not been used is that they are often a poor indicator of the rate of return to be expected from new investment, and only the latter is meaningful for the study of business fluctuations. Much of the investment in plant and equipment existing at any moment was purchased years ago when prices were different. Part of it has been written out of the basis of computation by cumulative depreciation. New property would often be more efficient than old.

APPENDIX A

SOURCE OF DATA

Manufacturing: Quarterly Data

QUARTERLY SALES, MARGINS, AND PROFITS

These data are from Federal Trade Commission and Securities and Exchange Commission, *Quarterly Financial Report for Manufacturing Corporations*. The FTC-SEC obtain income and balance sheet data from all large corporations, and from samples of small ones; the amounts reported by the sampled corporations are raised to provide estimates for all corporations in each industrial group. The sampling and estimating procedure has been revised twice. We may call figures based on the original procedure Series A, those based on the first revision Series B, and those based on the second revision Series C. They are available respectively, for 1Q 1947 to 4Q 1951; 3Q 1951 to 2Q 1956; and 1Q 1956 to date. Each later series therefore overlaps the preceding one by two quarters.[1] In many cases, the B sales estimates for the overlapping quarters are much larger than the A estimates, and those in C are larger than those in B (Table A – 1). Apparently A and B, at least in the later quarters of their periods, understate the true national totals. Many of the earlier figures should be raised to make them comparable with the later ones. But how? Each series might be accurate at the beginning of its period, losing coverage of an industry gradually. In that case, its successive quarterly figures should be raised by gradually increasing amounts. Or it may not have covered the industry completely even at the beginning, in which case it might be appropriate to raise all the figures by a uniform percentage.

In most cases we decided which method would be better by comparing the FTC-SEC sales of a group, quarter by quarter, with an alternative estimate of sales. For each group with data on prices received, we multiplied its price index by the most nearly corresponding Federal Reserve index of production. The FTC-SEC sales data were turned into index numbers and the index for each was divided by the corresponding alternative index. Although the latter has its own defects, the trend of the

[1]According to the text of the later reports, Series C was obtained only for 2Q 1956. But the 4Q 1956 report contains "new sample" as well as revised old sample figures for 1Q 1956.

ratios thus obtained is instructive. If the trend of the ratios for an industry from 1947 to 1951 was downward, the FTC-SEC sales presumably lost coverage gradually over that period. If the curve was level, the FTC-SEC figures were presumably too low and should be raised by about the same percentage, over the entire period.

If the C figures for a group exceeded the B in the overlaps by only a small percentage, or if the curve of the test ratios was flat, we increased all the B figures by the overlap percentage. If the overlap difference was large, and if the test ratio had a downward trend, we raised the B figures by a uniformly increasing percentage which at the end equaled the overlap percentage. We then applied the same procedure to the A figures to bring them up to the level of the adjusted B figures at the overlap.

TABLE A-1
Comparison of Sales as Reported in
Estimates Based on Successive Samples

	Ratio of Sales of	
	Sample B to Sample A (third and fourth quarters, 1951)	Sample C to Sample B (first and second quarters, 1956)
Food and beverages	1.24	1.02
Tobacco	1.01	1.00
Textiles	1.25	.96
Apparel	1.81	1.26
Lumber and products	1.58	1.11
Furniture and fixtures	1.63	1.07
Paper and products	1.02	1.00
Printing and publishing	1.22	1.10
Chemicals	1.10	1.02
Petroleum refining	a	1.00
Rubber	1.00	1.00
Leather and products	1.32	1.04
Stone, clay, glass	1.11	1.06
Primary iron and steel	1.04	1.01
Primary nonferrous metals	1.11	1.02
Fabricated metals	1.19	1.02
Machinery	1.09	1.12
Electric equipment	1.10	1.06
Motor vehicles	1.04	.99
Other transportation equipment	1.06	1.03
Instruments	1.10	1.07
Miscellaneous	1.53	1.22
All manufacturing	1.15	1.04

[a]Industry in Sample A included coal products.

In most cases we used a uniform percentage. [2] Graduated increases were made in the B figures for apparel, the A and B for stone, clay, and glass, fabricated metals, machinery, and the A for electric equipment. In the five industries for which there are no price data, and consequently no alternative sales estimates, uniform percentages were used. No adjustment seemed necessary for tobacco or petroleum products. We preferred, however, to have figures for the latter industry alone, rather than for the petroleum and coal products group. Petroleum refining is reported separately beginning with the B series. The overlap ratio of the new figure for petroleum only to the old figure for petroleum and coal products is .9574; we multiplied the A sales figures by this ratio.

The 1957 revision of the Standard Industrial Classification changed the content of some manufacturing groups. Beginning with the 1Q 1959 report, FTC-SEC followed the new classification. Back figures were given for each quarter of 1958. Group by group and quarter by quarter, we computed the ratio of the old to the new figure. After pondering the trend, if any, in these ratios, we raised or lowered the figures for 1Q 1959 and later to make them comparable with the figures based on the old classification. The largest percentage increase was in the miscellaneous group, where we multiplied the new figures by 1.1078. The largest decrease was in rubber, where we multiplied the new figures by 0.8811. In apparel, lumber, furniture, printing and publishing, chemicals, petroleum, leather, and total manufacturing, the differences were zero or negligible, and no adjustment was made.

Margins, as computed by FTC-SEC, were made comparable by a simpler procedure, using the absolute difference during the overlap. If the C overlap margin for a group was 6.0 and the B margin 5.8, we raised all B margins by 0.2. If the B figure as adjusted was 7.1 during its overlap with A, and the latter was 7.4, we reduced all A margins by 0.3. Margins of 1Q 1959 and later figures were adjusted similarly to make them comparable with C figures.

Sales and margins, after adjustment for comparability and seasonal variation, were multiplied together to estimate adjusted profits.

The sales and profits data used to compute margins for individual companies are described in Table A-2.

PRICE INDEXES

Price indexes of industrial products included in the Bureau of Labor Statistics index of wholesale prices appear to represent prices received by producers rather than by wholesalers. (Many of these products, indeed, do not pass through the hands of wholesalers.) In some cases, subindexes made by BLS appear to represent the products of an FTC-SEC manu-

[2]The B series of textile and motor vehicle sales were *reduced* by a uniform percentage.

facturing group as closely as possible. In other cases we could achieve a closer correspondence to an FTC-SEC group by recombining BLS components. In making such a combination, we divided the BLS 1947–49 value weight of each component by the sum of the weights of all components. Each component index for any month was multiplied by the fraction of 1.0000 thus obtained, and the products for the several ingredients were added. In some cases it proved simpler to delete an inappropriate item from a BLS grouping, which was accomplished by giving a negative weight to the item, keeping the algebraic sum of the weights at 1.0000 (a mathematically defensible procedure). Details are shown in Table A–3. Finally the monthly figures were averaged to get quarterly figures. The composite price index is an average of the price indexes for

TABLE A-2

Large Industrial Companies with Quarterly Sales and Profit Data, 1919–41

	Initial Date		Number of	
	Year	Quarter	Sales Expansions	Sales Contractions
Hercules Powder Company[a]	1919	1	4	4
Studebaker Corporation	1919	1	5	6
Air Reduction Company	1921	1	3	3
Skelly Oil Company	1922	3	5	5
Calumet & Hecla Consolidated Copper Co.	1924	1	2	2
General Motors Corporation	1924	1	2	2
Chrysler Corporation	1926	1	1	2
General Electric Company[b]	1927	1	1	2
Tide Water Associated Oil Company	1927	1	3	3
Yellow Truck & Coach Mfg. Company	1927	1	1	2
Houston Oil Company of Texas	1928	1	1	2
Johns-Manville Corporation	1928	1	1	2
Crown Cork & Seal Company	1928	3	1	2
Atlas Powder Company	1929	1	1	1
Kimberley-Clark Corporation	1929	1	0	1
Link-Belt Company	1929	1	1	1
Continental Oil Company	1930	1	1	1
Scott Paper Company	1930	1	0[c]	0[c]
Radio Corporation of America[d]	1930	3	1	1
Allis-Chalmers Mfg. Company	1931	1	1	1
Ohio Oil Company	1932	1	2	2
Liquid Carbonic Corporation	1932	4	0	1
Total	--	--	37	46

[a] Profits after taxes, 1919–28.

[b] Profits after taxes.

[c] Sales declined to 1Q 1933, rose thereafter.

[d] Through 3Q 1941.

TABLE A-3

BLS Wholesale Price Indexes Used to Construct Indexes of Prices Received by Fifteen FTC-SEC Manufacturing Industries

FTC-SEC Industry	BLS Code Number	BLS Description	BLS Weight
Food and beverages	02	Processed foods	.9168
	02-23	Unprocessed fin fish	-.0086
	14-4	Alcoholic beverages	.0701
	14-5	Nonalcoholic beverages	.0217
Tobacco	14-1	Cigarettes	.7183
	14-2	Cigars	.1969
	14-3	Other tobacco manufactures	.0848
Textiles	03	Textile products and apparel	1.6981
	03-31	Man-made filament yarns and fibers	-.0717
	03-51	Apparel, women's, misses'	-.3505
	03-52	Apparel, men's, boys'	-.2776
	03-54	Apparel, infants', children's	-.0349
	03-55-22	Underwear, shorts, men's, woven	-.0041
	03-61	Burlap	-.0208
	12-3	Floor coverings	.0615
Apparel	03-51	Apparel, women's, misses'	.5254
	03-52	Apparel, men's, boys'	.4161
	03-54	Apparel, infants', children's	.0524
	03-55-22	Underwear, shorts, men's, woven	.0061
Lumber and products	08	Lumber and wood products	
Paper and products	09	Pulp, paper, and allied products	1.0181
	09-2	Wastepaper	-.0181
Chemicals	06	Chemicals and allied products	
Petroleum refining	05-51	Gasoline	.5655
	05-52	Kerosene	.0624
	05-53	Distillate fuel oils	.1592
	05-54	Residual fuel oils	.1379
	05-55	Lubricating oils	.0750
Rubber	07	Rubber and rubber products	1.2118
	07-11	Crude, natural rubber	-.1149
	07-12	Crude, synthetic rubber	-.0969
Leather and products	04	Hides, skins, leather, and leather products	1.1906
	04-1	Hides and skins	-.1906
Stone, clay, glass	12-61	Dinnerware	.0506
	12-62	Household glassware	.0474
	12-63	Glass containers	.1749
	13	Nonmetallic minerals, structural	.8875
	13-21	Sand, gravel, and crushed stone	-.1604
Primary metals	10-13	Semifinished steel products	.0421
	10-14	Finished steel products	.4924
	10-15	Foundry and forge shop products	.1670
	10-22	Primary nonferrous metal refinery shapes	.0758
	10-24	Secondary nonferrous metal and alloy basic shapes	.0373
	10-25	Nonferrous mill shapes	.1519
	10-26-01	Copper wire, bare	.0335

(continued)

TABLE A-3 (concluded)

FTC–SEC Industry	BLS Code Number	BLS Description	BLS Weight
Fabricated metals	10	Metals and metal products	2.5875
	10-1	Iron and steel	-1.1321
	10-2	Nonferrous metals	-.5305
	10-66-01	Water heaters, domestic, electric	-.0074
	12-41	Household stoves	.0544
	12-41-31	Household range, electric	-.0151
	12-67	Cutlery	.0157
	12-68	Metal household containers	.0275
Machinery	11-1	Agricultural machinery and equipment	.1580
	11-2	Construction machinery and equipment	.0960
	11-3	Metalworking machinery and equipment	.1630
	11-4	General purpose machinery and equipment	.2812
	11-5	Miscellaneous machinery	.1860
	12-42	Household laundry equipment	.0419
	12-43	Household sewing machines	.0060
	12-45	Household refrigerators and freezers	.0611
	12-66	Lawnmowers	.0068
Electric equipment	10-26	Wire and cable	.2215
	10-26-01	Copper wire, bare	-.0838
	11-7	Electrical machinery and equipment	.5324
	12-41-31	Household range, electric	.0286
	12-44	Household vacuum cleaners	.0286
	12-46	Household small electric appliances	.0642
	12-5	Television, radio receivers, and phonographs	.1844
	15-55	Phonograph records and recording blanks	.0241

Source: Bureau of Labor Statistics, "Wholesale Price Index (1947–49 = 100): Abbreviated Specifications for Individual Commodities," issued May 1955, and "Wholesale Price Index (1947–49 = 100): Base Value Weights for Groups, Subgroups, Product Classes and Individual Commodities," issued April 1952.

the fifteen groups weighted by the percentage distribution of sales in 1947–49.

The index of prices paid by manufacturers for materials is a weighted average of the following BLS "sector" price indexes:

(1100) Crude foodstuffs and feedstuffs
(1210) Crude nonfood materials, except fuel, for manufacturing
(1310) Crude fuel for manufacturing industries
(2100) Intermediate materials and components for manufacturing
(2410) Processed fuels and lubricants for manufacturing industries
(2500) Containers, nonreturnable
(2610) Supplies for manufacturing industries

The first three groups comprise the index of crude materials; the last four comprise the index of manufactured materials. The composite index does not include prices of transport, public utility, or other services to business.

LABOR COST

The data on hours, earnings, and number of workers come from BLS: *Bulletin 1312, Employment and Earnings Statistics for the United States, 1909 – 60* and current issues of *Employment and Earnings*.

Construction, Manufacturing, and Trade: Annual Data

These data are from Internal Revenue Service (formerly Bureau of Internal Revenue), *Statistics of Income* (annual). Our "sales" are IRS (BIR) "gross sales" plus "gross profits from operations," 1922 – 31; and "gross sales" plus "gross receipts" from business in which inventories are not an income-determining factor, 1932 – 61. Both sales and deductions are too low, in the 1922 – 31 period, by the amount of cost assigned directly to "operations," which cost was not included anywhere on the tax return. Experiments with analogous figures after 1932 (cost of operations was included but not segregated in 1932) indicate that ratios of costs to sales are not, in manufacturing or trade, seriously affected by the omission. Our profit from sales is sales as just described minus IRS total deductions. Our profit before tax is IRS "compiled net profit."

Sales were estimated for the 1919 – 21 period by applying to BIR "gross income" the 1922 – 26 average ratio of sales to gross income (all manufacturing, 0.976; durables, 0.981; nondurables, 0.972; trade, 0.978).

For construction corporations, gross receipts, not reported before 1932, were large relative to gross sales. For example, gross *profit* from such receipts was $423 million in 1931, gross sales were $1,618 million. Gross receipts in 1933 were $502 million, and gross sales $477 million. Revenue figures comparable with expense and profit figures therefore were not available; data before 1932 were not usable.

Compiled net profit exceeds BIR "net income" by the amount of tax-exempt interest. Only net income was available for 1919 – 21; net profit was estimated from its ratio to net income in later years.

In 1925 BIR did not report gross profits from operations. It reported as "miscellaneous income" the total of items b and c in Table A – 4. For all manufacturing, we estimated gross profits from operations (to be added to "gross sales") and cost of operations (to be subtracted from total deductions) as indicated in the table. Similar estimates were made for manufacturing of durables and for trade.

In all years, figures for manufacturing of nondurables were obtained by deduction. Durables figures are totals for the following industrial groups under "Manufacturing." 1922 – 35: lumber and wood products or forest products; stone, clay, and glass products; metal and metal products. 1936 – 37: the same, plus motor vehicles, complete or parts. 1938 –

TABLE A-4
Estimated Cost of Operations, Manufacturing, 1925
(million dollars)

a.	Miscellaneous income as defined in 1925	3,430
b.	Interest, rents, royalties, and miscellaneous income as defined in other years: average of 1924 and 1926	1,150
c.	Estimated gross receipts from operations, 1925 (a - b)	2,280
d.	Estimated gross profits from operations, average of 1924 and 1926	1,074
e.	Estimated cost of operations, 1925 (c - d)	1,206

47: lumber and timber basic products; furniture and finished lumber products; stone, clay, and glass products; iron, steel, and products; nonferrous metals and their products; electrical machinery and equipment; machinery . . . ; automobiles and equipment . . . ; transportation equipment except automobiles. 1948–61: the same, except primary metal industries and fabricated metal products in place of iron, . . . and nonferrous metals . . . ; plus ordnance and accessories and scientific instruments. . . . In general, the new groups were created by fission from the old.

Railroads

All figures in Chapter 5 were from publications of the Interstate Commerce Commission or its Bureau of Transport Economics and Statistics. The sources of the revenue, expense, traffic, and labor data, needed to compute revenue per traffic unit, cost per traffic unit, and the operating ratio, are described in detail in my *American Transportation*, pp. 383–86. Data on federal income and excess profits taxes and net income after tax, needed to compute the final margin, were obtained from the Bureau's monthly *Selected Income and Balance-Sheet Items* (Class I Railways). Data on postwar cumulative increases in freight rates come from its *Transport Economics* (Monthly Comment), September 1958, p. 5. The list of railroads emerging from receivership, and the data on their long-time debt before and after, were compiled from various annual issues of *Statistics of Railways*. In some cases the source shows the debt just before the receivership ended and the reorganization became effective. In other cases the before-end figures refer to the December 31 preceding emergence from receivership. The after-end figures all refer to the December 31 following emergence. The average interest rate on December 31, 1943 is computed by weighting the rates for various classes of debt (*Statistics of Railways*, 1943, p. 108) by the amounts outstanding (p. 132). The average for December 31, 1949 is given in the 1949 issue, p. 114.

Heavy charges for amortization, allowed for income tax purposes, are included in operating expenses as reported for the last four months of 1945, and large amounts of retroactively awarded wage increases are included in March, April, and May, 1946. The amounts are stated in the source and we have deducted them, increasing operating and pre-tax profit correspondingly. Similar retroactive wage awards are included in the expenses for June 1918 and August 1920, but the amounts are not on record; they account for the two spires in the cost per unit and operating ratio curves.

Telephone Companies

Monthly number of messages, and income account data beginning January 1933, were obtained from the Federal Communications Commission. Operating data were from *Monthly Reports of . . . Telephone Carriers . . .* (title varies). Annual data in Table 72 are from the December 1959 issue of this publication. Number of companies included varies, but changes are not large enough to affect the figures seriously except at the beginning of 1949. At that time, the number was reduced from 114 in December 1948 to 53 in January by eliminating small companies. Data for the twelve months of 1948 are available for both the larger and the smaller group. Ratios of smaller-group to larger-group figures are as follows: total operating revenues, 0.96750; net operating income, 0.95086; depreciation, 0.95086; federal taxes, 0.94921; other taxes, 0.97001. Figures before 1948 were multiplied by these ratios to make them comparable with later data.

FCC operating revenue, 1933–41, includes license fees and rentals received by some telephone companies from others. Later data do not include them. Data including them and excluding them are available from 1942 to 1948. The ratio of 1942 revenue excluding them (and reduced as explained above) to revenue including them is 0.9440. Revenue as reported by FCC from 1933 to 1941 has been multiplied by this ratio.

The monthly number of messages and net income before or after taxes was not reported until 1948.

The FCC did not report depreciation or taxes in January–May 1933. We estimated them at the average for the remaining seven months.

Operating revenue, May 1915–December 1932, was obtained from Interstate Commerce Commission files. (FCC took over interstate regulation from ICC in 1934.) There are also ICC figures overlapping the FCC figures for January 1933–May 1934. The two sets of figures differ because of changes in the accounting regulations.

Net operating income was obtained from office records of the *Survey of Current Business*, 1915–22, 1931–33, and from the *Survey's Annual Supplement*, 1923–30. Data for other variants of profit were not available before 1933.

Annual data on number of messages are from FCC, *Statistics of the Communications Industry* (annual) and ICC, *Telephone Companies: Selected Financial and Operating Data* (annual). Early figures in the form of averages per day or per month were multiplied by 365, 366, or 12, as appropriate.

Comments on economic conditions affecting companies during and after World War II are based on remarks in annual reports of the American Telephone and Telegraph Company to stockholders. Data on hourly earnings of telephone workers were from BLS, *Employment, Hours, and Earnings, Telephone*, release number LS54–2884, April 1954. These mainly covered employees subject to the Fair Labor Standards Act. January–March 1945 figures for all employees, except executives, were multiplied by 0.973, the ratio of the new to the old basis in April 1945.

Electric Utilities

Monthly data on kilowatt-hours sold and electric income account were obtained from Federal Power Commission, *Sales, Revenues and Income of Privately Owned Class A and Class B Electric Utilities* . . . (monthly). Kilowatt-hour data begin in January 1944, income data December 1941. Kilowatt-hour, revenue, and expense figures include power sold by utilities to utilities.

Earlier monthly figures (mentioned in Chapter 6) were obtained as follows: electric power production, from University of Illinois, Bureau of Business Research, *Bulletin No. 16* and *Survey of Current Business* and its supplements. Original sources were U.S. Geological Survey March 1919–December 1938, FPC January 1936 onward. These data include publicly as well as privately owned utilities, and some electric railway power plants, etc. (in the Geological Survey data). Earlier monthly figures on electric revenue were obtained as follows: revenue from central station sales, 1913–33, from *Electrical World*, adjusted, 1913–22, to 100 per cent basis by SCB; revenue from sales to ultimate consumers, 1928 onward, including publicly owned utilities, from Edison Electric Institute, *Statistical Bulletin* (annual).

Annual electric income account figures are from the same source. Estimates by Edison Electric Institute for 1926–36 were based on FPC, with allowance for small companies from 1937 onward. Intercompany sales were excluded from revenues and expenses.

Annual kilowatt-hour data used to determine annual peaks and troughs in kilowatt-hours come from Edison Electric Institute. Public plants were included.

Annual data on total (including nonelectric) revenue and income are from FPC, *Statistics of Electric Utilities, Classes A and B Privately Owned Companies* (annual).

Beginning-of-year data on electric rates were from FPC, *Typical Electric Bills*, 1954, pp. iii, viii, ix.

Gas Utilities

Data were obtained from American Gas Association, *Historical Statistics of the Gas Industry, 1961*, and *Gas Facts* (annual). These data cover the "total gas utility and pipeline industry," and include gas operations of electric utilities. Intercompany sales were included in revenues and expenses, except as noted in Chapter 6.

All Domestic Business

Component items for the income statement, as illustrated in Table 90, were taken from Department of Commerce, Office of Business Economics, *National Income, 1954 Edition*, Tables 7, 9, 11, and 23. Figures for 1952–53 were from corresponding tables in July 1956 *Survey of Current Business*. Figures for 1954–56 were from July 1957, *Survey of Current Business*. Some component items were not available for years after 1956. Capital expense, item f of our table, includes change in book value of inventories.

APPENDIX B

BASIC TABLES

TABLE B-1
Manufacturing Industries: Cost, Price, and Profit Data, Fifteen-Industry Composite and All Manufacturing, 1947–61
(seasonally adjusted data)

Year and Quarter	Fifteen-Industry Composite						All Manufacturing		
	Sales (million dollars)	Profits Before Taxes (million dollars)	Ratio of Profits to Sales (per cent)	Index of Quantity Sold (1947–49 = 100)	Index of Prices Received (1947–49 = 100)	Total Cost Per Unit	Sales (million dollars)	Profits Before Taxes (million dollars)	Ratio of Profits to Sales (per cent)
1947 1	35,044	4,116	11.8	99.8	93.3	91.4	43,226	4,928	11.4
2	35,133	3,798	10.8	98.8	94.6	93.5	44,623	4,507	10.1
3	36,242	3,642	10.0	100.4	96.0	95.7	44,899	4,310	9.6
4	38,520	3,825	9.9	102.8	99.7	99.5	47,527	4,325	9.1
1948 1	39,216	4,170	10.6	101.6	102.8	101.7	48,721	5,116	10.5
2	39,801	4,246	10.7	102.2	103.7	102.5	49,355	4,985	10.1
3	40,284	4,148	10.3	101.1	106.0	105.3	50,346	5,035	10.0
4	39,687	3,927	9.9	100.2	105.2	105.2	49,799	4,930	9.9
1949 1	38,126	3,361	8.8	99.0	102.5	103.5	47,879	4,261	8.9
2	36,666	2,796	7.6	98.1	99.5	101.7	46,524	3,489	7.5
3	36,405	2,939	8.1	98.5	98.5	100.2	46,444	3,948	8.5
4	35,859	2,957	8.2	97.6	98.2	99.4	44,664	3,707	8.3
1950 1	37,328	3,300	8.8	100.9	98.7	99.4	46,747	4,254	9.1
2	41,487	4,377	10.6	110.7	99.8	98.8	52,337	5,652	10.8
3	46,423	5,715	12.3	117.1	105.6	102.5	58,469	7,309	12.5
4	47,864	6,706	14.0	115.0	110.5	105.5	60,044	8,346	13.9
1951 1	51,757	6,549	12.6	118.4	116.2	112.6	64,346	7,979	12.4
2	51,485	6,144	11.9	117.7	116.2	113.6	64,115	7,501	11.7
3	49,863	5,249	10.5	115.4	114.8	114.0	61,968	6,507	10.5
4	51,486	5,338	10.4	119.9	114.0	113.4	63,781	6,442	10.1

(continued)

TABLE B-1 (continued)

Year and Quarter	Fifteen-Industry Composite						All Manufacturing		
	Sales (million dollars)	Profits Before Taxes (million dollars)	Ratio of Profits to Sales (per cent)	Index of Quantity Sold	Index of Prices Received (1947-49 = 100)	Total Cost Per Unit	Sales (million dollars)	Profits Before Taxes (million dollars)	Ratio of Profits to Sales (per cent)
1952 1	51,234	4,956	9.7	120.2	113.1	113.5	63,580	6,167	9.7
2	50,482	4,356	8.6	119.7	112.1	113.6	63,180	5,686	9.0
3	51,181	4,501	8.8	120.8	112.6	113.9	64,249	5,718	8.9
4	54,038	4,804	8.9	128.3	111.7	113.1	68,469	6,162	9.0
1953 1	54,188	5,232	9.7	128.7	111.5	112.1	69,348	6,727	9.7
2	54,828	5,441	9.9	129.2	112.2	112.7	70,446	7,045	10.0
3	54,652	5,238	9.6	126.5	114.2	115.2	70,334	6,822	9.7
4	51,604	3,674	7.1	120.1	113.8	117.7	65,823	4,673	7.1
1954 1	50,467	4,113	8.2	118.0	113.5	115.8	63,942	5,243	8.2
2	50,640	4,226	8.4	118.6	113.5	115.3	63,970	5,437	8.5
3	50,856	4,164	8.2	119.2	113.6	115.4	64,174	5,391	8.4
4	51,987	4,438	8.5	122.0	113.4	114.9	65,642	5,711	8.7
1955 1	53,916	4,977	9.2	125.8	113.8	114.7	68,896	6,683	9.7
2	56,052	5,412	9.7	130.0	114.3	114.8	71,408	7,284	10.2
3	57,916	5,917	10.2	132.3	115.9	115.9	73,538	7,721	10.5
4	59,385	6,327	10.6	134.6	116.7	116.2	74,806	8,079	10.8
1956 1	60,685	6,135	10.1	136.4	117.6	117.9	75,270	7,602	10.1
2	61,233	6,093	10.0	135.8	119.2	119.7	75,821	7,582	10.0
3	61,456	5,755	9.4	135.9	120.1	120.8	76,849	7,070	9.2
4	63,421	6,212	9.8	138.1	121.4	122.2	79,184	7,522	9.5

(continued)

TABLE B-1 (concluded)

Year and Quarter	Fifteen-Industry Composite						All Manufacturing		
	Sales (million dollars)	Profits Before Taxes (million dollars)	Ratio of Profits to Sales (per cent)	Index of Quantity Sold (1947–49 = 100)	Index of Prices Received (1947–49 = 100)	Total Cost Per Unit	Sales (million dollars)	Profits Before Taxes (million dollars)	Ratio of Profits to Sales (per cent)
1957 1	64,208	6,256	9.7	138.2	122.7	123.6	80,372	7,796	9.7
2	63,653	5,738	9.0	137.0	123.1	124.6	79,747	7,337	9.2
3	64,232	5,640	8.8	137.4	123.9	125.7	82,084	7,141	8.7
4	62,176	4,859	7.8	133.6	123.9	126.5	77,803	5,913	7.6
1958 1	59,268	4,004	6.8	128.0	124.1	127.3	73,071	4,750	6.5
2	59,695	4,085	6.8	129.8	123.9	126.3	73,328	4,913	6.7
3	62,447	5,052	8.1	135.0	124.2	125.3	78,366	6,113	7.8
4	64,376	5,685	8.8	139.3	124.1	124.2	79,594	6,765	8.5
1959 1	65,963	5,919	9.0	141.8	124.5	124.8	81,346	7,321	9.0
2	69,787	6,666	9.6	148.8	125.1	125.1	87,115	8,799	10.1
3	67,001	5,372	8.0	145.4	124.7	125.0	85,761	7,118	8.3
4	67,567	5,686	8.4	146.1	124.4	124.8	83,504	6,513	7.8
1960 1	68,886	6,098	8.8	147.3	125.0	125.7	86,447	7,607	8.8
2	68,838	5,492	8.0	148.0	125.1	126.1	86,790	7,204	8.3
3	68,351	5,221	7.6	146.2	125.6	127.3	87,478	6,736	7.7
4	67,610	4,900	7.2	145.2	125.6	127.3	84,785	5,935	7.0
1961 1	67,663	4,673	6.9	145.2	125.7	127.9	83,258	5,495	6.6
2	70,482	5,381	7.6	152.8	124.6	125.6	88,519	6,993	7.9
3	71,752	5,570	7.8	155.2	124.5	125.7	91,578	7,143	7.8
4	73,849	6,371	8.6	159.8	124.6	124.5	92,743	7,790	8.4

TABLE B-2

Manufacturing Industries: Labor Data, Fifteen-Industry Composite, 1947–61

(seasonally adjusted data, 1947–49 = 100)

Year and Quarter	All Workers, Man-Hours	Production Workers		Quantity Produced	All Workers		Production Workers		
		Man-Hours	Payrolls		Man-Hours Per Unit	Labor Cost Per Unit	Hours Per Unit	Hourly Earnings	Payrolls Per Unit
1947 1	104.5	105.7	94.6	98.8	105.8	94.6	107.0	89.3	95.7
2	103.9	105.0	97.3	99.5	104.4	94.8	105.5	92.4	97.8
3	102.9	103.8	98.7	99.9	103.0	96.5	103.9	94.8	98.8
4	104.7	105.6	102.3	103.0	101.7	98.7	102.5	96.7	99.3
1948 1	104.6	105.2	104.0	102.4	102.1	100.1	102.7	98.6	101.6
2	103.8	104.0	104.4	103.1	100.7	100.7	100.9	100.2	101.3
3	103.5	103.6	107.4	102.3	101.2	105.0	101.3	103.4	105.0
4	101.3	101.0	106.3	101.2	100.1	105.7	99.8	104.9	105.0
1949 1	96.8	96.0	101.2	99.9	96.9	103.2	96.1	105.2	101.3
2	92.3	91.0	95.9	96.8	95.4	101.5	94.0	105.1	99.1
3	91.3	90.0	94.7	97.4	93.7	98.9	92.4	105.0	97.2
4	90.5	89.1	93.2	96.3	94.0	99.3	92.5	104.4	96.8
1950 1	94.1	93.0	99.1	101.0	93.2	101.0	92.1	106.3	98.1
2	98.8	98.0	106.3	110.9	89.1	96.9	88.4	108.2	95.9
3	104.5	104.1	114.9	117.9	88.6	98.2	88.3	110.2	97.5
4	107.6	107.2	122.5	116.1	92.7	107.0	92.3	114.0	105.5
1951 1	109.6	108.9	127.7	119.5	91.7	108.8	91.1	117.0	106.9
2	110.5	109.4	130.7	118.5	93.2	112.7	92.3	119.2	110.3
3	107.6	105.7	127.6	116.7	92.2	113.5	90.6	120.4	109.3
4	106.6	104.2	127.3	119.8	89.0	112.4	87.0	121.9	106.3

(continued)

TABLE B-2 (continued)

Year and Quarter	All Workers, Man-Hours	Production Workers		Quantity Produced	All Workers		Production Workers		
		Man-Hours	Payrolls		Man-Hours Per Unit	Labor Cost Per Unit	Hours Per Unit	Hourly Earnings	Payrolls Per Unit
1952 1	107.7	105.2	129.8	120.2	89.6	114.8	87.5	123.1	108.0
2	105.2	102.1	126.6	117.7	89.4	115.5	86.7	123.6	107.6
3	106.5	103.4	129.7	120.1	88.7	113.9	86.1	125.2	108.0
4	111.7	108.9	139.9	128.1	87.2	115.1	85.0	128.2	109.2
1953 1	113.6	110.8	144.9	129.6	87.7	117.9	85.5	130.4	111.8
2	114.1	111.1	146.7	130.3	87.6	118.7	85.3	131.7	112.6
3	111.7	108.3	144.7	129.0	86.6	118.4	84.0	133.3	112.2
4	107.1	103.0	138.2	123.1	87.0	121.8	83.7	133.9	112.3
1954 1	103.5	98.9	133.1	119.9	86.3	122.4	82.5	134.2	111.0
2	101.5	96.7	130.5	120.6	84.2	120.3	80.2	134.6	108.2
3	100.7	95.7	129.4	121.4	82.9	117.4	78.8	134.8	106.6
4	102.2	97.3	132.8	124.8	81.9	118.3	78.0	136.1	106.4
1955 1	104.9	100.2	138.0	129.7	80.9	116.8	77.3	137.5	106.4
2	108.1	103.5	144.8	134.7	80.3	117.6	76.8	139.6	107.5
3	108.9	104.1	147.9	136.7	79.7	117.8	76.2	141.8	108.2
4	111.2	106.3	153.4	139.5	79.7	120.8	76.2	143.9	110.0
1956 1	111.3	106.3	155.3	141.2	78.8	120.9	75.3	145.8	110.0
2	110.7	105.4	156.5	140.5	78.8	124.1	75.0	148.2	111.4
3	108.8	102.6	153.8	138.9	78.3	124.3	73.9	149.5	110.7
4	110.6	104.4	159.9	142.2	77.8	126.7	73.4	152.8	112.4
1957 1	110.3	103.8	160.5	141.8	77.8	127.9	73.2	154.3	113.2
2	108.8	101.8	158.3	141.2	77.1	128.7	72.1	155.2	112.1
3	107.7	100.4	157.9	141.0	76.4	129.1	71.2	156.9	112.0
4	104.1	96.4	152.8	136.4	76.3	131.5	70.7	158.1	112.0

(continued)

TABLE B-2 (concluded)

Year and Quarter	All Workers, Man-Hours	Production Workers		Quantity Produced	All Workers		Production Workers		
		Man-Hours	Payrolls		Man-Hours Per Unit	Labor Cost Per Unit	Hours Per Unit	Hourly Earnings	Payrolls Per Unit
1958 1	99.2	91.1	144.6	128.3	77.3	133.9	71.0	158.4	112.7
2	96.5	88.0	140.6	129.9	74.3	130.9	67.7	159.3	108.2
3	98.6	90.4	146.1	135.7	72.6	128.0	66.5	161.3	107.5
4	101.1	93.0	152.3	141.7	71.3	126.6	65.6	163.3	107.5
1959 1	104.6	96.6	160.5	146.0	71.6	128.6	66.2	165.8	109.9
2	108.7	100.8	169.8	154.2	70.5	128.8	65.4	168.1	110.1
3	105.9	97.3	162.7	147.4	71.8	130.3	66.0	166.7	110.4
4	106.3	97.5	164.8	149.8	71.0	130.1	65.1	168.6	110.0
1960 1	108.4	99.9	172.4	153.5	70.6	132.3	65.1	172.1	112.3
2	107.5	98.7	170.1	154.3	69.7	132.5	64.0	172.0	110.2
3	105.0	95.6	165.7	151.8	69.2	131.6	63.0	172.8	109.2
4	101.0	91.3	158.7	149.0	67.8	130.1	61.3	173.4	106.5
1961 1	99.8	89.8	156.9	148.3	67.3	129.9	60.6	174.2	105.8
2	102.6	92.8	163.9	155.6	65.9	130.3	59.6	176.2	105.3
3	103.6	93.9	167.7	158.3	65.4	129.5	59.3	178.2	105.9
4	105.1	95.2	172.0	162.5	64.7	128.0	58.6	180.2	105.8

TABLE B-3

Railroads: Traffic Units, 1938–61

(seasonally adjusted data, billion traffic units)

	January	February	March	April	May	June	July	August	September	October	November	December
1938	29.37	27.44	28.00	28.05	26.81	26.95	28.30	28.26	28.56	29.34	29.77	30.68
1939	30.73	29.42	30.37	29.09	28.82	31.63	32.27	32.24	35.28	35.98	35.97	34.08
1940	35.32	34.24	33.05	35.68	36.07	36.00	35.99	37.20	36.14	35.06	37.05	38.41
1941	39.39	39.52	43.25	38.73	47.06	48.79	46.66	49.11	49.89	51.42	49.70	50.67
1942	53.00	53.07	55.07	59.40	61.02	63.39	64.52	66.89	70.65	72.49	72.77	73.12
1943	72.98	75.58	76.04	76.68	75.93	75.97	79.08	80.15	80.57	80.50	80.43	83.48
1944	82.82	85.30	80.63	81.04	80.05	81.08	78.72	79.52	79.71	79.37	79.70	79.33
1945	78.42	79.43	80.50	79.34	78.66	80.96	75.78	71.48	70.11	66.25	70.99	69.66
1946	69.60	66.30	66.03	51.57	48.85	62.09	65.63	64.40	62.26	63.65	61.55	61.71
1947	65.81	64.60	65.26	61.53	63.80	63.25	61.62	63.68	62.85	64.80	63.54	64.91
1948	62.53	65.77	58.26	56.02	62.71	63.70	52.41	60.80	61.42	52.16	59.84	59.07
1949	56.24	55.78	51.19	55.84	53.51	52.47	50.10	49.34	46.92	41.43	48.81	50.86
1950	47.71	45.00	53.95	54.57	52.62	55.78	56.34	59.27	59.33	60.83	57.61	60.00
1951	63.60	58.76	63.09	62.68	61.23	61.17	58.23	60.33	59.85	61.65	60.19	59.45
1952	62.12	65.83	60.43	58.54	57.30	52.37	54.52	57.10	59.72	57.70	59.55	57.77
1953	58.36	58.33	57.32	58.65	58.25	59.48	58.76	57.19	55.74	56.42	52.89	51.19
1954	52.16	52.78	50.48	50.89	51.35	52.54	51.97	50.31	50.38	52.15	52.01	53.31
1955	54.28	55.93	55.09	56.76	57.86	59.51	58.81	57.69	58.46	59.42	58.35	59.30
1956	60.88	64.09	60.74	61.29	60.51	60.77	53.31	57.41	58.55	60.14	58.25	60.10
1957	57.87	60.00	60.42	59.21	58.53	58.46	56.44	57.62	54.39	54.84	52.33	51.43
1958	51.75	49.96	49.68	48.13	48.03	50.97	48.54	50.99	51.39	53.59	52.16	52.36
1959	52.79	54.56	54.91	56.01	56.20	57.30	50.40	47.19	46.71	48.79	50.82	54.63
1960	54.82	56.62	54.73	56.20	53.87	53.79	50.12	49.51	48.57	50.93	47.92	47.88
1961[a]		49.76			51.26			50.76			52.63	

[a] Beginning 1961, data are published quarterly.

TABLE B-4

Railroads: Operating Revenue Per Traffic Unit, 1938–61
(seasonally adjusted data, cents)

	January	February	March	April	May	June	July	August	September	October	November	December
1938	.9918	1.0197	1.0250	1.0282	1.0463	1.0605	1.0360	1.0708	1.0602	1.0539	1.0672	1.0469
1939	1.0387	1.0493	1.0524	1.0426	1.0802	1.0300	1.0077	1.0251	1.0142	1.0206	1.0170	1.0220
1940	1.0215	1.0210	1.0036	.9692	.9798	.9708	.9956	.9841	.9942	1.0322	1.0076	1.0034
1941	1.0000	1.0111	.9734	1.0411	.9669	.9576	.9736	.9549	.9924	.9822	.9516	.9809
1942	.9468	.9715	.9951	1.0364	1.0134	.9968	1.0088	.9810	.9274	.8998	.9427	.9702
1943	.9652	.9647	.9750	.9974	.9785	.9710	.9592	.9464	.9589	.9456	.9628	.9654
1944	.9384	.9472	.9691	.9573	.9829	.9734	.9853	.9967	.9976	.9856	.9949	.9836
1945	1.0047	.9862	.9901	1.0024	1.0233	.9998	1.0067	1.0010	.9635	1.0057	.9466	.9083
1946	.9664	.9599	.9594	1.1224	1.0667	.9729	.9848	1.0455	1.0554	1.0665	1.0868	1.0653
1947	1.0514	1.0967	1.0981	1.0625	1.1393	1.1055	1.1727	1.1178	1.1477	1.1253	1.1720	1.1926
1948	1.2480	1.2121	1.3290	1.3484	1.2725	1.3184	1.3809	1.3623	1.3645	1.2960	1.3588	1.3142
1949	1.4147	1.3492	1.4395	1.3868	1.3878	1.4046	1.4315	1.4368	1.4695	1.4369	1.4227	1.3451
1950	1.4316	1.4473	1.3737	1.3555	1.4194	1.3998	1.4029	1.4324	1.4581	1.3957	1.4746	1.4883
1951	1.3871	1.3565	1.3837	1.4079	1.4542	1.4017	1.4360	1.4396	1.4192	1.4373	1.4787	1.4606
1952	1.4512	1.4296	1.4446	1.5003	1.5223	1.5583	1.4844	1.5035	1.5651	1.5666	1.5023	1.5579
1953	1.5632	1.5520	1.5885	1.5772	1.5370	1.5267	1.5854	1.5372	1.5874	1.5347	1.5723	1.6007
1954	1.5196	1.5178	1.5677	1.5317	1.4740	1.4966	1.5095	1.5206	1.5193	1.4295	1.5234	1.5033
1955	1.4646	1.4479	1.4870	1.4334	1.4634	1.4500	1.4533	1.4914	1.4673	1.4157	1.4965	1.4545
1956	1.4446	1.4154	1.4491	1.4622	1.5179	1.4548	1.5234	1.5017	1.4613	1.4835	1.5215	1.4559
1957	1.5623	1.5145	1.4823	1.5310	1.5404	1.4607	1.5578	1.5361	1.5725	1.5693	1.5867	1.6140
1958	1.5929	1.5446	1.5298	1.5784	1.5690	1.5258	1.6160	1.5542	1.6126	1.5617	1.5504	1.6062
1959	1.5704	1.5269	1.5467	1.5617	1.5539	1.5426	1.6399	1.5597	1.6110	1.5352	1.5348	1.5557
1960	1.5223	1.5233	1.5333	1.4972	1.5291	1.5051	1.5237	1.5532	1.5199	1.4846	1.5770	1.5355
1961[a]		1.4986			1.4863			1.5112			1.4915	

[a] Beginning 1961, data are published quarterly.

TABLE B-5

Railroads: Operating Expenses Per Traffic Unit, 1938–61

(seasonally adjusted data, cents)

	January	February	March	April	May	June	July	August	September	October	November	December
1938	.7961	.8291	.8139	.8043	.8154	.8141	.7799	.8011	.8081	.7744	.7807	.7536
1939	.7615	.7916	.7876	.8041	.8296	.7692	.7447	.7574	.7086	.7073	.7159	.7262
1940	.7324	.7421	.7486	.7082	.7061	.7056	.7233	.7094	.7164	.7399	.7039	.6886
1941	.6865	.6829	.6516	.7294	.6347	.6246	.6309	.6237	.6715	.7349	.7486	.7102
1942	.6574	.6539	.6419	.6281	.6127	.6037	.6100	.5987	.5607	.5507	.5670	.5713
1943	.5807	.5724	.5800	.5865	.5959	.6014	.5948	.5848	.5879	.6116	.6338	.6941
1944	.6079	.6111	.6419	.6389	.6555	.6466	.6724	.6792	.6482	.6511	.6678	.6777
1945	.6752	.6662	.6639	.6815	.6932	.6763	.7300	.7676	.7328	.7562	.7401	.8000
1946	.7119	.7291	.6906	.9977	1.0016	.8426	.8329	.8658	.8434	.8413	.8843	.8616
1947	.8242	.8463	.8386	.8997	.8671	.8677	.9046	.8731	.9426	.9116	.9448	.9353
1948	.9909	.9567	1.0578	1.0644	.9748	.9799	1.0064	1.0298	1.0171	1.0122	1.0739	1.0564
1949	1.1024	1.0921	1.1440	1.0838	1.1140	1.1176	1.1407	1.1698	1.1605	1.2141	1.1098	1.0747
1950	1.1528	1.1949	1.0604	1.0498	1.0946	1.0523	1.0309	1.0380	1.0185	1.0076	1.0825	1.0343
1951	1.0193	1.1127	1.0701	1.0831	1.1195	1.1007	1.1731	1.1372	1.1059	1.0912	1.1216	1.0902
1952	1.1101	1.0591	1.1129	1.1611	1.1716	1.2297	1.1671	1.1413	1.1365	1.1835	1.1192	1.1838
1953	1.1407	1.1425	1.2109	1.1697	1.1590	1.1548	1.1972	1.1843	1.2151	1.1872	1.2532	1.3090
1954	1.2090	1.1885	1.2383	1.2197	1.1875	1.1825	1.1940	1.2171	1.2130	1.1323	1.1571	1.1339
1955	1.0919	1.0851	1.1085	1.0810	1.0911	1.0837	1.0990	1.1399	1.1209	1.0897	1.1338	1.1266
1956	1.0935	1.0738	1.1124	1.1140	1.1494	1.1251	1.2302	1.1622	1.1296	1.1215	1.1882	1.1022
1957	1.1961	1.1512	1.1385	1.1892	1.2112	1.1712	1.2378	1.1973	1.2467	1.2292	1.2847	1.2780
1958	1.2657	1.2874	1.2502	1.2904	1.2836	1.2135	1.2965	1.2136	1.2335	1.1730	1.2055	1.2047
1959	1.2283	1.1979	1.1890	1.1868	1.1790	1.1731	1.3105	1.3102	1.3248	1.2382	1.2247	1.1521
1960	1.1634	1.1764	1.1986	1.1489	1.1940	1.1937	1.2582	1.2836	1.2600	1.1842	1.2694	1.2322
1961[a]		1.2221			1.1828			1.1998			1.1431	

[a]Beginning 1961, data are published quarterly.

TABLE B-6

Railroads: Operating Ratio, 1938–61

(seasonally adjusted data, per cent)

	January	February	March	April	May	June	July	August	September	October	November	December
1938	80.6	81.9	79.0	78.5	77.4	76.3	75.0	74.4	75.9	74.0	73.5	73.1
1939	73.7	76.0	74.5	77.3	76.3	74.2	73.7	73.4	69.5	69.7	70.7	72.2
1940	72.1	73.2	74.2	73.3	71.6	72.2	72.4	71.7	71.7	72.1	70.2	69.7
1941	69.0	68.0	66.4	70.3	65.2	64.8	64.6	64.9	67.3	75.3	74.6	73.6
1942	69.4	67.3	64.5	60.6	60.5	60.6	60.5	61.0	60.5	61.2	60.1	58.9
1943	60.2	59.3	59.5	58.8	60.9	61.9	62.0	61.8	61.3	64.7	65.8	71.9
1944	64.8	64.5	66.2	66.7	66.7	66.4	68.2	68.1	65.0	66.1	67.1	68.9
1945	67.2	67.6	67.1	68.0	67.7	67.6	72.5	76.7	76.1	75.2	78.2	88.2
1946	73.6	76.0	72.0	88.9	93.9	86.6	84.6	82.8	79.9	78.9	81.4	80.9
1947	78.4	77.2	76.4	77.4	76.1	78.5	77.1	78.1	82.1	81.0	80.6	78.4
1948	79.4	78.9	79.6	78.9	76.6	74.3	72.9	75.6	74.5	78.1	79.0	80.4
1949	81.6	80.9	79.5	78.2	80.3	79.6	79.7	81.4	79.0	84.5	78.0	79.9
1950	80.5	82.6	77.2	77.5	77.1	75.2	73.5	72.5	69.9	72.2	73.4	69.5
1951	73.5	82.0	77.3	76.9	77.0	78.5	81.7	79.0	77.9	75.9	75.9	74.6
1952	76.5	74.1	77.0	77.4	77.0	78.9	78.6	75.9	72.6	75.6	74.5	76.0
1953	73.0	73.6	76.2	74.2	75.4	75.6	75.5	77.0	76.5	77.4	79.7	81.8
1954	79.6	78.3	79.0	79.6	80.6	79.0	79.1	80.0	79.9	79.2	75.9	75.4
1955	74.6	74.9	74.5	75.4	74.6	74.7	75.6	76.4	76.4	77.0	75.8	77.5
1956	75.7	75.9	76.8	76.2	75.7	77.3	80.8	77.4	77.3	75.6	78.1	75.7
1957	76.6	76.0	76.8	77.7	78.6	80.2	79.5	77.9	79.3	78.3	81.0	79.2
1958	79.5	83.3	81.7	81.8	81.8	79.5	80.2	78.1	76.5	75.1	77.8	75.0
1959	78.2	78.5	76.9	76.0	75.9	76.0	79.9	84.0	82.2	80.7	79.8	74.1
1960	76.4	77.2	78.2	76.7	78.1	79.3	82.6	82.6	82.9	79.8	80.4	80.2
1961	81.2	82.7	80.8	81.5	79.2	78.2	80.2	78.3	79.7	77.0	76.6	76.2

TABLE B-7

Railroads: Pre-Tax Margin, 1931–61

(seasonally adjusted data, per cent)

	January	February	March	April	May	June	July	August	September	October	November	December
1931	5.39	3.00	2.98	3.92	5.06	4.83	4.34	3.16	1.33	-.95	-.48	-1.52
1932	-3.79	-.97	-2.47	-3.75	-9.16	-9.96	-14.21	-7.26	-.97	-.76	-2.55	-4.28
1933	-6.41	-8.89	-15.04	-6.59	.41	6.02	9.84	4.71	2.66	-2.52	-.67	.41
1934	1.39	.57	3.51	.00	.33	1.19	-1.79	-1.64	-3.20	-4.50	-3.57	-2.17
1935	-1.57	.11	-.17	1.25	.66	-2.38	-5.50	-1.25	1.72	3.26	3.25	2.02
1936	3.80	3.64	-.35	3.59	2.99	3.37	5.34	5.66	4.59	5.97	7.62	8.01
1937	5.06	6.75	9.37	6.67	4.98	6.27	4.62	1.46	.83	-2.68	-4.28	-5.41
1938	-6.02	-7.92	-6.81	-5.58	-4.57	-5.11	-3.11	-1.20	-2.68	-.30	.25	1.39
1939	2.14	.40	.15	-2.43	-2.05	.05	.48	1.48	6.47	8.16	7.83	6.49
1940	5.95	5.04	2.48	3.88	4.32	2.84	3.12	4.33	4.90	6.87	7.95	12.30
1941	11.10	11.98	13.22	7.58	13.66	14.63	14.79	14.56	13.46	9.47	7.26	14.56
1942	13.21	14.96	17.00	20.61	20.86	22.51	23.35	23.33	24.69	27.24	26.90	23.23
1943	25.82	26.64	27.16	27.86	25.94	24.21	25.16	25.33	23.27	21.30	21.29	18.90
1944	21.92	22.36	20.37	20.32	20.61	20.44	19.37	19.61	20.89	20.29	20.98	22.15
1945	19.66	19.58	19.88	20.82	20.68	19.84	16.57	11.46	10.26	10.44	9.65	-2.00
1946	10.64	10.13	12.37	-.95	-8.59	.58	4.33	5.94	6.59	7.33	6.34	7.63
1947	10.47	9.47	9.87	11.08	10.22	7.48	6.64	8.12	4.90	8.50	8.68	13.06
1948	9.03	10.27	8.00	9.24	12.31	16.36	14.66	13.28	13.70	13.30	11.17	7.78
1949	8.16	9.63	9.37	10.68	8.36	8.17	7.59	6.41	7.06	4.37	9.72	8.76
1950	8.30	7.54	11.47	11.10	11.00	13.43	15.75	16.99	18.00	17.80	15.78	18.99
1951	16.27	9.27	12.12	11.86	12.42	11.34	8.38	10.23	9.24	13.50	13.07	14.70
1952	13.24	17.20	12.93	11.86	12.50	10.72	11.29	13.41	15.39	13.91	14.97	14.81
1953	15.12	16.00	14.33	15.84	14.65	14.67	15.36	13.03	12.66	11.38	8.42	5.57
1954	8.37	9.20	9.74	9.05	7.91	9.77	10.19	8.68	8.10	9.39	12.02	12.89
1955	12.96	12.71	13.88	13.18	14.59	14.39	14.32	13.24	12.80	11.35	12.80	11.42
1956	12.07	12.57	11.98	13.00	13.31	11.89	9.36	11.45	11.79	12.79	11.08	12.02
1957	11.83	13.31	12.20	11.25	10.16	8.72	10.50	10.34	8.68	8.51	7.47	7.09
1958	8.14	5.00	5.74	5.24	5.12	7.31	8.10	9.25	10.84	11.23	10.61	9.91
1959	9.99	11.47	11.66	12.33	12.08	10.25	7.58	1.84	3.80	3.92	6.46	9.30
1960	10.82	12.08	9.83	10.44	8.41	6.24	4.16	3.03	3.34	4.77	5.60	1.11
1961	5.47	5.16	5.83	4.05	6.28	6.73	6.55	8.02	6.16	8.19	10.62	5.75

[a]After-tax margin prior to June 1934.

TABLE B-8

Railroads: Man-Hours Per Traffic Unit, 1938–61

(seasonally adjusted data, per 1000 traffic units)

	January	February	March	April	May	June	July	August	September	October	November	December
1938	5.80	6.18	6.08	5.80	5.81	5.98	5.57	5.84	5.88	5.69	5.84	5.65
1939	5.55	5.93	5.87	5.83	6.04	5.72	5.38	5.57	5.15	5.18	5.35	5.39
1940	5.37	5.44	5.47	5.15	5.14	5.14	5.29	5.17	5.17	5.49	5.23	5.00
1941	4.84	4.87	4.70	5.94	4.97	4.80	4.87	4.60	4.69	4.57	4.57	4.63
1942	4.37	4.33	4.23	4.15	3.98	4.03	3.94	3.82	3.74	3.66	3.63	3.79
1943	3.71	3.65	3.67	3.68	3.61	3.79	3.58	3.51	3.56	3.46	3.58	3.46
1944	3.49	3.60	3.67	3.60	3.68	3.69	3.64	3.72	3.69	3.64	3.71	3.71
1945	3.86	3.78	3.74	3.74	3.76	3.71	3.81	4.03	3.94	4.20	4.00	4.05
1946	4.08	4.13	4.04	5.11	4.95	4.08	3.96	4.10	4.16	4.25	4.31	4.15
1947	4.07	4.13	3.96	4.26	4.16	4.07	4.26	4.05	4.18	4.09	4.01	4.00
1948	4.26	4.12	4.42	4.37	4.03	4.03	4.11	4.18	4.18	4.09	4.23	4.22
1949[a]	4.32	4.28	4.40	4.13	4.32	4.31	4.31	4.51	4.13	4.24	3.82	3.77
1949[a]	4.69	4.65	4.81	4.49	4.68	4.68	4.68	4.90	4.51	4.65	4.17	4.11
1950	4.46	4.61	4.02	3.87	4.23	4.02	3.80	3.98	3.89	3.90	4.14	3.83
1951	3.83	4.02	3.77	3.72	3.92	3.72	3.89	3.91	3.68	3.78	3.78	3.71
1952	3.75	3.57	3.59	3.86	3.90	4.03	3.84	3.68	3.74	3.94	3.56	3.83
1953	3.71	3.69	3.73	3.72	3.73	3.70	3.82	3.70	3.89	3.77	3.86	4.00
1954	3.73	3.71	3.83	3.73	3.58	3.60	3.55	3.67	3.69	3.43	3.49	3.50
1955	3.35	3.28	3.36	3.18	3.27	3.25	3.19	3.45	3.36	3.21	3.34	3.23
1956	3.14	3.10	3.13	3.05	3.23	3.09	3.33	3.22	3.03	3.13	3.15	2.94
1957	3.21	3.01	2.89	3.05	3.13	2.94	3.15	3.04	3.14	3.16	3.10	3.11
1958	3.12	3.20	2.95	3.09	3.05	2.81	3.04	2.81	2.89	2.80	2.69	2.83
1959	2.81	2.73	2.67	2.67	2.67	2.63	2.99	2.91	2.97	2.81	2.67	2.64
1960[b]	2.55	2.65	2.68	2.52	2.64	2.64	2.67	2.80	2.69	2.55	2.71	2.70
1961[b]		2.59			2.47			2.42			2.39	

[a] The figures for 1938-49 include only occupations for which hours were reported; the 1949-1961 figures include all workers.

[b] Beginning 1961, data are published quarterly.

TABLE B-9
Railroads: Hourly Earnings, 1938–61
(seasonally adjusted data, cents per hour)

	January	February	March	April	May	June	July	August	September	October	November	December
1938	88.1	84.6	86.6	89.1	89.6	87.2	91.4	87.9	88.6	88.6	86.2	87.0
1939	87.8	84.2	86.0	89.1	88.0	86.5	89.8	87.4	87.7	86.6	85.5	86.7
1940	86.5	85.9	87.1	89.0	88.8	88.5	88.9	87.8	87.4	85.1	86.2	85.9
1941	88.4	86.4	86.4	81.0	82.6	83.9	83.9	86.7	88.4	89.8	89.0	96.6
1942	97.7	96.7	96.8	92.8	95.7	95.5	96.4	98.5	99.7	100.8	99.9	96.4
1943	96.8	95.6	96.0	93.7	96.9	96.0	97.5	99.7	100.0	101.7	101.6	100.5
1944	106.6	106.9	108.2	106.1	107.2	108.0	109.7	110.5	110.8	112.1	112.3	110.9
1945	114.9	109.2	109.2	106.9	109.0	110.7	111.5	112.5	112.9	111.5	111.6	112.8
1946	111.0	110.3	111.1	120.1	127.3	135.5	138.5	133.5	131.9	129.4	130.4	134.9
1947	131.7	134.3	136.4	131.5	132.3	139.0	136.5	134.5	144.4	144.2	148.7	152.1
1948	149.1	151.1	151.7	150.1	150.7	154.4	153.8	152.7	151.4	153.5	154.1	159.2
1949[a]	156.8	158.5	161.5	165.1	163.6	167.8	170.2	165.1	183.7	187.6	184.5	189.7
1949[a]	144.4	145.9	147.7	151.9	151.0	154.5	156.7	152.0	168.2	171.0	169.0	174.0
1950	168.2	170.7	171.6	175.2	168.3	172.2	175.0	169.2	171.7	169.8	170.4	175.8
1951	169.7	177.1	186.5	190.3	185.4	193.5	194.3	190.2	193.8	189.6	191.2	194.9
1952	194.8	196.9	202.1	199.0	195.3	202.7	202.1	203.3	199.8	201.2	205.8	201.6
1953	204.7	207.4	207.0	208.5	205.8	207.6	205.3	205.6	201.8	208.1	207.9	203.7
1954	214.7	215.3	211.9	215.2	216.7	216.8	216.3	211.7	213.6	220.3	218.2	212.5
1955	219.0	224.3	215.0	222.2	222.4	220.5	225.3	211.8	211.8	220.7	219.4	224.7
1956	238.5	239.6	234.3	240.2	239.5	240.9	242.8	230.6	234.6	234.8	242.8	243.5
1957	249.6	253.6	248.0	251.0	256.3	260.2	258.6	250.8	248.7	252.7	268.3	263.6
1958	272.7	272.9	271.7	273.3	282.5	283.4	281.9	274.2	268.6	274.4	288.8	281.3
1959	290.9	293.4	284.9	289.3	289.9	290.8	287.0	284.1	280.0	287.3	291.9	283.4
1960	299.1	296.7	287.9	296.6	299.3	297.1	305.3	288.5	291.2	300.7	298.2	296.1
1961[b]		305.4			309.4			310.2			302.1	

[a] The figures for 1938–49 include only occupations for which hours were reported; the 1949–1961 figures include all workers.

[b] Beginning 1961, data are published quarterly.

TABLE B-10
Railroads: Labor Cost Per Traffic Unit, 1938–61
(seasonally adjusted data, cents per traffic unit)

	January	February	March	April	May	June	July	August	September	October	November	December
1938	.5111	.5228	.5268	.5166	.5208	.5214	.5089	.5134	.5207	.5043	.5032	.4918
1939	.4873	.4994	.5049	.5197	.5315	.4949	.4833	.4866	.4518	.4486	.4574	.4671
1940	.4645	.4673	.4765	.4585	.4566	.4549	.4703	.4541	.4519	.4672	.4506	.4297
1941	.4277	.4206	.4063	.4812	.4107	.4027	.4085	.3990	.4146	.4105	.4066	.4474
1942	.4270	.4187	.4096	.3852	.3809	.3849	.3799	.3764	.3727	.3690	.3627	.3653
1943	.3593	.3491	.3522	.3449	.3499	.3639	.3492	.3498	.3560	.3518	.3639	.3466
1944	.3720	.3848	.3972	.3820	.3945	.3984	.3992	.4110	.4089	.4082	.4129	.4116
1945	.4235	.4126	.4084	.3998	.4098	.4106	.4247	.4534	.4450	.4684	.4463	.4569
1946	.4527	.4557	.4487	.6136	.6302	.5530	.5486	.5474	.5485	.5501	.5619	.5597
1947	.5362	.5545	.5401	.5602	.5502	.5659	.5813	.5446	.6035	.5899	.5962	.6083
1948	.6353	.6225	.6705	.6560	.6073	.6224	.6321	.6384	.6329	.6278	.6518	.6717
1949	.6772	.6784	.7105	.6819	.7067	.7232	.7334	.7447	.7587	.7953	.7048	.7150
1950	.7503	.7871	.6899	.6779	.7121	.6922	.6649	.6736	.6678	.6624	.7054	.6733
1951	.6499	.7118	.7032	.7079	.7269	.7200	.7558	.7435	.7133	.7167	.7228	.7231
1952	.7305	.7029	.7255	.7683	.7616	.8167	.7759	.7480	.7471	.7928	.7324	.7720
1953	.7595	.7653	.7722	.7756	.7676	.7683	.7842	.7607	.7851	.7847	.8024	.8147
1954	.8007	.7986	.8115	.8028	.7757	.7803	.7695	.7771	.7882	.7557	.7614	.7439
1955	.7337	.7356	.7225	.7066	.7272	.7167	.7187	.7306	.7117	.7085	.7329	.7258
1956	.7490	.7429	.7335	.7325	.7736	.7443	.8086	.7424	.7109	.7348	.7649	.7158
1957	.8012	.7633	.7167	.7656	.8022	.7650	.8146	.7623	.7808	.7984	.8317	.8199
1958	.8507	.8733	.8016	.8445	.8615	.7963	.8571	.7706	.7763	.7683	.7770	.7962
1959	.8175	.8011	.7607	.7725	.7739	.7647	.8581	.8268	.8315	.8073	.7793	.7483
1960	.7626	.7863	.7715	.7475	.7901	.7843	.8151	.8077	.7834	.7669	.8080	.7996
1961[a]		.7909			.7641			.7508			.7220	

[a] Beginning 1961, data are published quarterly.

TABLE B-11

Telephone Companies: *Local and Toll Calls, 1948–61*

(seasonally adjusted data, million calls)

LOCAL CALLS

	January	February	March	April	May	June	July	August	September	October	November	December
1948	4,681	4,702	4,660	4,673	4,709	4,773	4,813	4,760	4,822	4,866	4,884	4,919
1949	4,978	5,008	5,048	5,110	5,074	5,112	5,130	5,192	5,243	5,224	5,266	5,278
1950	5,267	5,276	5,426	5,437	5,532	5,513	5,532	5,637	5,591	5,538	5,595	5,618
1951	5,560	5,604	5,556	5,411	5,502	5,529	5,498	5,560	5,508	5,589	5,764	5,461
1952	5,730	5,764	5,667	5,715	5,745	5,633	5,775	5,714	5,794	5,862	5,707	5,838
1953	5,908	5,713	5,816	5,879	5,859	5,906	5,950	5,901	5,932	5,973	5,864	5,925
1954	5,885	5,866	6,014	5,999	6,036	6,046	6,064	6,055	6,219	6,136	6,246	6,231
1955	6,170	6,317	6,231	6,317	6,182	6,441	6,380	6,491	6,509	6,471	6,574	6,632
1956	6,403	6,672	6,749	6,647	6,773	6,819	6,730	7,075	6,763	6,922	6,975	6,836
1957	7,273	7,118	7,156	7,282	7,302	7,229	7,465	7,386	7,369	7,497	7,505	7,438
1958	7,542	7,494	7,452	7,626	7,656	7,586	7,664	7,672	7,757	7,742	7,655	7,846
1959	7,911	7,827	7,929	7,887	7,888	8,065	8,080	8,077	8,145	8,145	8,244	8,231
1960	7,994	8,461	8,611	8,282	8,368	8,505	8,193	8,693	8,511	8,361	8,640	8,552
1961	8,283	8,584	8,607	8,435	8,737	8,790	8,379	8,913	8,586	8,724	8,928	8,597

TOLL CALLS

	January	February	March	April	May	June	July	August	September	October	November	December
1948	147.7	149.0	147.2	148.7	148.8	151.4	154.0	151.2	152.8	152.8	152.7	155.2
1949	157.1	156.4	157.8	158.4	157.9	158.8	156.8	159.1	160.5	157.9	159.2	157.0
1950	155.6	157.1	159.1	158.4	157.0	154.5	153.6	154.8	152.3	153.4	152.7	153.8
1951	153.5	151.0	151.3	147.1	151.9	151.5	151.5	154.9	150.5	156.0	157.6	155.6
1952	156.0	160.3	152.4	151.1	156.5	154.9	157.5	155.7	158.0	159.6	154.9	159.2
1953	160.5	159.5	158.9	162.7	159.5	161.8	162.3	156.8	160.2	159.3	158.2	159.4
1954	158.2	157.0	161.3	163.4	159.7	164.2	165.4	165.4	168.4	166.7	170.2	171.6
1955	170.7	172.1	175.0	173.0	175.8	178.1	174.7	184.7	183.8	180.1	184.3	186.3
1956	187.6	193.3	192.9	190.7	194.4	193.7	192.0	196.4	191.4	197.5	199.8	194.9
1957	205.5	199.9	199.0	206.5	207.1	202.6	208.2	207.0	201.3	209.4	207.0	207.5
1958	209.8	210.6	206.1	209.1	210.0	210.9	213.1	212.7	216.8	217.3	213.1	224.1
1959	223.1	223.2	229.7	230.1	229.1	235.6	231.0	229.6	231.9	228.8	232.2	234.0
1960	230.0	247.1	243.0	240.1	242.5	245.3	231.8	249.8	243.8	235.9	243.8	246.2
1961	246.4	245.6	249.0	242.1	255.5	255.2	240.4	262.3	249.8	253.4	261.4	252.9

TABLE B-12
Telephone Companies: Operating Revenues, 1947–61
(seasonally adjusted data, million dollars)

	January	February	March	April	May	June	July	August	September	October	November	December
1947	190.5	191.7	192.3	150.0[a]	176.5[a]	194.5	200.7	199.8	205.7	209.2	208.6	214.1
1948	216.4	220.3	221.9	228.4	227.4	228.3	230.0	231.5	234.8	234.8	239.1	240.6
1949	242.4	242.5	246.0	252.4	252.5	255.1	255.1	259.4	262.2	262.7	267.1	268.3
1950	268.9	270.8	276.4	278.2	284.1	287.0	292.3	298.4	296.1	299.3	300.1	304.3
1951	312.7	311.7	315.0	315.0	316.6	318.3	320.5	325.3	324.7	330.5	337.0	333.5
1952	337.7	342.4	342.1	345.8	350.2	351.6	353.8	354.9	362.6	365.1	361.7	370.8
1953	373.3	375.4	375.6	381.4	383.8	386.4	391.4	384.6	390.3	394.6	397.2	399.7
1954	398.5	400.8	406.8	409.5	409.2	415.0	418.4	421.6	427.0	426.8	433.2	436.9
1955	440.5	442.5	449.6	450.4	454.9	460.3	459.0	472.9	473.9	470.9	479.7	484.5
1956	487.3	497.3	498.5	499.5	506.0	508.9	511.1	517.5	512.7	524.5	527.3	528.2
1957	536.8	536.7	538.4	548.7	551.9	549.1	559.0	560.1	556.1	565.9	570.1	570.0
1958	576.0	576.1	577.0	581.3	585.0	591.0	594.5	598.4	607.7	611.6	610.6	623.6
1959	625.3	627.6	636.2	641.6	644.4	651.5	654.6	654.6	659.4	658.7	666.8	666.8
1960	670.4	682.4	684.1	686.8	693.1	698.0	686.4	714.2	708.2	703.3	718.0	709.5
1961	721.7	719.1	726.4	717.9	740.4	740.2	727.3	755.3	745.7	758.7	774.5	757.2

[a]Figures were affected by a strike during these months.

TABLE B-13

Telephone Companies: Operating Profit, 1947–61

(seasonally adjusted data, million dollars)

	January	February	March	April	May	June	July	August	September	October	November	December
1947	61.46	64.42	66.37	40.00	49.17	58.11	57.38	58.60	59.31	60.99	64.44	68.20
1948	66.86	70.84	70.45	70.53	74.02	73.64	73.64	75.50	75.24	75.24	73.43	72.18
1949	75.57	75.43	76.49	79.91	81.76	85.03	88.85	89.29	91.45	94.96	96.46	97.82
1950	98.19	99.86	103.56	106.28	107.95	110.81	120.48	120.73	119.52	118.97	115.40	120.72
1951	122.96	122.25	123.28	122.58	122.45	122.77	121.83	122.26	126.31	126.14	128.91	130.64
1952	129.65	132.81	136.39	138.46	136.63	137.93	133.23	136.92	139.67	140.46	142.04	143.97
1953	146.01	150.23	148.17	150.64	152.54	152.28	153.18	154.76	154.16	158.18	160.73	160.47
1954	161.02	160.98	161.79	164.44	169.27	168.41	172.84	175.50	173.25	178.51	179.49	180.34
1955	187.74	188.14	189.29	190.73	193.34	196.65	200.30	199.42	203.97	204.85	205.17	205.80
1956	205.74	208.64	211.98	214.90	214.10	217.24	218.50	221.19	226.61	225.38	219.17	240.76
1957	244.12	248.18	248.38	250.96	252.43	254.84	257.56	260.43	262.10	263.60	268.11	263.18
1958	265.78	273.18	277.66	283.00	292.42	300.05	304.54	308.36	310.83	314.90	318.33	324.73
1959	324.40	326.07	332.53	335.27	336.83	335.60	338.19	341.26	343.01	346.00	348.09	348.39
1960	355.12	355.54	355.74	367.44	363.75	363.76	375.12	370.25	372.33	380.29	373.87	377.21
1961	380.60	379.88	380.16	387.96	387.78	392.72	404.76	396.78	402.20	415.73	409.88	425.26

TABLE B-14

Telephone Companies: Operating Margin, 1947–61

(seasonally adjusted data, per cent)

	January	February	March	April	May	June	July	August	September	October	November	December
1947	32.26	33.60	34.51	26.67	27.86	29.88	28.59	29.33	28.83	29.15	30.89	31.85
1948	30.90	32.16	31.75	30.88	32.55	32.26	32.02	32.61	32.04	32.04	30.71	30.00
1949	31.18	31.11	31.09	31.66	32.38	33.33	34.83	34.42	34.88	36.15	36.11	36.46
1950	36.52	36.88	37.47	38.20	38.00	38.61	41.22	40.46	40.36	39.75	38.45	39.67
1951	39.32	39.22	39.14	38.91	38.68	38.57	38.01	37.58	38.90	38.17	38.25	39.17
1952	38.39	38.79	39.87	40.04	39.01	39.23	37.66	38.58	38.52	38.47	39.27	38.83
1953	39.11	40.02	39.45	39.50	39.74	39.41	39.14	40.24	39.50	40.09	40.47	40.15
1954	40.41	40.16	39.77	40.16	41.37	40.58	41.31	41.63	40.57	41.83	41.43	41.28
1955	42.62	42.52	42.10	42.35	42.50	42.72	43.64	42.17	43.04	43.50	42.77	42.48
1956	42.22	41.95	42.52	43.02	42.31	42.69	42.75	42.74	44.20	42.97	41.56	45.58
1957	45.48	46.24	46.13	45.74	45.74	46.41	46.08	46.50	47.13	46.58	47.03	46.17
1958	46.14	47.42	48.12	48.68	49.99	50.77	51.23	51.53	51.15	51.49	52.13	52.07
1959	51.88	51.96	52.27	52.26	52.27	51.51	51.66	52.13	52.02	52.53	52.20	52.25
1960	52.97	52.10	52.00	53.50	52.48	52.11	54.65	51.84	52.57	54.07	52.07	53.17
1961	52.74	52.83	52.33	54.04	52.37	53.06	55.65	52.53	53.94	54.80	52.92	56.16

TABLE B-15
Telephone Companies: Net Operating Income, 1947–61
(seasonally adjusted data, million dollars)

	January	February	March	April	May	June	July	August	September	October	November	December
1947	19.59	20.62	22.00	5.35	10.78	17.05	14.61	16.20	16.74	17.47	19.14	19.67
1948	20.76	22.59	22.20	21.92	23.69	23.44	22.92	24.37	23.29	23.97	22.32	19.64
1949	22.11	21.50	22.02	23.46	24.33	26.39	28.27	29.05	30.09	31.94	31.88	32.02
1950	32.81	33.57	35.75	36.52	36.95	39.49	46.02	36.80	40.82	39.73	40.13	39.51
1951	40.76	39.59	40.32	39.41	39.75	39.16	38.13	38.64	29.87	37.30	38.34	38.67
1952	39.03	40.27	42.12	42.49	41.14	41.51	39.82	42.23	42.55	42.88	43.31	48.19
1953	45.30	46.82	45.49	46.45	47.20	46.97	45.93	47.64	46.89	49.09	50.12	49.76
1954	50.04	48.74	48.94	49.99	52.20	49.32	65.07	56.20	54.27	57.92	57.95	56.03
1955	61.88	60.79	60.32	61.01	61.80	63.51	64.40	63.90	65.93	66.24	65.36	65.47
1956	66.64	66.88	67.63	69.28	68.31	69.51	70.44	71.05	72.61	71.38	68.05	77.78
1957	74.88	77.34	77.36	76.33	76.01	77.11	75.09	79.47	80.04	79.72	82.61	78.32
1958	80.76	83.54	85.93	87.96	92.79	95.40	97.42	97.79	99.54	99.92	101.53	98.09
1959	104.24	104.45	106.72	106.99	106.99	105.46	106.90	107.76	108.54	109.97	110.88	118.67
1960	113.61	112.90	112.46	117.43	114.76	113.98	120.60	118.05	116.93	122.75	119.70	116.47
1961	123.07	121.31	121.10	125.80	123.56	124.13	137.51	124.90	123.49	131.68	130.62	132.64

TABLE B-16

Telephone Companies: Operating Income Ratio, 1947–61

(seasonally adjusted data, per cent)

	January	February	March	April	May	June	July	August	September	October	November	December
1947	10.28	10.76	11.44	3.57	6.11	8.77	7.28	8.11	8.14	8.35	9.18	9.19
1948	9.59	10.25	10.00	9.60	10.42	10.27	9.97	10.53	9.92	10.21	9.34	8.16
1949	9.12	8.87	8.95	9.29	9.64	10.34	11.08	11.20	11.48	12.16	11.94	11.93
1950	12.20	12.40	12.93	13.13	13.01	13.76	15.74	12.33	13.79	13.27	13.37	12.98
1951	13.03	12.70	12.80	12.51	12.56	12.30	11.90	11.88	9.20	11.29	11.38	11.60
1952	11.56	11.76	12.31	12.29	11.75	11.81	11.25	11.90	11.73	11.74	11.97	13.00
1953	12.14	12.47	12.11	12.18	12.30	12.16	11.73	12.39	12.01	12.44	12.62	12.45
1954	12.56	12.16	12.03	12.21	12.76	11.88	15.55	13.33	12.71	13.57	13.38	12.82
1955	14.05	13.74	13.42	13.55	13.59	13.80	14.03	13.51	13.91	14.07	13.63	13.51
1956	13.68	13.45	13.57	13.87	13.50	13.66	13.78	13.73	14.16	13.61	12.91	14.73
1957	13.95	14.41	14.37	13.91	13.77	14.04	13.43	14.19	14.39	14.09	14.49	13.74
1958	14.02	14.50	14.89	15.13	15.86	16.14	16.39	16.34	16.38	16.34	16.63	15.73
1959	16.67	16.64	16.77	16.68	16.60	16.19	16.33	16.46	16.46	16.70	16.63	17.80
1960	16.95	16.54	16.44	17.10	16.56	16.33	17.57	16.53	16.51	17.45	16.67	16.42
1961	17.05	16.87	16.67	17.52	16.69	16.77	18.91	16.54	16.56	17.36	16.87	17.52

TABLE B-17

Telephone Companies: Net Income Before Taxes, 1948–61

(seasonally adjusted data, million dollars)

	January	February	March	April	May	June	July	August	September	October	November	December
1948	27.18	31.25	30.58	30.11	33.46	30.36	28.51	29.68	28.61	29.90	25.73	24.12
1949	25.44	24.85	26.12	28.13	29.36	31.16	33.55	33.93	35.36	38.12	39.86	42.32
1950	41.40	42.94	46.09	48.05	49.35	51.78	61.36	60.04	58.11	56.54	58.36	61.78
1951	63.33	62.26	62.88	60.93	59.26	60.87	59.72	59.72	63.02	61.99	64.67	66.86
1952	65.89	69.59	73.78	72.08	71.29	71.10	66.70	68.62	71.40	72.77	75.05	70.36
1953	78.28	81.25	78.71	81.87	83.34	82.41	81.98	83.96	82.18	86.40	88.81	90.84
1954	87.34	86.38	86.43	89.07	93.65	93.75	97.39	98.46	93.54	98.94	99.59	101.74
1955	110.71	108.88	109.88	108.16	110.70	112.05	119.54	114.77	119.83	119.76	117.50	119.72
1956	121.46	121.28	123.34	125.80	123.18	126.56	128.36	129.62	132.70	132.27	126.03	152.72
1957	138.34	142.78	138.31	139.14	138.83	139.35	133.64	141.63	141.65	141.05	145.20	142.97
1958	142.06	147.96	149.37	152.95	160.64	167.66	174.73	173.20	178.51	176.26	180.46	183.98
1959	185.67	185.63	191.81	194.34	194.62	190.30	191.44	193.90	189.22	196.20	197.24	192.08
1960	201.45	200.40	201.47	210.71	205.94	203.75	215.69	208.39	210.33	217.71	208.70	220.72
1961	215.98	212.00	212.83	216.42	216.28	216.56	220.99	218.86	223.14	232.46	227.63	251.29

TABLE B-18

Telephone Companies: Pre-Tax Margin, 1948–61

(seasonally adjusted data, per cent)

	January	February	March	April	May	June	July	August	September	October	November	December
1948	12.56	14.19	13.78	13.18	14.71	13.30	12.40	12.82	12.18	12.73	10.76	10.02
1949	10.50	10.25	10.62	11.15	11.63	12.21	13.15	13.08	13.49	14.51	14.92	15.77
1950	15.40	15.86	16.68	17.27	17.37	18.04	20.99	20.12	19.63	18.89	19.45	20.30
1951	20.25	19.97	19.96	19.34	18.72	19.12	18.63	18.36	19.41	18.76	19.19	20.05
1952	19.51	20.32	21.57	20.84	20.36	20.22	18.85	19.34	19.69	19.93	20.75	18.98
1953	20.97	21.64	20.96	21.47	21.71	21.33	20.95	21.83	21.06	21.90	22.36	22.73
1954	21.92	21.55	21.25	21.75	22.89	22.59	23.28	23.35	21.91	23.18	22.99	23.29
1955	25.13	24.61	24.44	24.01	24.34	24.34	26.04	24.27	25.29	25.43	24.49	24.71
1956	24.93	24.39	24.74	25.19	24.34	24.87	25.11	25.05	25.88	25.22	23.90	28.91
1957	25.77	26.60	25.69	25.36	25.15	25.38	23.91	25.29	25.47	24.92	25.47	25.08
1958	24.66	25.68	25.89	26.31	27.46	28.37	29.39	28.94	29.37	28.82	29.55	29.50
1959	29.69	29.58	30.15	30.29	30.20	29.21	29.25	29.62	28.70	29.79	29.58	28.81
1960	30.05	29.37	29.45	30.68	29.71	29.19	31.42	29.18	29.70	30.96	29.07	31.11
1961	29.93	29.48	29.30	30.15	29.21	29.26	30.38	28.98	29.92	30.64	29.39	33.19

TABLE B-19

Telephone Companies: Net Income After Taxes, 1948–61

(seasonally adjusted data, million dollars)

	January	February	March	April	May	June	July	August	September	October	November	December
1948	18.91	21.33	21.27	21.21	23.00	20.60	19.58	20.36	19.86	20.58	17.58	16.79
1949	17.36	16.80	17.80	19.01	19.35	20.76	21.95	22.59	23.31	24.96	26.08	27.01
1950	26.96	27.73	29.52	30.36	31.31	32.83	38.33	29.38	32.68	32.53	33.34	34.57
1951	34.91	33.83	34.17	33.53	33.13	32.81	32.02	33.05	23.41	31.80	32.80	32.69
1952	33.87	35.57	37.67	36.25	36.04	36.04	34.21	35.50	36.26	37.85	38.69	38.98
1953	40.35	41.32	40.33	42.67	42.77	42.22	41.18	43.22	43.15	44.78	45.78	46.83
1954	44.26	43.48	44.07	45.28	47.21	47.60	60.86	51.48	49.26	51.94	52.48	52.18
1955	57.41	56.44	58.01	55.78	57.47	58.08	60.79	59.80	62.06	62.06	60.85	63.20
1956	63.64	63.13	63.94	65.48	64.83	66.73	66.85	68.91	69.57	69.80	67.02	78.79
1957	72.69	75.14	73.55	73.72	74.26	74.17	70.22	75.32	74.44	75.09	76.80	74.75
1958	75.26	77.54	78.12	79.61	83.56	86.88	90.10	88.80	91.77	90.59	92.95	91.09
1959	96.02	95.85	98.53	100.16	99.64	97.56	99.38	100.54	99.68	102.70	103.42	105.00
1960	104.34	104.29	104.75	109.10	106.48	106.18	111.58	110.20	110.83	114.13	110.59	113.77
1961	113.45	110.60	110.64	112.72	112.39	112.69	117.52	113.48	115.13	120.89	119.33	129.08

TABLE B-20

Telephone Companies: After-Tax Margin, 1948–61

(seasonally adjusted data, per cent)

	January	February	March	April	May	June	July	August	September	October	November	December
1948	8.74	9.68	9.59	9.29	10.11	9.02	8.51	8.79	8.46	8.76	7.35	6.98
1949	7.16	6.93	7.24	7.53	7.66	8.14	8.61	8.71	8.89	9.50	9.76	10.07
1950	10.03	10.24	10.68	10.91	11.02	11.44	13.11	9.85	11.04	10.87	11.11	11.36
1951	11.16	10.85	10.85	10.64	10.46	10.31	9.99	10.16	7.21	9.62	9.73	9.80
1952	10.03	10.39	11.01	10.48	10.29	10.25	9.67	10.00	10.00	10.37	10.70	10.51
1953	10.81	11.01	10.74	11.19	11.14	10.93	10.52	11.24	11.06	11.35	11.53	11.72
1954	11.11	10.85	10.83	11.06	11.54	11.47	14.55	12.21	11.54	12.17	12.11	11.94
1955	13.03	12.75	12.90	12.38	12.63	12.62	13.24	12.65	13.10	13.18	12.69	13.04
1956	13.06	12.69	12.83	13.11	12.81	13.11	13.08	13.32	13.57	13.31	12.71	14.92
1957	13.54	14.00	13.66	13.44	13.46	13.51	12.56	13.45	13.39	13.27	13.47	13.11
1958	13.07	13.46	13.54	13.70	14.28	14.70	15.16	14.84	15.10	14.81	15.22	14.61
1959	15.36	15.27	15.49	15.61	15.46	14.97	15.18	15.36	15.12	15.59	15.51	15.75
1960	15.56	15.28	15.31	15.89	15.36	15.21	16.26	15.43	15.65	16.23	15.40	16.04
1961	15.72	15.38	15.23	15.70	15.18	15.22	16.16	15.02	15.44	15.93	15.41	17.05

TABLE B-21
Electric Utilities: Kilowatt-Hours Sold, 1944–61
(seasonally adjusted data, million kwh)

	January	February	March	April	May	June	July	August	September	October	November	December
1944	16,884	17,229	17,334	17,186	17,121	17,144	17,022	17,306	17,356	17,377	17,303	17,326
1945	17,461	17,445	17,472	17,474	17,633	17,501	17,331	16,794	16,155	16,251	16,280	16,095
1946	15,902	15,505	15,943	16,153	16,294	16,621	17,093	17,409	17,473	17,823	17,837	17,804
1947	18,343	18,485	18,485	18,850	19,154	19,056	19,062	19,306	19,691	19,812	19,843	20,041
1948	20,041	20,452	20,723	20,442	20,710	20,372	20,951	21,078	21,315	21,414	21,654	21,737
1949	21,467	21,436	21,312	21,229	21,030	21,045	21,382	21,444	21,267	20,732	21,100	21,752
1950	22,000	22,221	22,701	22,396	23,269	23,690	23,856	24,172	24,514	24,856	25,019	25,024
1951	25,458	25,650	25,631	26,011	26,094	26,164	26,015	26,269	26,158	26,655	27,061	26,904
1952	27,052	27,196	27,070	26,920	26,951	26,427	26,972	27,711	28,264	28,419	28,641	28,950
1953	28,907	29,012	29,470	30,016	29,968	30,251	30,435	30,079	30,022	29,800	29,745	29,696
1954	29,954	30,035	30,243	30,432	30,514	31,071	31,460	31,288	31,459	32,000	32,261	32,394
1955	32,844	33,633	34,207	34,629	35,333	35,495	36,014	37,224	37,358	37,392	37,899	38,203
1956	38,435	38,686	38,834	38,926	39,206	39,295	38,892	39,266	39,492	40,207	40,382	40,286
1957	40,739	40,962	40,845	41,241	41,202	41,258	41,851	41,549	41,549	41,597	41,671	41,538
1958	41,476	41,278	41,261	40,837	40,940	41,659	42,194	43,004	43,359	43,537	43,659	44,133
1959	44,594	44,901	45,584	46,026	46,486	46,912	46,954	46,448	46,970	46,947	47,404	48,016
1960	48,189	46,681	49,571	49,367	48,931	48,399	48,819	50,403	50,143	49,910	49,806	48,870
1961	49,731	49,540	50,226	50,712	52,129	52,063	51,712	54,013	54,347	55,139	55,163	54,251

TABLE 'B-22

Electric Utilities: Electric Operating Revenue, 1944–61

(seasonally adjusted data, million dollars)

	January	February	March	April	May	June	July	August	September	October	November	December
1944	252.5	257.5	260.5	259.3	259.6	260.1	257.7	259.0	259.1	259.0	258.4	255.9
1945	264.3	265.0	264.0	262.6	266.1	267.3	265.1	262.4	256.7	260.3	262.9	263.4
1946	264.9	264.7	265.7	268.1	269.2	270.9	274.6	278.0	278.9	283.2	285.6	287.7
1947	293.1	295.6	297.7	302.1	305.0	305.1	302.8	308.3	315.7	320.1	322.5	327.6
1948	328.9	333.6	338.4	336.9	338.3	343.8	347.8	351.4	357.2	359.1	361.1	361.9
1949	359.9	359.8	360.2	360.6	360.8	362.7	368.1	368.3	365.8	363.1	366.8	372.8
1950	376.7	378.9	386.1	389.9	393.8	397.0	399.0	401.7	405.6	413.0	413.6	415.6
1951	421.1	425.3	426.2	430.6	433.3	434.7	435.1	437.8	442.0	444.9	452.2	451.4
1952	454.5	457.5	459.1	457.7	459.4	460.3	467.3	475.7	480.4	485.4	490.1	495.6
1953	496.7	496.5	502.6	508.1	512.3	515.9	518.8	517.6	517.9	520.1	520.2	520.2
1954	527.1	526.5	529.8	534.9	537.4	542.2	549.6	549.0	552.5	559.4	562.0	566.6
1955	565.6	575.1	581.9	587.3	592.4	593.4	597.7	610.8	615.9	616.5	620.4	629.0
1956	632.1	634.4	638.3	640.8	644.5	650.0	647.6	648.4	653.1	659.5	663.8	663.8
1957	671.7	677.4	678.0	685.5	689.4	691.7	700.0	700.9	697.8	698.9	704.4	704.2
1958	706.0	708.9	712.3	711.3	712.5	717.8	724.4	736.6	739.0	743.3	744.6	752.6
1959	759.9	761.4	768.4	775.3	784.9	791.9	794.4	795.7	803.7	804.9	808.2	811.2
1960	809.8	814.9	832.8	836.4	831.9	835.5	840.7	852.7	852.3	849.9	851.4	844.5
1961	853.5	854.0	860.9	871.3	884.4	886.4	887.3	908.0	917.1	920.5	917.6	911.7

APPENDIX B

TABLE B-23

Electric Utilities: Electric Operating Margin, 1944–61

(seasonally adjusted data, per cent)

	January	February	March	April	May	June	July	August	September	October	November	December
1944	53.70	53.28	54.32	55.65	54.58	54.44	54.68	53.78	54.42	54.09	53.75	53.89
1945	54.07	54.15	54.02	53.73	54.00	54.25	54.13	55.22	55.09	54.44	54.13	51.97
1946	54.32	54.17	53.71	52.33	50.85	51.61	51.46	51.22	51.24	50.85	50.39	50.16
1947	48.62	48.99	48.61	48.13	48.36	48.71	46.14	45.77	45.39	45.36	46.67	46.43
1948	42.93	44.66	44.65	44.29	44.75	42.87	43.47	43.80	44.09	44.52	45.31	45.68
1949	51.57	46.30	46.42	47.17	46.95	46.84	47.87	47.65	48.28	48.50	48.01	48.07
1950	47.78	47.93	47.71	49.09	48.83	49.29	49.70	48.67	49.24	49.73	48.72	48.94
1951	48.11	49.35	49.01	49.09	48.40	49.18	49.30	48.26	50.14	49.56	50.09	51.26
1952	49.75	50.12	51.10	49.95	50.13	50.23	49.35	50.05	49.38	49.05	49.91	50.12
1953	50.78	50.88	50.70	50.23	50.73	50.15	49.81	50.56	50.24	50.68	50.83	50.75
1954	51.24	51.57	51.09	51.73	52.31	51.99	52.75	52.81	52.54	52.86	52.74	51.34
1955	52.93	52.76	52.72	53.19	52.77	53.19	53.24	52.60	53.22	53.84	52.90	53.28
1956	53.16	52.47	53.08	53.28	53.02	53.18	53.34	51.94	53.36	52.30	52.62	53.34
1957	51.76	53.07	52.97	52.25	52.34	52.78	52.34	52.82	52.81	52.54	52.91	54.13
1958	53.37	53.25	53.47	53.59	53.77	53.69	53.87	54.24	54.11	54.18	54.69	54.18
1959	54.52	54.44	54.20	54.40	54.66	54.67	54.97	54.86	55.32	55.78	55.21	55.36
1960	55.67	54.29	54.51	55.97	55.27	55.32	56.57	54.69	55.36	55.58	54.69	55.25
1961	54.90	55.00	54.68	55.96	55.44	55.65	56.52	55.22	55.92	55.95	54.93	56.97

TABLE B-24

Electric Utilities: Electric Net Revenue Ratio, 1944–61

(seasonally adjusted data, per cent)

	January	February	March	April	May	June	July	August	September	October	November	December
1944	21.15	21.51	23.07	22.37	21.46	22.41	22.70	22.90	22.85	23.09	24.77	26.38
1945	21.94	22.34	21.21	23.08	24.05	23.01	22.52	23.67	26.02	26.97	21.53	35.00
1946	25.67	25.20	24.39	23.65	23.63	23.62	23.05	23.60	22.41	21.82	21.39	19.95
1947	22.55	22.23	21.97	21.09	21.31	21.67	19.78	19.88	19.58	19.06	20.00	18.96
1948	19.00	19.03	19.03	18.85	19.04	17.68	18.26	18.70	18.84	18.71	18.97	18.90
1949	19.51	19.84	19.79	20.22	19.84	20.07	20.76	20.85	21.35	20.90	20.53	20.39
1950	20.92	20.14	20.18	21.24	20.82	20.73	20.88	19.09	18.34	20.24	19.37	18.89
1951	18.38	18.65	18.21	18.60	18.32	18.73	18.52	17.95	17.90	17.71	19.02	20.16
1952	19.12	19.26	19.91	19.14	19.44	19.73	18.96	19.78	19.59	19.06	19.40	20.24
1953	20.01	20.04	20.00	19.70	19.91	19.46	19.55	19.92	19.97	20.17	20.03	19.84
1954	20.26	20.30	20.29	20.43	20.84	20.21	21.03	21.55	20.85	21.42	20.89	19.82
1955	21.06	20.69	20.60	20.98	20.85	21.52	20.88	20.56	20.83	20.89	20.33	20.32
1956	20.46	20.30	20.38	20.68	20.45	20.46	20.57	20.10	20.79	20.38	20.46	21.09
1957	19.90	20.71	20.68	20.26	20.23	20.47	20.54	20.76	20.66	20.50	20.71	20.83
1958	20.93	20.96	21.28	21.19	21.33	21.55	21.44	21.72	21.56	21.44	21.82	21.80
1959	21.50	21.57	21.43	21.49	21.70	21.59	21.82	21.77	21.94	22.15	21.80	21.55
1960	22.08	21.70	21.39	22.11	21.93	22.05	22.45	21.70	21.86	22.23	21.71	22.27
1961	21.91	22.03	21.56	22.23	22.04	22.29	22.60	22.04	22.09	22.23	21.64	22.13

TABLE B-25

Electric Utilities: Electric Net Operating Revenue, 1944–61

(seasonally adjusted data, million dollars)

	January	February	March	April	May	June	July	August	September	October	November	December
1944	53.4	55.4	60.1	58.0	55.7	58.3	58.5	59.3	59.2	59.8	64.0	67.5
1945	58.0	59.2	56.0	60.6	64.0	61.5	59.7	62.1	66.8	70.2	56.6	92.2
1946	68.0	66.7	64.8	63.4	63.6	64.0	63.3	65.6	62.5	61.8	61.1	57.4
1947	66.1	65.7	65.4	63.7	65.0	66.1	59.9	61.3	61.8	61.0	64.5	62.1
1948	62.5	63.5	64.4	63.5	64.4	60.8	63.5	65.7	67.3	67.2	68.5	68.4
1949	70.2	71.4	71.3	72.9	71.6	72.8	76.4	76.8	78.1	75.9	75.3	76.0
1950	78.8	76.3	77.9	82.8	82.0	82.3	83.3	76.7	74.4	83.6	80.1	78.5
1951	77.4	79.3	77.6	80.1	79.4	81.4	80.6	78.6	79.1	78.8	86.0	91.0
1952	86.9	88.1	91.4	87.6	89.3	90.8	88.6	94.1	94.1	92.5	95.1	100.3
1953	99.4	99.5	100.5	100.1	102.0	100.4	101.4	103.1	103.4	104.9	104.2	103.2
1954	106.8	106.9	107.5	109.3	112.0	109.6	115.6	118.3	115.2	119.8	117.4	112.3
1955	119.1	119.0	119.9	123.2	123.5	127.7	124.8	125.6	128.3	128.8	126.1	127.8
1956	129.3	128.8	130.1	132.5	131.8	133.0	133.2	130.3	135.8	134.4	135.8	140.0
1957	133.7	140.3	140.4	138.9	139.5	141.6	143.8	145.5	144.2	143.3	145.9	146.7
1958	147.8	148.6	151.6	150.7	152.0	154.7	155.3	160.0	159.3	159.4	162.5	164.1
1959	163.4	164.2	164.7	166.6	170.3	171.0	173.3	173.2	176.3	178.3	176.2	174.8
1960	178.8	176.8	178.1	184.9	182.4	184.2	188.7	185.0	186.3	188.9	184.8	188.1
1961	187.0	188.1	185.6	193.7	194.9	197.6	200.5	200.1	202.6	204.6	198.6	201.8

TABLE B-26

Electric Utilities: Electric Operating Profit, 1944–61

(seasonally adjusted data, million dollars)

	January	February	March	April	May	June	July	August	September	October	November	December
1944	135.6	137.2	141.5	144.3	141.7	141.6	140.9	139.3	141.0	140.1	138.9	137.9
1945	142.9	143.5	142.6	141.1	143.7	145.0	143.5	144.9	141.4	141.7	142.3	136.9
1946	143.9	143.4	142.7	140.3	136.9	139.8	141.3	142.4	142.9	144.0	143.9	144.3
1947	142.5	144.8	144.7	145.4	147.5	148.6	139.7	141.1	143.3	145.2	150.5	152.1
1948	141.2	149.0	151.1	149.2	151.4	147.4	151.2	153.9	157.5	159.9	163.6	165.3
1949	185.6	166.6	167.2	170.1	169.4	169.9	176.2	175.5	176.6	176.1	176.1	179.2
1950	180.0	181.6	184.2	191.4	192.3	195.7	198.3	195.5	199.7	205.4	201.5	203.4
1951	202.6	209.9	208.9	211.4	209.7	213.8	214.5	211.3	221.6	220.5	226.5	231.4
1952	226.1	229.3	234.6	228.6	230.3	231.2	230.6	238.1	237.2	238.1	244.6	248.4
1953	252.2	252.6	254.8	255.2	259.9	258.7	258.4	261.7	260.2	263.6	264.4	264.0
1954	270.1	271.5	270.7	276.7	281.1	281.9	289.9	289.9	290.2	295.7	296.4	290.9
1955	299.4	303.4	306.8	312.4	312.6	315.6	318.2	321.3	327.8	331.9	328.2	335.1
1956	336.0	332.9	338.8	341.4	341.7	345.7	345.4	336.8	348.5	344.9	349.3	354.1
1957	347.7	359.5	359.6	358.2	360.8	365.1	366.4	370.2	368.5	367.2	372.7	375.6
1958	376.8	377.5	380.9	381.2	383.1	385.4	390.2	399.5	399.9	402.7	407.2	407.4
1959	414.3	414.5	416.5	421.8	429.0	432.9	436.7	436.5	444.6	449.0	446.2	449.1
1960	450.8	442.4	454.0	468.1	459.8	462.2	475.6	466.3	471.8	472.4	465.6	466.6
1961	468.6	469.7	470.7	487.6	490.3	493.3	501.5	501.4	512.8	515.0	504.0	519.4

TABLE B-27

Electric Utilities: All Operations, Revenue, Profits, and Margin, 1937–61

Year	Operating Revenue	Operating Expenses	Operating Income	Profits Before Taxes	Operating Margin	Pre-Tax Margin
	(million dollars)				(per cent)	
1937	2,532	1,187	1,345	565	53.12	22.31
1938	2,549	1,177	1,372	550	53.83	21.58
1939	2,647	1,192	1,455	624	54.97	23.57
1940	2,797	1,257	1,540	683	55.06	24.42
1941	3,029	1,379	1,650	757	54.47	24.99
1942	3,216	1,461	1,755	823	54.57	25.59
1943	3,464	1,620	1,844	886	53.23	25.58
1944	3,615	1,741	1,874	882	51.84	24.40
1945	3,682	1,780	1,902	879	51.66	23.87
1946	3,815	1,936	1,879	945	49.25	24.77
1947	4,291	2,382	1,909	942	44.49	21.95
1948	4,830	2,826	2,004	983	41.49	20.35
1949	5,069	2,821	2,248	1,129	44.35	22.27
1950	5,528	2,979	2,549	1,313	46.11	23.75
1951	6,058	3,216	2,842	1,482	46.91	24.46
1952	6,549	3,449	3,100	1,740	47.34	26.57
1953	7,136	3,734	3,402	1,895	47.67	26.56
1954	7,588	3,863	3,725	2,049	49.09	27.00
1955	8,361	4,181	4,180	2,308	49.99	27.60
1956	9,054	4,521	4,533	2,475	50.07	27.34
1957	9,670	4,875	4,795	2,576	49.59	26.64
1958	10,195	5,036	5,159	2,711	50.60	26.59
1959	11,129	5,404	5,725	2,989	51.44	26.86
1960	11,920	5,778	6,142	3,193	51.53	26.79
1961	12,604	6,048	6,556	3,343	52.02	26.52

220

TABLE B-28

Electric Utilities: Electric Departments' Revenue, Operating Margin,
and Net Revenue Ratio, 1926 – 46

Year	Operating Revenue (million dollars)	Operating Margin	Net Revenue Ratio
		(per cent)	
1926	1,415	56.96	39.01
1927	1,567	58.33	40.65
1928	1,689	60.33	41.86
1929	1,817	60.98	42.93
1930	1,894	61.83	43.56
1931	1,874	62.97	44.02
1932	1,713	63.92	42.79
1933	1,640	63.41	40.37
1934	1,710	62.87	38.54
1935	1,785	62.52	38.15
1936	1,911	62.27	37.26
1937	2,031	61.55	35.75
1938	2,018	62.24	35.03
1939	2,148	62.85	34.87
1940	2,277	62.10	32.94
1941	2,467	61.61	29.23
1942	2,609	61.59	26.37
1943	2,816	59.98	24.93
1944	2,955	58.54	24.84
1945	3,012	58.20	25.86
1946	3,127	55.71	24.75

TABLE B-29
Gas Utilities: Quantity Sold, Revenue, Operating and Pre-Tax Margins, 1937 – 61

Year	All Gas Utilities[a]		INVESTOR-OWNED GAS UTILITIES (PER CENT)			
					Pre-Tax Margin	
	Quantity Sold (billion therms)	Revenue (million dollars)	Operating Margin	Before All Taxes	Before Federal Income Taxes	Before Federal and State Income Taxes
1937	15.8	802	39.70	22.61		
1938	14.7	777	39.73	21.78		
1939	15.9	814	40.10	23.90		
1940	17.2	872	42.50	26.66		
1941	19.0	914	41.97	26.44		
1942	20.8	994	42.51	27.27		
1943	23.4	1,064	43.12	28.16		
1944	25.1	1,108	43.50	28.06		
1945	25.9	1,153	41.31	27.73		
1946	26.4	1,213	38.02	26.89	19.80	
1947	29.9	1,396	34.24		18.65	
1948	33.9	1,579	32.75		17.09	
1949	35.8	1,689	33.11		16.91	17.24
1950	42.1	1,948	34.31			19.51
1951	48.2	2,228	35.31			19.91
1952	52.4	2,466	33.88			18.37
1953	56.1	2,716	32.94			17.28
1954	61.0	3,049	32.42			17.33
1955	66.6	3,450	33.18			18.41
1956	72.5	3,850	33.32			18.92
1957	77.0	4,134	32.40			17.58
1958	80.3	4,568	32.04			17.04
1959	87.9	5,065	31.99			16.87
1960	92.9	5,617	31.57			16.93
1961	95.9	5,993	31.44			16.10

[a]Excludes gas sold for resale and revenue from such sale.

TABLE B-30

Construction Corporations: Sales, Profits, and Margin, 1932–61

Year	Sales (million dollars)	Profits Before Taxes (million dollars)	Margin (per cent)	Year	Sales (million dollars)	Profits Before Taxes (million dollars)	Margin (per cent)
1932	1,363	−88	−6.46	1947	6,929	392	5.66
1933	1,026	−53	−5.17	1948	9,228	577	6.25
1934	1,217	−26	−2.14	1949	9,739	518	5.32
1935	1,455	3	0.21	1950	11,358	562	4.95
1936	1,967	38	1.93	1951	14,011	560	4.00
1937	2,417	49	2.03	1952	15,052	599	3.98
1938	1,927	26	1.35	1953	15,959	514	3.22
1939	2,208	33	1.49	1954	17,215	488	2.83
1940	2,473	68	2.75	1955	19,741	478	2.42
1941	3,452	178	5.16	1956	23,183	678	2.92
1942	4,678	340	7.27	1957	26,675	741	2.78
1943	4,247	268	6.31	1958	28,148	661	2.35
1944	3,111	139	4.47	1959	31,682	581	1.83
1945	2,872	113	3.93	1960	32,362	382	1.18
1946	4,220	232	5.50	1961	36,743	512	1.39

TABLE B-31
Trade Corporations: Sales, Profits, and Margin, 1919–61

Year	Sales (million dollars)	Profits Before Taxes (million dollars)	Margin (per cent)	Year	Sales (million dollars)	Profits Before Taxes (million dollars)	Margin (per cent)
1919	24,878	1,379	5.54	1940	46,478	1,084	2.33
1920	30,820	572	1.86	1941	56,919	2,082	3.66
1921	26,742	-55	-0.21	1942	55,066	2,571	4.67
1922	28,133	736	2.62	1943	57,518	3,094	5.38
1923	31,727	983	3.10	1944	60,895	3,255	5.35
1924	34,595	845	2.44	1945	65,742	3,364	5.12
1925	38,635	1,045	2.70	1946	95,488	5,583	5.85
1926	39,886	902	2.26	1947	121,867	6,082	4.99
1927	40,049	865	2.16	1948	135,861	5,759	4.24
1928	42,380	966	2.28	1949	130,629	3,842	2.94
1929	42,709	801	1.88	1950	153,196	6,315	4.12
1930	36,505	-15	-0.04	1951	166,250	5,498	3.31
1931	29,870	-506	-1.69	1952	166,657	4,421	2.65
1932	22,586	-756	-3.35	1953	167,963	3,934	2.34
1933	23,699	9	0.04	1954	171,027	3,650	2.13
1934	32,427	398	1.23	1955	205,152	5,126	2.50
1935	36,933	548	1.48	1956	215,373	5,246	2.44
1936	42,583	930	2.18	1957	229,076	4,717	2.06
1937	44,705	837	1.87	1958	225,737	4,433	1.96
1938	38,375	418	1.09	1959	252,868	5,573	2.20
1939	42,061	815	1.94	1960	265,363	4,535	1.71
				1961	266,419	4,573	1.72

224 APPENDIX B

TABLE B-32

All Domestic Business: "External" Sales, "External" Cost, and Cost Ratio, 1929–56

Year	Sales (million dollars)	Cost (million dollars)	Cost Ratio (per cent)	Year	Sales (million dollars)	Cost (million dollars)	Cost Ratio (per cent)
1929	99,096	74,668	75.3	1943	167,619	116,863	69.7
1930	81,664	68,548	83.9	1944	179,180	124,405	69.4
1931	67,423	59,187	87.8	1945	178,446	125,049	70.1
1932	51,344	48,507	94.5	1946	195,426	136,233	69.7
1933	53,009	45,802	86.4	1947	222,707	156,357	70.2
1934	59,322	50,154	84.5	1948	242,974	174,179	71.7
1935	66,614	53,765	80.7	1949	234,828	175,529	74.7
1936	76,011	58,694	77.2	1950	270,768	194,513	71.8
1937	84,049	65,524	78.0	1951	304,330	222,119	73.0
1938	75,535	61,295	81.1	1952	314,223	236,666	75.3
1939	83,733	65,050	77.7	1953	332,794	254,509	76.5
1940	92,344	70,019	75.7	1954	327,865	255,318	77.9
1941	119,467	84,427	70.7	1955	358,220	276,008	77.0
1942	144,658	100,707	69.6	1956	380,268	298,347	78.5

INDEX